BIBLICAL INTERPRETATION:
A ROADMAP

BIBLICAL INTERPRETATION: A ROADMAP

Frederick C. Tiffany

and

Sharon H. Ringe

ABINGDON PRESS
Nashville

Library of Congress Cataloging-in-Publication Data

Tiffany, Frederick C., 1941–
  Biblical interpretation: a roadmap / Frederick C. Tiffany and Sharon H. Ringe.
     p.   cm.
  Includes bibliographical references.
  ISBN 0-687-01608-8 (alk. paper)
  1. Bible—Hermeneutics.   2. Bible—Criticism, interpretation, etc.
I. Title.
BS476.T534   1996
220.6'01–dc20   95-52737
                                                                    CIP

Unless otherwise noted, all scripture quotations are from The New Revised Standard Version Bible, copyright © 1989 by the the Division of Christian Education of the National Council of the Churches of Christ in the USA. Used by permission.

This book is printed on acid-free, recycled paper.

96 97 98 99 00 01 02 03 04 05 — 10 9 8 7 6 5 4 3 2 1

MANUFACTURED IN THE UNITED STATES OF AMERICA

To
Linda L. Tiffany
and
Hilda F. Ringe

Thanks Giving!

Contents

PART 3: ISSUES AND RESOURCES
IN INTERPRETATION

Abbreviations

For the convenience of the reader, we will use the following abbreviations for the most commonly used English translations of the Bible:

JB   *The Jerusalem Bible*

KJV   The King James Version of the Bible

NAB   *The New American Bible*

NEB   *The New English Bible*

NIV   *The Holy Bible, New International Version*

NJB   *The New Jerusalem Bible*

NRSV   The New Revised Standard Version Bible

REB   *The Revised English Bible*

RSV   The Revised Standard Version of the Bible

JPS   *Tanakh: A New Translation of the Holy Scriptures According to the Traditional Hebrew Text* (Jewish Publication Society)

TEV   *The Bible in Today's English Version*

All quotations from these Bible translations are reprinted by permission.

Preface

This book testifies to the power of community.

It began when we taught a course together at the Methodist Theological School in Ohio and discovered common concerns about pedagogy and power. These concerns came into focus in the search for better ways to introduce students to the Bible—literally to lead them into it, and to find in that process excitement, challenges, and a sense of their own authority as interpreters. Writing this book so fully in common that we can no longer remember who wrote the initial drafts of each chapter has taught us to rely on one another, not just to catch errors, but also to expand each other's insights and understandings at every step along the way.

Our two-person community grew to include the students in our classes and the pastors and lay people in the churches with whom we tested the roadmap. That community was greatly enriched by the involvement of Professors Bruce C. Birch, Denise Dombkowski Hopkins, David C. Hopkins, and James T. Clemons of Wesley Theological Seminary, who have also used the roadmap in the seminary's "Practicum for Biblical Interpretation" and in other classes. Members of the faculty and students of Seminario Bíblico Latinoamericano are significant teachers and learners with us, about the "text" of the world as well as about that of the Bible. Organizations as diverse as the Society of Biblical Literature, the Lilly Endowment, Vanderbilt University, Loyola Marymount University, and the Association of Theological Schools have sponsored a variety of gatherings and forums that have allowed our community of study and learning to include greater numbers of persons from historically excluded communities in the United States and from other areas of the world. To all of these colleagues and conversation partners, we express our heartfelt thanks. We are also grateful for the assistance generously provided by members of the staff of Abingdon Press.

Important members of the community in which this book was written are Marilyn and Robert Lohr, innkeepers of the Bayberry Inn in Somerset, Pennsylvania—halfway between our homes in Columbus, Ohio, and Washington, D.C.—where our families gathered often. Their gracious hospitality (and Marilyn's spectacular breakfasts) heightened the pleasure already endemic to this work.

Our warmest thanks go to our families. Sharon's mother, Hilda, and Fred's wife, Linda, endured the endless conversations and long sieges of writing through which this project evolved. They arranged family holidays around our work, and endured mealtime conversations that were frequently derailed into unfinished discussions or sudden ideas related to "the book." How could we not dedicate it to them?

Frederick C. Tiffany
Sharon H. Ringe
May 1, 1995

An Introduction to This Roadmap

The Bible is an open book. Women and men from a variety of theological traditions, ethnic communities, economic strata, ages, physical conditions, and sexual orientations have been reading it for centuries. At different times, people in all of these circumstances have found themselves empowered by the Bible, challenged by it, confused by it, restricted by it, and harmed by it. They have sought to understand it, to interpret it, to control it, to obey it, and to escape it. People love the Bible as a source of life and light and truth and hope. And sometimes they hate its power.

The task of biblical interpretation daunts and sometimes distresses people who love the Bible and people who are alientated from it alike. Many feel trapped by the alternative of simply accepting or rejecting the interpretations of the Bible which are dominant within the church or the academic community. On the other hand, sorting out the growing variety of interpretations coming from different social, theological, or methodological perspectives can feel overwhelming. Faced with that disempowering dilemma, some assemble as many possible interpretations as they can find, and try valiantly to harmonize them. Others simply choose the one that best meets their needs of the moment. In the midst of this cacophany of voices, one question dominates: How can anyone know what is "right" and what is "wrong" anymore?

This book has grown out of our experiences in seminary classrooms and with gatherings of church people, as questions such as these have been on the agenda either openly or secretly. The book presents a process by which people can study the Bible in ways that allow them to take advantage of the expertise and authority of their own life experiences and context, as well as those of other readers in other cultural contexts—including those of academic biblical scholars. In addition, we provide some guidelines to help interpreters who are not "experts" in the technical disciplines of biblical study identify and explore literary clues to how and why various biblical passages function as they do, and clues to the social world that formed the contexts of the communities that gave rise to, preserved, amended, and transmitted the biblical texts.

Basic Assumptions Underlying the Process of Reading

It is important to be up-front about our assumptions underlying this particular roadmap of biblical interpretation. First among them is the recognition that the Bible is a collection of documents written by human authors for specific human communities struggling to understand and express their own identity in relationship with each other and with God. That means that these documents are historically and culturally relative, and we must respect the specific social institutions and world views that underlie them. For modern readers in Europe and North America, those institutions and world views, the perception of how religion and other socio-political institutions are related, and even the images of God underlying the texts can seem foreign indeed. Yet we must recognize the continuing power of the biblical texts as places where we are encountered or addressed by God even in the midst of that foreignness, as well as in the intimacy of common joys, fears, and longings that find their home in God.

A second assumption—one that parallels the first—is that the perspective of every reader is also historically and culturally relative. All people are influenced by the place and time in which they live; by the economic, social, political and religious factors shaping their lives; and by the communities to whose well-being they are committed. It is important to become aware of the cultural assumptions that shape the readings of texts, and to acknowledge, as best one can, the world-construct—in Spanish, *cosmovisión*—that shapes our approaches to the biblical texts.

A third assumption is that while no reading can claim special privilege, neither does any reading function in isolation from other persons and communities. An important step in responsible interpretation is learning to be attentive to readings from many distinct persons and communities. Engaging this wider community of interpreters will have an impact both on the content or meaning encountered in the text, and on the approaches and methods of interpretation that are used.

Openness and receptivity to a variety of readings does not, however, mean that anything goes. Some readings may incorporate errors in understanding the language of the text or the circumstances of the historical context, and those readings must be corrected. Many such errors are not value-neutral, but rather they build into one's reading of a text conclusions that are prejudicial and often harmful. For example, historians and biblical interpreters used to assume that the Levitical purity laws pertained equally to all Jewish women's lives in first century Palestine. Recent work by Jewish feminist interpreters and historians has corrected that misconception, making clear the differences that existed, for example, between the lives of women from families closely linked to the Jerusalem temple, who would have been concerned about cultic purity, and the lives of women in rural Galilee, where the strict adherence to purity regulations would not have been a daily requirement. Not surprisingly, these scholars have also been able to document considerable differences in all aspects of women's life circumstances that reflected a woman's economic class. In short, women's lives *then* exhibited as much variety as do women's lives *today*. To posit Jesus and the movement he led as offering an unusual openness to women, in contrast to his "Jewish background" (as the old language of Christian scholars often put it), is doubly problematic. In the first place, it perpetuates an inaccurate picture of the world from which Jesus came, and, at the same time, it removes Jesus from his own religious, social, and cultural roots. In the second place, these errors portray women's lives as merely an abstraction that is a projection of patriarchal values, and they equate Judaism with misogyny, thus supporting Christian prejudice against Judaism and the Jewish people.

At other times a reading may not represent a historical inaccuracy, but it still may be destructive or harmful in its effects on some persons or groups. Such readings too must be confronted with an appropriate response. One important example of such an occurrence has its roots in a problem of translation. The Gospel of John identifies the principal group of Jesus' opponents as *hoi Ioudaioi*, a Greek word usually translated into English as "the Jews" (and into other modern languages by the equivalent term). Within the Gospel it is clear that this term does not refer to the religio-ethnic group usually designated by that word, for Jesus himself is sharply distinguished from that group (see, for example, John 7:1). Instead, the word appears to refer on one level to "Judeans"—people from the southern part of the country close to Jerusalem, who are described as opposing Jesus and his largely Galilean followers. In the drama of the life of the Gospel writer's own community, the term appears to identify, *not* the Jewish people as a whole, but only the group of the synagogue officials who were in opposition to that particular Christian community. The continued translation of the term *hoi Ioudaioi* as "the Jews," however, has given biblical warrant to vicious expressions of anti-Judaism on the part of Christians through the centuries.

Learning to "Love the Questions"

This is not the first generation to struggle with how to read and understand the Bible. For present-day interpreters, many of the earlier struggles are masked by the fact that history has usually preserved only the points of view of persons and groups that won the battles—or at least continued to have powerful supporters. Those ways of reading, and the conclusions reached by them, have been remembered in the dominant histories of church and synagogue and in historical accounts of the development of biblical interpretation. Examples of those readings include the theological and doctrinal commentaries written by the "Fathers" of the early church and by other church leaders and scholars through the centuries. These same works, however, often preserve the only remaining traces of other perspectives and interpretations from the same historical periods, which are noted as errors or even "heresies" that the writer corrects. Other interpretations of biblical texts by peoples and communities not given voice in the standard histories have been preserved in other media than formal publications. For example, sermons by preachers who addressed their enslaved sisters and brothers on the plantations of the southern United States in the eighteenth and early nineteenth centuries provide an important record of some approaches to the Bible that differed markedly from those heard in the white congregations of the period, or read in the published commentaries. Other interpretations are recorded in personal diaries and letters carefully preserved by family and friends through the years. Unfortunately, many other ways of reading have been lost to conscious memory, as the chains of transmission of oral histories were interrupted by the violence and suffering that have marked the history of those peoples.

In all of these approaches it is clear that people read the Bible to seek answers to questions—both questions about life situations of the readers and questions about the text itself. Methods of reading are really nothing more than organized efforts to respond to the questions that arise in the reading of texts in particular contexts. The methods and the values the interpretations embody grow out of the questions. For example, a reader who is curious about the worship practices in the earliest churches will approach 1 Corinthians 11 using tools of historical investigation that will get as descriptively accurate a picture of what was taking place in Corinth as it is possible to get. If the same reader has further shaped the question to focus on women's roles in those churches, the tools of gender analysis will have to come into play. If the real question underlying the study is what historical and theological affirmations undergird the current practice of a particular church, the methods will have to be adapted further.

It is important to keep in mind the fact that the methods used in pursuing one's questions are themselves not disinterested and neutral. Instead, they embody the values of the social locations in which they were developed (often the church or the university). The choice of particular methods already implies a set of assumptions and, in turn, limits the range of questions that one might likely ask or entertain. Questions that these methods cannot answer will be ruled out of bounds. It is important, therefore, to be open to a wide range of approaches, in order to allow as much freedom as possible for questions to emerge.

More fundamental than the answers at which one arrives in the process of biblical interpretation, or than the particular methods one uses, are the questions themselves that one brings to the text. The step of clarifying initial questions and the further questions that arise as one works with a given text is crucial for several reasons. Once the questions have been sharpened and clarified, it is easier to turn to appropriate tools and to engage helpful strategies to get at their answers. One may also more readily recognize how it is that the questions raised by others have led them to follow different strategies and methods, which might, in turn, yield new insights or a fresh angle of vision on one's own questions.

The discipline of paying attention to and refining questions also serves as a reminder that every project of interpretation is undertaken within a particular social location and is guided by the interpreter's prior experiences. To accept this reality of human limitation is not to confess a weakness or imperfection that must be overcome. Instead, it is to claim the freedom that comes from acknowledging the uniqueness of the interpreter's own self that God has created and is creating, and of the particular communities to which one is accountable. It is to open oneself to the possibility of genuine dialogue with and within the diversity and the fullness of God's created world.

The Design of This Roadmap

We begin, then, from these three fundamental assumptions that govern our approach to reading the Bible: (1) that the text arises from particular social settings, (2) that the reader likewise reads from specific settings, and (3) that neither the diversity of texts nor the multitude of readers stand in isolation one from another. We have also suggested that each reader or community of readers should begin the process by asking questions. A critical goal from the very beginning of one's reading of a text is to formulate good questions—questions that arise out of particularities of the interaction of readers and texts. Moving too quickly to answers may well deny the integrity of both reader and text.

Interpretive approaches always develop in the dialogue between texts and interpreters. There is no "pure" method that is not shaped by the texts being read and the agenda and social location of the interpreter. Based on that premise, in this guide we have interwoven a description of each phase of the process with our own work on a specific text, Luke 14:25-35. We do this not simply, or even primarily, to use the text as an illustration of the application of the method. We do this to allow the method to emerge from our interaction with the text. This does not mean that we approach the text without any preconceived methodological principles. We have both been trained in the accepted methods of twentieth century, Euro-American, academic biblical interpretation. Neither the content and methods we have learned, nor the values inherent in that training, can be erased from our minds and hearts, nor would we want them to be. We have also both learned about the reading of texts from a variety of faith communities. That too is a continuing memory of both mind and heart. We bring our own questions, together with our learnings and experiences. All of this has helped shape the particular approach to biblical texts which we follow, and which we offer here.

In the first five chapters of the book, we set out the process in considerable detail. The five chapters represent the principal dimensions of the interaction between readers and text envisioned in the roadmap. Each chapter is divided into some of the specific stages by which that interaction can take place. At each stage we will sketch some "tips for travelers" in the form of preliminary descriptions of what that stage entails, and of the underlying rationale. After unfolding a section of the roadmap, we will then follow those travel hints through the biblical text we have chosen. In the process, we will try to stay open to new paths that may appear on the horizon, and to unexpected discoveries of details that would enhance both our work on the specific passage and the guide itself.

Instead of simply reading the material we offer, as if it were our travel diary from an exotic trip, we ask that you join us on the journey. We invite you to read the text with us for yourself. Allow and encourage your own interpretation to materialize. Let your own adaptation of this method develop and take shape as it evolves in interaction with the text, with this roadmap, with other interpreters, and with other approaches.

Part 2 of the book provides examples of how this approach might be adapted to work with other types of literature found in the Bible. The five chapters illustrate adaptations of two general sorts. The most common sort deals with the particular literary and historical concerns that are introduced by the various types of biblical literature and the themes they emphasize. For example, to read the Psalms and other poetic literature requires attention to literary conventions and rules and to different techniques for identifying the contexts that gave rise to the texts. Not form and function, but content and context command one's attention in the case of letters and prophetic writings. These writings are so tightly linked to the contexts and events that gave rise to them that discerning their historical circumstances requires more precise attention than is necessary or even possible for other types of texts.

The second sort of adaptation deals with the sequence in which the various steps of the process are carried out. In letters and prophetic books, for example, the importance of the originating context—why Paul wrote a particular letter, or why Amos spoke so harshly—might lead you to reference books early in the process of interpretation. Such basic research, which is not discussed until chapter 4 of Part 1, might well follow the initial encounter with a text (chapter 2), and precede the "close reading" of the text (chapter 3).

In both the initial discussion of the roadmap and the additional sample texts, we raise or point to a number of underlying questions and issues in interpretation. Some of the principal issues are addressed in Part 3, which also includes a chapter that identifies resources with which to investigate specific questions of background and interpretation, and to expand the community of interpreters.

This book is of necessity linear in its presentation: One page follows another. We recognize, however, that the order we have chosen for the material is not the best one for all readers. We encourage you, therefore, to use the book in whatever way is most helpful for you. For example, if you like to explore the broader theoretical issues underlying a project before examining the specific details, you might find it helpful to begin your reading with chapter 11. If work on one example leaves you with a string of questions that begin "OK, but what about . . . ?," you will probably want to skip to other sample texts before you finish part 1. (We have no illusions of having covered every type of biblical text, but we hope that the ones we discuss will provide suggestions for you to continue to adapt this process.)

Individual learning styles also influence how readers will choose to work with this book. We have begun each chapter in Part 1 with a discussion of what we envision that step of the process to involve, and then we have taken that step with the sample text. On the other hand, if you know that you learn best from concrete examples, you might find it most helpful to read all of the sections that present work on the text (set off by horizontal rules and distinguished by a different typeface) *before* you go back to the more theoretical descriptions of the various steps in the process.

This book grants priority to verbal media, both oral (discussion) and written (reading and note-taking), as tools for biblical interpretation. The age of group members, the range of literacy levels, the agenda or purpose of the group's study, the formality or informality of the setting, and the comfort of group members with each other may necessitate other alternatives. For instance, where some or most members of a group are unable to read, the leader will need to find ways to evoke analogies with the participants' own experience and context in order to get at dimensions of the social world of the text being studied. You—or the group with whom you plan to work—might find it helpful to incorporate a more extensive use of graphic arts, movement, drama, or other media to get at fresh responses to a text. If you are working alone, and especially if you are well-practiced in traditional academic methods of biblical interpretation, the use of non-verbal media can be very helpful in allowing you to identify and express new questions about and reflections on a text.

The purpose for which the study is carried out also shapes the process. If the purpose of the study is to provide the background for a sermon for a specific occasion or for a paper in a seminary course in biblical exegesis, the process will need to be focused through that lens. A study of the same passage carried out in a group in which the study itself is the end product might prove much more wide-ranging. Such a Bible study might lead to a general sense of where the passage is leading, rather than to a theme or conclusion of the text itself, or a principal connection of the text to the contemporary context. A group that engages in Bible study as part of its common work on a problem or project in the community, and that is looking to the Bible to guide its action or fortify its commitment in the face of a challenge or threat, will bring a different investment in the process from that of a group that gathers only for Bible study.

In other words, this roadmap is intended not to define or limit one's options in working with biblical texts, but rather to provide a general orientation to the territory readers have chosen to explore. Each "traveler's" or "tour group's" particular identity, interests, purpose, resources, and sense of adventure will determine how the map will best be used. We encourage you to adapt this process. Develop it, work with it, and play with it in whatever ways are necessary to make it your own. Many of these explorations will lead to exciting encounters with biblical texts and with a growing community of partners in interpretation. Some of the experiments may prove less successful, or simply fall flat. Those too, like getting lost in a new part of the countryside or in a city where one has just arrived, can lead to important learnings both about the territory one is exploring and about the travelers themselves—the Bible and its interpretation in your own context.

¡Buen viaje! Bon voyage!

PART 1

The Roadmap

Chapter 1

Locating the Readers
and the Reading Context

Beginning the Journey at Home

The journey of biblical interpretation begins at home, with attention to the immediate contemporary environment in which the biblical text is encountered. This might seem like an odd place to begin a process of biblical study. Would it not make more sense to begin with the biblical text and information about the biblical world, which is to say the world within which the text originated? Is that not the world the interpreters want to explore and understand? Why start with the world of the readers of the biblical text?

One reason for the decision to begin at home is that every journey into and with the biblical texts will be new, principally because each community of interpreters at every moment of its life is unique. Even if a person or group returns to a text studied earlier, that return trip will not be exactly like any previous ones. Each person will have changed, the composition of the group may have varied, and the wider historical and social context will be different. Because of those changes and the uniqueness of each particular moment of interpretation, each encounter with the text will be a distinct and distinctive adventure. Thus, to start with the readers' circumstances affirms this diversity and this dynamic of change in the study of biblical texts.

The decision to begin at home also grows out of the conviction that the world in which we all live is God's creation, and that God is present through and active within that world. In and through this world God reveals God's self. This was true in biblical times; it is true today. Thus the world is a primary "text" within which one can discern God's word. The Bible is also God's "text" or word—a record given a place of privilege by historic decisions of the church, and a record that itself represents the discernment of God's presence and action in the world by a number of particular communities at specific moments in history. The church affirms, and the experience of many people confirms, that reading this record guides efforts to discern and interpret God's more immediate word received through the text of the present world.

A third factor in the decision to begin the journey at home is a consideration of the nature of texts that have been recorded in writing or other media. It is the very nature of any recorded text that it does not remain confined to its original context. Once recorded, any text takes on a life of its own, such that its meaning or significance is no longer defined by or limited to the context of recording. It certainly is not limited by the historical facts about the event which it purports to describe or record.

Even oral communications function in this sense as recorded texts. A conversation between two people is context-specific, and meaning occurs principally at the moment when the communication takes place. Despite that primary meaning, later reflections on the event and on what was said and heard can lead to new perceptions. These understandings are derived from the memory of the communication (in a sense from the recording of that communication event on the memory of participants), more than from the original communication itself.

Even in such a context-specific communication as an oral message, the transmitting and receiving of meaning are complex functions. There is the intended meaning of the speaker, signer, singer, or writer, and there is the message received by each person or group present in that moment. Experience teaches how perplexing the process of communication is. Even in situations where the participants are relatively homogeneous and share common cultural assumptions, primary language, general history, and similar expectations, what the speaker intends and what the audience receives may differ substantially. Words have particular associations in the minds of each person, and those associations influence what is perceived in the communication. A word that is commonly assumed to convey happiness—the word "picnic," for example—may trigger memories of a tragic accident or other event, or years of buried sadness at the picnics one was not able to attend. In other words, the word may have no positive meaning at all for someone, or it may suggest media pictures portraying a fun thing that *other* people do. Similarly, the word "family" may conjure images of good times and security for many, while for others it evokes feelings of pain and abuse. Meaning thus occurs not in isolated words or signs, but in the relationships of those words with each other and in the interaction of those words within and between the worlds of experience of the communicator and the receivers.

It is important, therefore, even in the immediacy of face-to-face exchanges, for the communicator to seek to understand as fully as possible the experiences of the receivers. The receivers, in turn, will want to understand where the communicator is coming from. What is common in their experiences? What values or understandings are assumed? What are presumed to be shared perceptions of a given situation? Where and in what ways are their experiences and perceptions different?

Communications that are recorded in more lasting forms, such as a written document, an audio recording, a video recording, or some other medium of preservation and transmission, are even more complex. These records—or, in general terms, "texts"—can and will be transported into new settings, each of which gives rise to a new communication event. Though the words (and in the case of a voice recording, even the tones and inflections of the speech) are transmitted faithfully from one context to another, the changed contexts within which a text is received affect the meaning of the communication in such a way that it is as if the text itself has become new. Since meaning occurs in the interaction between the text and those who receive it, and is not defined or delimited by the text alone, each new occasion with a text will create new meanings. A common experience of this shift of meanings comes when one reads a novel or sees a movie for a second time, and finds in it meanings, delights, or disappointments that were not apparent in the first encounter. A more dramatic instance of new meanings comes when one rereads a book like Winnie the Pooh as an adult after having loved it as a child, or when one rereads the moving *Diary of Anne Frank* after visiting the Franks' home in Amsterdam or after a pilgrimage to one of the concentration camps where Jews and others were imprisoned and killed. Examples such as these make it clear that a recorded text, though fixed in form, is not a static entity.

"Contexts" of Biblical Interpretation

An important aspect of beginning the journey of biblical interpretation "at home," with attention to the identity and circumstances of the interpreters, is the role of various contexts in biblical interpretation. As a recorded text, any passage in the Bible has been interpreted and granted meanings in many and widely varied contexts. At least three basic types of context can be distinguished, each of which plays a distinct role in biblical studies. One of these types (which will be explored in chapter 4) consists of the contexts within and for which the biblical texts themselves were developed. A second is the specific context of the current interpreters—your context and ours. Finally there are all those other contexts within which individuals and communities, both past and contemporary, engage in interpreting that same text. Each of these contexts is important, and information gleaned about each type of context, and from each of them about the text itself, has an impact on any effort to understand a biblical text. It is important to distinguish among these types, even while recognizing that none stands in isolation from the others. In particular, it is important to remember that perceptions of and responses to all contexts are filtered through the perspectives and experiences of each immediate interpreter.

Speaking of the world of the immediate interpreter as one context of the biblical texts does not thereby separate the interpreter from the text. On the contrary, to begin at this place is to recognize that the text itself forms a part of the interpreter's immediate world. This is not to deny the obvious fact that biblical texts were written at particular times and places in history, and that they were written out of and for particular communities. Contemporary interpreters do not belong to that same world of understanding. This is one reason that biblical texts often appear strange. References are made to foreign places, names, customs and practices. The biblical languages themselves are foreign. Even in translation, particular phrases, literary allusions, or symbols are often obscure.

On the other hand, though contemporary readers are not part of the social worlds of the Bible, the Bible does belong to the social worlds of any and all interpreters. Its specific role and function in particular communities, however, will vary considerably. Some individuals and groups belong to those religious traditions in which the Bible has been preserved, and in which it functions as sacred scripture. In such communities biblical texts are often read as a regular part of worship. The language of ritual and prayer is shaped by the language of Bible translations, oftentimes from the language of a "classic" translation, such as the King James Version in English, the *Reina Valera* in Spanish, or Luther's German translation. Sermons expound on the reading from a biblical text recognized as "sacred." Selected Bible stories are re-counted for and sometimes re-enacted by children. Various groups gather to study the scriptures. In all of these, and still other ways, the Bible lives in the world of such persons.

Some of these religious communities also exist in a culture that has shared in a long history of contact with the Bible. The influence of the Bible can be seen in virtually all aspects of the culture, whether literature, art, social structures, holidays, festivals, philosophy, or law. In fact, these cultures cannot be understood apart from some knowledge of the biblical traditions. In such a setting one simply absorbs certain biblical stories and images through the culture itself. Even persons who do not belong to a religious community shaped by particular biblical traditions will still know some of these traditions by way of the larger cultural context.

Indeed, the apparent familiarity of the Bible becomes a roadblock to interpretation among the members of those communities whose religion and culture have been so thoroughly infused with the biblical tradition. In such contexts, the Bible becomes so identified with the particular cultural or religious tradition that the Bible tends to be assumed to express that culture's values. Conversely, the culture is assumed to express biblical norms, and only those religious and cultural expressions that have arisen from the dominant culture or system of beliefs are recognized as "biblical"—and hence legitimate.

Awareness of and concern about these dynamics of cultural and confessional captivity have sometimes prompted interpreters to react by insisting on reading the Bible in its own context—that is, in the context of the origin, transmission, or editing of a particular book or other identifiable section. Such an approach does have merit. The "historical-critical method" that is still the basis of many university and seminary courses in Bible sought initially to offer an alternative to readings that were doctrinally and culturally shaped. It reminds the student that the Bible is a collection of foreign documents, as well as being a familiar book. That method, however, like any method, is a product of its own social setting of origin, and any effort to reconstruct the world of the Bible is shaped by the social location of the scholar. The historical-critical method in particular has been shaped by the values and norms of post-Enlightenment western Europe and North America. This approach is in danger of perpetuating an even more subtle form of cultural captivity than those that openly promote the doctrines or values of a "Christian"—or, more broadly, a "biblical"—culture. Scholars who use the historical-critical method have always been aware that they hold presuppositions, and they might even have identified them. But these presuppositions have usually been identified as a problem to be compensated for or overcome, rather than as an important aspect of the interpretive process that generates meaning in the encounter between text and interpreter. When they are viewed as a problem, the interpreter's goal has been to bracket these assumptions in such a way that they would contaminate as little as possible the results of the historical study. In contrast, the approach proposed here is to honor such presuppositions by taking them seriously as a dynamic in the process of interpretation. This does not mean that they are accepted without question. Instead, they are examined critically as, in a real sense, part of the interpreter's interaction with the text of God's creation, and hence also with the biblical text.

Other individuals and groups engage the Bible from a context in which the Bible is a recent addition to a culture already shaped by religious traditions based on other sacred texts or traditions. In such a context, readers are often struck initially by a sense of the foreignness of the Bible and the biblical world as it has been conveyed to them. What is less clear to them is how the Bible can have a positive role in their self-understanding and in the life of their communities.

In some such cases, the world of the interpreter may actually have considerable congruence with the worlds of the Bible in terms of their assumptions about technology, economic models, and social values and institutions. However, the fact that the Bible was carried into their world by representatives of Western civilization, who brought it to them wrapped in the packaging of their own cultures, has obscured these similarities. For example, some African and African American scholars note the geographic relationship of Africa and the lands of the

30

Bible. They also find positive correlation between practices and values reflected in the biblical records and those of African traditions. Some missionaries from the Western world were also aware of some of these similarities. For cultural reasons, such observations were valued negatively and used as an excuse to impede people's access to the biblical text—for example, by a reluctance to translate the Old Testament into African languages. The values and ideology expressed in such decisions also influenced the selections of texts for public reading, and the interpretation of those texts in the missionaries' preaching and teaching.

Contexts Within Contexts: Readings and Counter-Readings

Understanding a community's historical experience with the biblical tradition thus includes exploring the role of the Bible within that context, and in particular examining the social and political role that the Bible has played. It is also important to recognize a diversity of contexts and roles within that community, along with their social implications and conflicts. For example, plantation owners in the southern United States read and interpreted the Bible (or had the Bible read and interpreted to them and to those persons they held as slaves) to convey the message that slaves must obey their masters, and to enforce the notion of the masters' own racial superiority. In these hands the Bible functioned to construct and reinforce a particular social order that encompassed plantation owners and their families, those employed or supported by the owners, and those enslaved by the owners. At the same time, and in the same plantations, however, communities of enslaved persons, acting against the rules of plantation society, gathered secretly for worship in the forest, creating an alternative church structure that has been called "the Invisible Institution." There the biblical story of an enslaved people whose cry was heard by God was recognized as a commentary on the readers' own experience. For them the Bible also became a resource for hope and a stimulus to action.

These communities of enslaved persons knew full well the role that the social location of the interpreter played in creating the meanings of biblical texts, and they understood the conflict generated by those different readings. Preachers in the owners' churches, on the other hand, were less likely to acknowledge or even to recognize how their social location was shaping their readings. Their interpretation of the Bible was, they presumed, universally true. Given their position of power, they presumed that the world which they had constructed and the meaning they had given to that world would be accepted by everyone. They needed only to enforce conformity to the truth as they knew it. In so doing, they confused the world of their creation with the world of God's creation. They assumed that the primary text of their life experience was the only such text and, therefore, that the commentary of the Bible on their life experience was its only true meaning.

Similar patterns of reading and counter-reading occur between the dominant and various marginalized cultures of today's world—between readings framed by the values of Euro-American, middle class, patriarchal, able-bodied, hetero-sexist society on the one side, and readings stemming from historically excluded racial or ethnic communities, women of all cultures, persons who are disabled, or gay men and lesbians of all cultures. More will be said later about the importance of attention to a diversity of voices in order to uncover the assumptions and values of the dominant culture, which often wield their power through the collusion of power and invisibility.

It is important to note that socially or contextually distinguished readings and counter-readings occur within the dominant culture as well. Several brief examples from the authors' own experience will serve to illustrate how that works. Our seminary students regularly tell us that they could not do in a church the kind of biblical study that is required of them in seminary. Responses to this concern by academic theologians and biblical scholars are often cast in terms of the universal applicability of their methods and of insights derived from using them. Such responses fail to acknowledge or address issues of social location that underlie the students' questions. The students are then left to assume that something is wrong with their questions. They draw the inevitable conclusion that to acknowledge the impact of social context on their reading somehow compromises the value or truth of their interpretation. In fact, however, the opposite is the case: To fail to acknowledge the social context is itself the first compromise of truth.

Social location can be seen to enter the process of interpretation as persons define their location relative to the recognized experts in the field of biblical interpretation. Often a participant in a Bible study either defers to the experts (consequently disparaging his or her own comments and those of other non-experts in the group), or else identifies with the experts' privileged position. Thus, one may begin by apologetically acknowledging one's own lack of knowledge or expertise, or by asserting authority claims, saying, for example, "scholars tell us that. . . ." The function of such a remark too often does not identify the source of this information or, in particular, the social location of that source. Its authority is simply assumed. Because the authority is not itself identified as a category of social location, the role that such comments play in the interpretive process is not openly recognized, even though everyone understands their meaning. The appropriateness of such forms of social identification, therefore, is not questioned.

Sometimes the power of social location within a group is established implicitly, by the dynamics of the group process. For example, a woman in a predominantly male group may be ignored, because her remarks find no resonance in the experience of the men, who assume their experience to be universal and normative. Or persons may be functionally excluded from participation and ignored because their culture teaches different group behaviors from those of the dominant culture represented in the group. Such culturally conveyed values, for example, underlie the perceived shyness of many Asian or Indigenous people who find themselves in the midst of a group dominated by people of European culture and ancestry.

Until the existence and role of such factors of social location are recognized, interpretations that emerge within groups will reflect only the social location of those with authority, either formal or informal, to participate and to be recognized. Failure to attend to the social locations of each of the diverse individuals within the group, and of the group itself as a corporate entity, allows unacknowledged dynamics to govern the process of interpretation. Furthermore, if a group does not acknowledge such elements of its own diversity, it is unlikely to recognize other dimensions of diversity—of race, class, gender, marital status, sexual orientation, or able-bodiedness—which are not represented in its circle. Without that recognition, any group can too easily grant universal significance to its own readings.

Biblical Interpretation as a Group Project

Clearly the global dominance of Euro-American culture and its attendant institutions accounts for the difficulty that many who share in or who have adopted that culture have in recognizing its presence and its power. Its presence is so pervasive that recognizing it is like becoming aware of the earth's atmosphere that surrounds us, and it seems so powerful that raising a counter-voice feels rather like trying to contradict the law of gravity! A specific aspect of that culture that relates directly to the task of biblical interpretation is the value placed on individualism and privatization in the society at large. In communities of the dominant culture, the way in which the Bible has been privatized has tended to obscure the social role that book plays in offering support or critique to the institutions and values that structure their world. Within these communities the Bible is commonly viewed as a personal document. Bible reading is viewed as an individual undertaking, whether in the practice of personal devotional reading or in the study of the isolated scholar. In both cases the typical pattern has been that of the private encounter of an individual with the printed text. When the text is expounded in a public setting (whether as a sermon in corporate worship or as a lecture in a classroom), that exposition is usually a pronouncement of the insights of one individual, drawn from that person's private study of the text—a way of working that feeds the granting of prestige to experts.

Even "group" Bible study most frequently moves in one of two directions, both of which focus on the individual. It becomes an exercise in presenting and defending one's own interpretation, or it is an occasion for participants to share, one after the other, personal interpretations. In neither case is the agenda guided by an appreciation of others' approaches and perspectives, even when the membership of the group includes persons from a wide variety of perspectives, nor is the goal a common search for understanding or for motivation to take action together. There is no expectation that the views of each person will be transformed, or that the biases of each person will be made visible within the community of interpreters, nor is it anticipated that the community's understanding will be influenced by each member and by the dynamics within the group. There is very little sense that the group gathers to seek a wisdom that is other than that of any individual or of the combined insights of the gathered individuals that are assembled with no interaction between them, like beads on a string.

Movements like Christian base communities in Latin America have given new vision and visibility to the dynamics of communal interpretation of the Bible. In such contexts attention is paid to the social reality of the community undertaking the Bible study, as well as to the interpretations by the community. Such communities, like the "Invisible Institution" mentioned above, are well aware that their reading is not the only way texts can be interpreted. As a consequence of both secular and church power structures, those communities have been subjected to the biblical interpretations of the dominant culture and of persons and groups with political and economic hegemony. They have also come to recognize that those readings reflect and help to maintain social structures that have had powerful and often negative consequences for their lives.

The Christian base communities thus begin with a recognition that social world impacts interpretation. Their own process of communal study begins with an explicit review and reminder of those consequences. Their interpretation of their life experience—their "reading" of this primary text of God's activity—informs their reading of the Bible. In the witness of the biblical traditions, they find congruence between that record of God's action and the experience of God's project in their own social reality and experiences. In turn, then, their reading of the Bible instructs their understanding of their present reality. In that dialogical process, which Latin American theologians call "hermeneutical circulation," the power of the God of the biblical traditions enlivens the life and witness of the community.

In similar ways, the social realities of women in Euro-American as well as other cultures have led them to recognize the support, strength, and insight that often are the result of conversations among groups of women. These group discussions, in which women have shared stories of the joys, worries, burdens, thoughts, and dreams that shape their lives, have sometimes been trivialized by being called "coffee-klatches" or "tea parties." Such gatherings, however, have provided a life-line for women whose work in the home or in their jobs outside the home otherwise would keep them isolated from other women, and from the empowering recognition that they are not alone in their experiences or feelings about their lives. It is also in such groups, in morning Bible study classes, or in church women's circles, that women have learned to raise questions of the Bible and of the dominant culture's interpretations of those scriptures that have such a powerful effect on their lives for both good and ill. In the midst of praying the Psalms and finding strength for their lives in the stories and affirmations found in the Bible, many women have recognized that the Bible is a book in which women are left on the margins if not completely off the page. Sometimes their absence is striking. Where was the mother when the prodigal came home? What did Sarah say when Abraham took Isaac to the mountain? Sometimes the marginalization is more subtle, as when women are present, but only as background characters, and not as active participants. Even stories about women seem to be told from outside of women's experience, and in terms of their importance for a man's story. For example, stories about Sarah and Hagar and about Rachel and Leah are told to introduce their sons whom God has promised to Abraham and Jacob, not to tell us about these women. Similarly, the narratives at the beginning of Luke's Gospel introduce Mary and Elizabeth only as the mothers of Jesus and John the Baptist. After the births of their sons, both fade from importance in the story. The narratives convey men's views of women's realities, and the social norms that are assumed or prescribed are those of a patriarchal society—men's prescriptions for how women ought to behave.

By and large, the interpretations of the dominant culture do not even take notice of such biases built into the biblical texts, and of the added task necessary for women to translate themselves into many parts of the Bible. Women meeting in groups to study the Bible often recognize that this book, complete with its usual interpretations, is a commentary on their own life experiences within the dominant, patriarchal social structure. However, within these groups many women have been able to draw on their own and each other's experiences to raise questions, both of the biblical record and of interpretations of that text. In so doing they have realized that the recognized commentators and official interpreters do not speak for them. On the other hand, they have also realized the extent to which they have internalized that official interpretation, in as much as it has been accepted as "natural" or "normal." Finding support in such groups, women have found the courage to engage the Bible in relation to their own social contexts.

As they have come to recognize the importance of social location in shaping the reading of texts, these women have articulated and demonstrated the importance of this step for all interpreters. As they have come face to face with the rich diversity of stories and realities of women's lives in their own group of conversation partners, many have become increasingly sensitive to the factors that separate as well as those that unite them as women. They have come to appreciate differences of race, class, age, able-bodiedness, marital status, or sexual orientation, for example, as important shapers of their contexts and of their insights as interpreters of the Bible.

Insights that come to us from communities such as these—communities that recognize so clearly the impact of social location on biblical interpretation—have informed our decision to begin the journey at home. Experiences of the vitality of communal study in these communities prompt us to encourage the study of biblical texts in and by groups. As we have already noted above, such a communal approach already challenges a major premise of the worldview of the dominant Western culture. The process of communal study itself thus serves as a reminder that each interpretation is the product of the social context of a given reading. By acknowledging that each person brings a unique and valued insight to the understanding of the text, a group begins to experience the impact of social location on interpretation. By participating in a process that seeks a communal understanding of the text, the group struggles with the tension between the recognition that each interpretation offered must be taken seriously by all others in the group, the knowledge that no reading is definitive, and the awareness that not every reading has a creative or life-affirming impact on the lives of the interpreters themselves, or on others whose lives they touch. This dynamic demands an effort to understand both the world of each individual reader in the group and the world of the group as a community that struggles with a particular biblical text.

Selecting the Biblical Text

At this point it is time to turn attention to the selection of the biblical text that will be the focus of the study. That may seem a strange addition to this section on locating the readers, but it is appropriate for three reasons. First, the particular text under consideration brings into focus specific aspects of the readers' contexts that are relevant to it. A healing story in one of the Gospels, for example, calls attention to the readers' assumptions about health and illness, and their experiences with formal and informal resources for medical care. One's identity as a descendant of persons held as slaves in the southern United States or as a member of one of the nations of native peoples on that continent will affect whether the story of Israel's journey out of Egypt and into the "promised land" is experienced as a story of liberation or a saga of conquest and oppression. Second, the biblical text itself becomes very much a part of the context of this world in which the community lives. Particularly for people who recognize the Bible as Scripture and thus as in some sense authoritative, any given text chosen from the Bible provides a significant framework for interpreting their world. Third, the social context of the interpreters plays an important role in determining the process and criteria by which the text is selected.

Texts for reading or study may be selected in various ways. In some instances the text has been pre-determined. For example, scriptures for reading in worship and for preaching may be set by a lectionary, which is a list of readings (from both Testaments, and in some traditions also from the collection of "Deuterocanonical" or "Apocryphal" books) assigned by the church for each Sunday of the church year and for special holidays. A text, a biblical book, or a theme may be assigned by a professor in a class, or by a church school curriculum.

In other situations the text may be selected by those who will be studying it. A study group may choose to explore a particular book (Genesis, Jeremiah, Luke, or Revelation), a particular type of material (parables, healing stories, lament psalms, trickster tales, or apocalyptic literature), or a particular theme (discipleship, women and the Bible, or stewardship). There may be a text that one wants to study out of some particular interest, or that one simply feels led to study. One might seek a text from the Bible that seems appropriate or relevant to a particular issue or concern that one is seeking to understand—a text that would appear to provide some commentary on the situation, or that might help one discern God's presence or will in it. Or one might search for a text that would help one speak "God's word" as a word of judgment or a word of hope to a community in a particular situation. Of course, another approach to selecting a text is simply to drop the

Bible and see where it opens! The results of such a process could be both interesting and bizarre!

The advantage of working with assigned texts like lectionary readings is that it pushes people to explore unfamiliar territory and to struggle with "difficult" texts. There is less of a tendency to work only with favorite themes. But it is important to remember that someone or some group has selected these assigned texts too. In that process some "difficult" texts may have been omitted, or only those texts may have been chosen that support the interests and values of those doing the selecting.

In a classroom, the instructor typically makes selections according to criteria that may not be made explicit to the students. The instructor may be aware of some of those criteria, such as requiring students to deal with different types of literature or to deal with a variety of theological concerns. Other criteria may be unconscious, such as the unexamined dynamics of gender, racial, ethnic, class, or theological bias embedded in the professor's own education, preferred methodologies for biblical interpretation, politics, or confessional stance.

In the case of a lectionary, a church committee has made the selections. In that process, liturgical, theological, and sociological factors have influenced the committee and formed the criteria of selection. Again, some of these factors are stated explicitly, while others are not articulated. The membership of the selection committee, for example, already makes its own statement about whose agendas are and are not important to consider. Assumptions that are politically and theologically significant, such as the committee's understanding of the nature of the relationship between the two Testaments or prior ideas about thematic associations, influence the grouping of texts that are assigned to be read on a given day.

The lectionary also assumes congruence between the biblical texts and the contemporary context. This can lead a preacher to adopt a process of "application": Discover what the text says, and apply it to the immediate situation. In such a process, it is often tempting to focus on an apparent similarity of words or on abstract ideas, without examining more carefully differences in context or situations, or without considering the possible negative effects of such readings for some readers. Following such a procedure is, of course, not limited to work with lectionary texts. It is equally tempting, and perhaps even more so, when a preacher works with a text that seems to fit the particular issue or concern to be addressed.

When the group or individual selects the text for study, it is easier to get at the criteria on which the selection is based. But precisely because of this immediacy and familiarity, both individuals and groups are often tempted to take them for granted and not examine them. Some factors, of course, will be known and probably easily stated. Some question or some principle has led to the selection. But it is equally important to think about those dynamics that may not be as readily conscious, such as the cultural assumptions discussed earlier, and the role played by social location.

It is important to remember that engagement with the text begins with this very process of selection, which itself emerges from and is influenced by the social context of the interpreters. It is also important to remember that any individual passage belongs to a larger canonical literary composition. Not only is a unit that is selected for study or reading removed from its canonical literary context, it is also given a different immediate context. For example, if the text is read in a worship service, that setting becomes a new context of the text—a context that, in turn, has its own social role and origins. The text is now surrounded, not by the literature that surrounds it in the Bible, but by the language and actions of the particular liturgy, which include such elements as other Bible texts (with which it is now placed in immediate juxtaposition), prayers, responses, musical selections, and the sermon. Or, in a quite different situation, if the chosen text is placed in the context of a study on parables, for example, it is now read with the collection of parables selected for study and any study books used as secondary resources. This new setting for the text also conveys its own methods of interpretation and its own social setting.

This is the first of several sections, woven into the chapters of this book but distinguished by a different typeface, in which we—Fred and Sharon—become interpreters with you, and demonstrate this method of biblical interpretation by doing the steps just described.

We have chosen Luke 14:25-35 as the central text for our study. We have deliberately selected a text on which we have not led numerous Bible studies. Our conviction is that this general roadmap can guide one through any text, and thus our goal has been to challenge ourselves with a text on which neither of us had worked extensively. It is also a text that is not an obvious "form" or literary type. It is not quite narrative, yet it has narrative qualities and a narrative context. It presents itself as a unit, yet the basis of its cohesion is not immediately obvious. Its subject matter is not explicitly Christology, yet it has christological implications. It deals with a common and popular theme within religious communities, yet it does so in language that we would rather avoid. It does not present itself as overtly "multi-cultural," yet, like all texts, it must be read with an awareness of cultural diversity.

There was also a specific occasion that called attention to this text. A pastor, having heard an exposition of the first part of Luke 14, said to Sharon: "It is the end of that chapter [verses 25-35] with which I need some help. No one ever talks about those sayings. But that is the material that I find troubling in my pastoral work." A later check of the commentaries and other study materials with which we are familiar confirms the fact that virtually no one comments on this text—at least not much. This pastor's plea, coming as it did from a particular church context, seemed to be an important challenge to the two of us, persons whose professional life is set in academic classrooms.

Factors That Define the Context of a Group

What questions, then, does one ask to probe the social location of the reader and the reading community as they confront any given text? One set of questions will be posed in terms of general social categories, such as nationality, gender, race, ethnic identity, class and economic status, age, sexual orientation, religious affiliation, and cultural assumptions. Obviously one cannot be exhaustive in this process of self-identification. Thus, being attuned to the issues of the text that will be read is particularly important. The specific issues and characteristics to be identified as forming one's context will be determined in some measure by the text under study.

If you have not yet done so, take time to read though the text on which you will be working (or the sample text for this study, Luke 14:25-35). Be particularly attentive to the spheres of life addressed and the particular issues raised. For example, if one issue on which the text appears to focus is the family, attention to one's own experiences of family and to one's cultural assumptions about families will be especially significant in one's interaction with that text. On the other hand, one must be cautious about assuming too quickly that one can identify the issues of a text. For example, as the sample text will illustrate, what look initially like family issues may turn out to address another arena of life entirely, such as economic security and social status. For such reasons, it is important to be suspicious of the issues which are usually or immediately identified as the focus of a text, for those very issues, and the ways they are formulated, are themselves a product of the reader's social location and over-riding concerns.

With some texts it might be important to acknowledge as part of one's context the assumptions one brings about such issues as the relationship between religious and secular arenas of life, economic systems, political structures, the origin and treatment of disease, or the importance of communal stability and security. In Euro-American contexts, for example, primary value in the economic arena is granted to private property, but that is not a value shared by many other cultures where questions of community well-being are paramount, and where the plenty or scarcity of resources defines the well-being of the entire society. Attitudes toward such issues and values inevitably affect one's reading of biblical texts dealing with land tenure, wealth and poverty, work and idleness, or economic suffering and marginalization.

To cite another example of the complex dimensions of the context that affects one's reading, if a biblical text deals with healing, it is important to identify assumptions about health, illness and health care delivery. Do you share the assumptions of modern Western medicine that injury, a specific virus or bacterium, a genetic irregularity, or a biochemical disorder lies at the root of most forms of illness and disability? What awareness and appreciation do you hold for the wisdom inherent in many of the traditional healing arts, which are more attuned to the role of the human psyche and spirit in both illness and well-being? What has been your own experience with illness? Do you or the other members of the study group have access to adequate health care? Are any of you unable to get medical insurance because of the cost of the coverage or because of an existing illness? Do you know of families whose resources have been depleted as a result of a catastrophic illness or injury? How have you experienced the social dimensions of illness and injury? Has injury or illness resulted in a physical condition that has limited public access for you or a person close to you? Have you experienced, directly or indirectly, the social responses to a person living with AIDS?

It is not easy to begin to assess and define such cultural assumptions. These assumptions are so much a part of the environment that they are accepted as "reality." They define the way things really are. One way that people often begin to recognize the particularity and peculiarity of their own cultural assumptions is through an encounter with cultural realities that other communities take for granted. Another way is through a deliberate process of "conscientization," such as that described earlier in relation to Christian base communities and women's groups. One's cultural assumptions are so thoroughly a part of everyone's reality—like the very air that one breathes—that participants within groups must help each other to recognize what they are breathing so naturally and normally. Like the air itself, an enveloping culture is necessary for life, but it can become toxic, and it is crucial to know the difference!

A second set of questions examines what is going on generally in the world of current events. What are the issues presenting themselves in the news media? What issues are brought to our attention by such other means as newsletters of organizations, the "alternative press," community associations, or global connections and contacts? Are some of these issues not discussed in the public media? Why? How are such issues handled by the media? What impact do these issues have on one's community today? Attention should be paid to global, national, regional, and local concerns; and efforts should be made to comprehend the impact both of local events, actions, and decisions on the larger society and the world, and of global decisions on local conditions.

In addition, it is important to pay attention to what is happening in the lives of individual members of the group. Perhaps an individual interpreter will want to acknowledge matters of concern in her or his own life. Has a plant closing meant unemployment for a member of the group, or a farm foreclosure resulted in the loss of a home and livelihood? Or perhaps a member is struggling with a decision about a career change, or an illness in a family has left them facing financial ruin. What larger economic and structural issues are raised by these personal dilemmas? For example, in the United States the larger framework surrounding the issue of the accessibility of treatment for an illness is political wrangling over a national plan for health insurance.

Some of the matters that affect the people who constitute a particular group of interpreters belong to the common human experience shared by people of all economic classes, all racial or ethnic groups—in short, all social categories. Such experiences include the dynamics of interpersonal relationships, illness, birth, death, and violence in the home or as part of most urban and many suburban communities. Despite the fact that these are realities common to most if not all people, the range of responses to these human situations will be set by such factors as cultural norms, social and economic resources, and personal experiences. For example, women who have experienced some measure of social and economic independence (often through the experience of working outside the home) and women who lack such resources may both know the pain of domestic violence. That common suffering is a point of human contact between them. On the other hand, the way in which that common pain is experienced and the options for response are influenced significantly by social and economic resources, by other life experiences, and by the attitudes of and resources provided by the larger community. The specific dimensions of these common human experiences that make each of them unique cannot be ignored. Each person's story, each community's story, and each people's story must be attended to as making a unique contribution to a group's understanding of the world in which they live. Each particular story suggests the distinctive perspective and the special contribution that each reader brings to the encounter with texts.

Even when a group of interpreters has done the basic work of identifying their context, aspects of that step need to be reviewed each time the group gathers, or each time an individual interpreter sits down to work. Some factors of that identity and context obviously remain constant, but others can undergo both subtle and dramatic shifts in a relatively short time. For example, relationships begin or end or undergo crises. Economic security can vanish with the sudden loss of a job. Illness or an accident can strike without warning to create a crisis related to health care. A local or neighborhood occurrence—a vicious crime or the hope-filled opening of a new school—can change one's sense of the safety or desirability of one's immediate environment.

Events around the world can have a stunning impact, as news media bring immediate awareness of the effect that civil wars, "natural" disasters, or economic shifts can have on loved ones in other regions, on persons and groups with whom one is in solidarity, and on one's own sense of living in a secure world.

In an important sense, the step of re-establishing the interpreters' context reflects the principle attributed to Karl Barth, that one should always do theology with the Bible in one hand and the daily newspaper in the other. That advice is particularly wise in light of connections that can be recognized between contemporary events and the specific themes or motifs of texts to be studied. In fact, those contemporary events and experiences can influence what is deemed important or even what details one notices in a biblical passage.

Sometimes the specific agenda of the passage or even the type of passage one is studying makes that connection particularly vivid. For example, if a group is studying the story of the healing of the man beside the pool in John 5 soon after a member of the community has died of AIDS, questions will likely focus sharply on such issues as why some are healed and others not, and how illness and healing—or the absence of healing—figure in God's will for human lives. News of escalating violence and suffering in a war or in civil unrest in some region of the world will shape the reading of a psalm of lament or the narratives of Israel's "conquest" of Canaan. News of moral scandals in high places of the government will influence a group's response to narratives of King David's exploits and chicanery.

Similarly, personal events in the lives of interpreters shape their particular sensitivities. A new grandchild born to a member of the group will clearly shape the reading of the story of the birth of Samuel. That reading will be shaped in another way by the presence in the group of someone experiencing difficulty in conceiving or bearing a long-desired child, or someone having recently aborted a fetus. If someone in the group, or someone known to them, is caught in the web of family violence, the "household codes" (Col. 3:18–4:1; Eph. 5:22–6:9; 1 Pet. 2:18–3:7) with their injunctions of submission and obedience will present particular problems of interpretation. If someone has just received a promotion, or lost a job, or had a mortgage foreclosed, that experience may affect how thoroughly an interpreter will be able to accept Paul's indictment of a merit system of "works," in favor of

45

"justification by grace." Such experiences, or a recent (or freshly remembered) experience of discrimination or harassment in one's place of work, can alter one's reading of the parable of the workers in the vineyard (Matt. 20:1-16) or of the prophets' many cries for justice toward the poor and vulnerable members of their society.

In addition to the content of texts, the type of literature one is studying might also highlight certain aspects of one's context. For example, if the focus of the study is to be a psalm, the role of hymns and other music in the interpreters' lives becomes an important factor of the context. In addition, the particular role the Book of Psalms has played in the worship, devotional, or pastoral experiences of members of the group will shape their expectations of any particular psalm. Cultural attitudes toward the expression of anger or grief or other emotions will also have relevance for one's work on these poems, and it will be helpful to identify these attitudes at the beginning of the process. If the study is to focus on one of Paul's letters, people's experiences with different types of letters become important. Have official letters from a government communicated welcome or dreaded news affecting one's own circumstances or the lives of loved ones? Have personal letters been a vital link to family members in a land from which members of the group are in exile? Is someone waiting or longing for such a letter that never comes?

In a process of group Bible study, it is thus crucial that each individual be encouraged to acknowledge the life experiences and specific cultural contexts that he or she brings to that process. In the sharing of personal stories, individuals begin to locate themselves in relation to the group as well as to the text. Such sharing is especially important, given the fact that many groups turn out to be relatively homogeneous. The richness of the diversity that can be recognized when particular life experiences are shared will be evident even in an apparently homogeneous group, and it will enrich even further those groups with greater diversity.

The growing sense within the group of the diversity of contexts and perspectives present, and of the richness that diversity brings, prompts an awareness also of the diversity which is not present—of the absent or silent voices. Later in this guide we will talk about the need to find ways to be attentive to those voices as well. The purpose is not simply to multiply information, to accumulate a variety of

46

interesting perspectives, or to collect exotic ideas from different people and places. The goal is rather that each participant's world be transformed through the encounter with the worlds of other interpreters, as they come into dialogue with the biblical text.

It is important also to recognize that any group in which one is working is more than the sum of its members. The group also has a corporate identity and history that must be acknowledged. What is the history of the group? What was the occasion for its formation, or what is the purpose of its existence? Does the group have a long history of work together, or has it come together for this particular study? Is it part of a larger community that has a shared history? Is the group seeking to discern its own particular mission within a congregation? Is it a group that is newly formed, but composed of long-time members of a congregation? Is the group gathered around a particular professional task, such as a clergy group that has gathered for a lectionary Bible study as part of their sermon preparation? Or is this a group brought together at a regional gathering, so that the participants and their local situations are basically unknown to each other? Do members of the group share in a common worship life? Do they belong to a common worshiping tradition, even if members worship in different congregational settings? Or do they come from dramatically different liturgical experiences or, perhaps for some, from none at all? Is the group relatively homogeneous in terms of class, gender, racial and ethnic identity, nationality, culture, religious identity, able-bodiedness, occupation, sexual identity, family status, age, and life experiences, or is it somewhat diverse?

The answers to these questions will help determine the kinds of questions that need to be addressed in identifying the world of the readers. A group with a long history will have stored in its collective memory considerable information about the social realities of individuals and about the group's shared experiences. For example, a church will carry memories associated with its building or with key leaders, or memories of important decisions and the dynamics that surrounded them (including, perhaps, strong feelings about their consequences). In such instances what is needed may be more a process of recalling, reminding, and updating. In a newly formed group much more information will need to be shared, but in such a group there is also more room for the group to define its identity, purpose, and task, at least initially, though with the recognition that that self-presentation will be modified in and by the experience of the group. This process of unfolding of the group's identity is ongoing and continuing, just as the world of the interpreters and the very people themselves are not static. Each new occasion creates a new constellation of factors that define the social location of the group.

The Role of the Spirit in Interpretation

A conviction which we share and which undergirds this study guide is a belief that the Spirit is at work within the particular and concrete lives of individuals and groups. Thus, to deny the important perspective and insights that each individual brings would be to limit a group's access to the wisdom of the Spirit. On the other hand, any individual's or any group's ability to grasp the teachings of the Spirit is shaped by their peculiar social contexts. They perceive the Spirit through the lenses of personal experience and awareness. This is not a criticism, nor a negative judgment, but rather an acknowledgment that all persons are finite creatures. However, if one person or group invokes the Spirit in a claim to speak universally—that is, presumes to speak as if they are privileged to mediate the divine voice on behalf of all, and to deny that other points of view or other voices might be equally valid bearers of God's creative presence—the Spirit's role is thwarted.

Worship, prayer, or meditation can convey deep significance to the reader or reading community, and can allow them to experience God's presence in the process of reading and interpreting the Bible. Such acts of devotion or spiritual discipline, however, are not substitutes for study. Rather, the Spirit is active in both approaches to biblical texts. It is also important to remember that worship and prayer themselves are not individual or private phenomena, even when they are intensely personal, but instead they have a communal origin and context. Worship and prayer life grow out of specific traditions and reflect the tastes, beliefs, and practices of specific communities. People pray in the languages and forms they have been taught. Thus, while prayer and worship offer neither a "pure" encounter with God nor unmediated insight into a biblical text, the spirit of one's worship and prayer life—including its openness or closedness to the Spirit's presence in other voices—constitutes an important part of a community's or a

48

person's self-understanding and identity. It is part of the definition of the "home" where this particular journey of biblical interpretation begins.

In this section we will locate ourselves in relation to two related but distinct endeavors. One is the writing of the book; the other is our study of the specific biblical text, Luke 14:25-35. It seems important to share something of the context within which the "road-map" itself emerged, and within which it continues to develop, as well as to describe something of our setting for the interpretation of the biblical text. Many of the factors are common to the context of both endeavors, but there are also some factors which are of particular significance to the discrete tasks.

The movement toward the writing of this book began for us when we team-taught a foundational class in biblical studies at the seminary where we were both members of the faculty. At that time we did share a common institutional setting, with its liturgical life, governance, mission, and social context. Soon after that, however, Sharon moved to a different seminary, though a seminary affiliated with the same denomination. Thus our reading community (of two persons) is one in which we each share some knowledge about the other's context—and, indeed, the two seminaries share many common characteristics—but we no longer live and teach in the same immediate community.

Both of us also bring experiences of teaching in seminaries of other traditions. Fred has taught for a number of years at a Quaker seminary, with its "free-church" polity and its identity as a historic "peace church." Sharon is currently an adjunct professor at an ecumenical seminary in Central America, whose students work at the graduate, undergraduate, and "popular" levels of theological education. The context of ministry in the midst of the liberation struggles of the students' and other faculty members' home countries shapes the educational and theological task even more powerfully than do the academic standards of the university system to which the school relates.

In addition, we share another common community, that of the "academy." This includes both the formally organized professional guild of biblical scholars (the Society of Biblical Literature) and the more informal network of academic associations, publication systems, and other methods of interchange, and the scholarly norms of accountability that characterize theological education in the United States.

As individuals we share several common characteristics, enough so that we are a relatively homogeneous reading community. We are of a similar age, which is to say that we were both shaped by the events of the 1960s—the civil rights movement, the anti-war movement, and the assassinations of Martin Luther King, Jr., Malcolm X, and John and Robert Kennedy. We were involved in the civil rights and anti-war movements as middle class Euro-Americans—activities that reflected early stages of our awareness of race, class, and political analysis. We are both ordained clergy in mainline (though different) denominations, both hold Ph.D.s, and both hold tenured positions in seminaries related to a major Protestant denomination. Thus we share privileged status economically and professionally. We did, however, both choose to "interrupt" our educational journeys (at a time when this was less common than it is today), in the one instance during seminary, in the other early in a doctoral program. In both instances that decision grew out of a dis-ease with the educational process that we were undergoing. Both have enjoyed extended travel, study and work in Europe, the Middle East, Africa, and Latin America, and each has developed fluency in languages other than English. Neither of us comes from a family with professional connections to academy or church.

There are also important differences, for example of childhood experiences, gender, marital status, and the composition of the households in which we currently live. Sharon spent her childhood as an only child, living for a number of years in Europe on military bases, and the rest of the time in a small town in New Hampshire. Fred is the oldest of eight children, growing up in a small Kansas town. Both, however, have experienced a network of extended family relationships.

Sharon entered seminary and was ordained at a time when women in these ranks were rare. Fred experienced the same educational and vocational realities as a member of the dominant gender group. Our paths to an awareness of the importance of gender analysis were thus quite different.

The composition of our immediate households also differs, though in both cases there have been recent transitions. Fred and Linda, his wife, are now "empty nesters," having recently watched their only child leave home to attend college. Sharon and Hilda, her mother, now live together, after the death of her father. In both cases we are talking about small households. On the other hand we are aware of and have been involved as friends, colleagues, and pastors with persons living out other household patterns, both within our own society and in other cultures.

All of these family experiences and circumstances influence our attitudes and understanding of "family," which is one sphere of life addressed by the text we are studying (see Luke 14:26). Our experiences in the 1960s and 1970s, as well as in Latin America, Africa, and the Middle East, play a significant role in shaping attitudes about war and peace, and we read of the king "going out to wage war" (see Luke 14:31-32) through lenses molded by those events. We have grown up in a culture that places high value on pragmatic planning for the future (compare Luke 14:28-30), and a society in which success is measured by possessions—"The one who dies with the most toys wins!" (in contrast to Luke 14:33). Neither of us is hearing impaired, so we can respond to Luke 14:35b without feeling excluded by the assumption of "hearing."

We write this book at a time when we perceive within religious communities a growing hunger for Bible study, which is reflected in the development of many new programs and study materials, such as the *Disciple* Bible Study program of The United Methodist Church. This hunger is often coupled with an alienation from traditional methods by which Bible study has been conducted. It is not so much that the methods do not offer important insights or information, but that these methods seem not to connect to people's lives. They also perpetuate an authoritarian approach that defers to the experts to determine both the questions to be asked and the answers to be given. Too often the questions have not been those of the groups engaged in Bible study in the churches.

Within the arena of academic theology there has been a proliferation of new scholarly methods. Even more significant, the gender and racial or ethnic composition of the theological academy has begun to change dramatically. This is true of our particular seminaries and of the scholarly guild alike. No longer are these exclusively—though they still are predominantly—composed of Euro-American males. As persons from other social and cultural contexts have joined their voices to the conversation, they have identified, both explicitly and implicitly, the role that social location plays in determining the approaches used, the questions asked, and the perspectives brought to bear on biblical texts (as well as on other aspects of the theological

51

task). By raising these questions they have also reminded us anew that many interpreters of the Bible are not members of the academic guild.

We have already noted important learnings from non-academic or "popular" contexts, such as the "Invisible Institution" within the culture of enslaved persons in the United States or from the Christian base communities in countries of Latin America. Some of these groups, such as some women's groups or caucuses of historically excluded groups, have functioned on the margins of the academic community. It is not yet clear whether the academic guild will be transformed by their presence, or whether it will simply be expanded to make room for these other interpreters without truly engaging them.

We are also aware of historical factors that urge us to take seriously the global dimensions and inter-connected dynamics of the world in which we live. We experience the paradox of growing tribalism and growing internationalism, both in local communities and in global politics and economics. We struggle with the tension between the temptations of rigid dogmatism and the flight to total relativism, both within and between religious groups and within and between other social and political organizations.

In terms of the biblical text (Luke 14:25-35), we find ourselves struggling with issues of discipleship in relation to the very issues identified above. We are also aware that these questions are being asked in and for a world that often feels as if it is falling apart. We feel more strongly called to "rescue" the family, rather than to hate family members. In fact, the media report far too many instances of violence and abuse within the family, and of violence done to families by the institutions of society.

We also live in a society that claims to be dealing with ever more limited resources. Thus there is an ever greater pressure to "count the (ecological as well as the financial) costs" before beginning any new undertaking. Human costs are less frequently a part of the formula. Our own seminaries struggle constantly with economic realities that confront both the institutions themselves and the people involved in them. Increasingly the costs of seminary education are being carried by the students, through higher tuition. What does one say about discipleship to a student who feels caught between a clear sense of call to pastoral ministry and a growing indebtedness? Will the programmatic decisions made by our institutions be governed only by the pragmatic criteria of financial calculations? What does discipleship mean in such a context, and what is the particular voice of our passage in that conversation?

Taking Stock of Where We Are

This journey, then, begins at home, but it does not begin in isolation. In fact, that beginning point serves as a reminder of the many persons and factors that participate in creating this place called "home." The text to be studied itself participates in creating that environment, and the environment gives an immediate context to the text. To ignore that context is truly to neglect an important aspect of the reality of the text. A text does not have meaning apart from the context in which it communicates, and that communication will be shaped by the context in which it takes place. Thus the interpreters' context must be described.

Beginning at home also serves as a reminder that this social context is but one of a multitude of homes. To acknowledge the specificities of the interpreters' immediate context is also to recognize that neither it nor any setting is universal. "Home" is not only the starting place of one's own work, but also the basis for relating to other persons and their starting places. Any home context, though distinguishable from all others, is not separable from those others. To begin at home opens the expectation that new horizons will be encountered and that home itself will be transformed in the process of one's interaction with a biblical text and other readers.

Chapter 2

Encountering the Biblical Text: Read, Feel, Question, React

First Impressions

The first step in encountering a biblical text is similar to the early stages of a relationship with a person. When you meet a person, you form initial impressions, become aware of feelings, and begin to recognize questions you want to ask in order to get to know the person. These initial responses often change over time as the relationship grows, and questions that once seemed significant fade into the background as others prove to be more important. Yet first impressions usually set the tone of a relationship. Acknowledging them allows you to test them against the data of further experience with a person, and to recognize how those initial reactions might be affecting how you process subsequent information and experiences.

In the case of a biblical text, the first step toward interpretation is to *read the passage carefully*, and to read it or hear it read aloud, or to see it signed. Even—perhaps especially—when it is a passage with which you are already familiar, pay close attention to the specific words and details by which it unfolds. Take time to acknowledge aloud or to make notes of your initial impressions, reactions, and questions in response to the passage.

It is important to keep a record of work on a text, beginning from these very first impressions. This sort of Bible study is best done with a group of people committed to sharing the process together. The conversations themselves can serve as a community record, or you may want to have one of the participants jot down key ideas on newsprint or in a notebook. If you find yourself having to work alone, a pile of scrap paper on which you can keep track of questions and responses along the way is one of the most important tools for biblical interpretation. As your work on a passage progresses, you will never again be able to recover the freshness of the questions and insights of the earlier stages, and it is important not to lose them, even if eventually you decide they were unhelpful. If *you* began there, chances are that others may also, and you will have a bridge over which to cross to meet them where they are, even after you become an expert on a passage. On the other hand, it is important to talk with others and recognize the very different places from which people begin in their interaction with a text. What seems obvious to you may be a fresh insight to someone else, and conversely, their reactions can open up new angles of vision on the text for you.

Being Attentive to the Biblical Text

Read the passage several times, until its themes and its language are so familiar to you that you can paraphrase it or even recite it. Read it in different ways. For example, a group might want to read a psalm antiphonally and in unison, or you might read a narrative as a drama in which different members of the group take the various characters' parts. Read the passage in different translations. If you know other languages, read the passage in those languages as well. Are you aware of different nuances of meanings of words, or different feelings evoked by the various translations? Again, make notes of those differences, perhaps in the form of questions you might want to explore later.

Pay attention to the feelings the passage evokes. What details prompt those feelings—specific words, affirmations, questions, characters, situations? What is it about the passage itself or in your own experience that lies behind those feelings? Do your feelings differ from the ones you think the author may have intended (for instance, do you find yourself getting angry at a story or a theological affirmation that is presented in a positive light)? Do your responses differ from the ones you have been told were intended? Think about why you may have been instructed to respond in these specific ways. Again, make notes to yourself about all of these steps, or take time to share them aloud in the group with which you are working.

As you carry out these repeated readings of the text, be on the alert for "speed bumps" in the text—details that catch your attention and demand closer inspection because they have evoked particularly strong feelings, or because they seem unclear, especially vivid, out of place, or inconsistent. Some of those speed bumps may have to do with the meanings of words that seem unusual, unclear, or especially important in the passage. Others may concern characters, customs, activities, institutions, or relationships that are foreign or troubling to you. Still others may result from the juxtaposition of steps in an argument that do not seem to fit together, or from an unusual sequence in a narrative. For example, what is not said that you expect will be? What is said that seems out of place, or that you were not expecting? Make notes of these points, because they will provide a way to focus your subsequent research about the passage.

If you are working alone or in a group that appears to be fairly homogeneous, try to imagine how people from other racial, ethnic, economic, or cultural backgrounds, or whose life experiences have been different, might read this text. Of course none of us can read *for* other people, but it is important to develop sensitivity to issues that may be of concern, and to images or situations that may be problematic to others. Note these points as questions that will serve as reminders to engage other readers—as, in fact, you will be instructed to do in a later step in this process. For example, the stories of Israel's flight from Egypt and journey into the promised land clearly assume the perspective of that "chosen people," and portray God's ways of blessing them and bringing about what has been promised to them. The other peoples the Israelites encounter on the way are barely noticed by most readers of the stories. For Native Americans and other Indigenous peoples, however, the fate of these "–ites," as one woman calls them (referring to the frequently cited lists of peoples such as the Hittites, the Girgashites, the Amorites, the Canaanites, the Perizzites, the Hivites, and the Jebusites), tells their own story. Not only does the callous treatment of these tribal peoples resident in the land reflect the Indigenous peoples' own pain, but the general silence about the lives and cultures of these groups leaves many Indigenous people with a deep longing to hear these missing stories.

You will not even recognize some of the questions others bring instinctively from their own experience and identity, and their concerns and problems will probably not even occur to you, but this initial exercise of a sympathetic imagination is an important place to begin. Knowing that the text evokes feelings and concerns within yourself, you will want to read in a way that allows room for the responses of others. This is particularly important for those interpretations that have the privilege of public authority, such as in preaching or in teaching.

Be alert also for images, phrases, or words whose meanings are puzzling to you as a modern reader. Are there allusions to cultural or ritual practices which would probably have been familiar to the early audiences, but which are no longer readily recognizable by most modern readers? It is important not to assume that we understand what was meant in a text by words that have become common in the life of the church. Their meanings may have changed since a word was used in the Gospels, for example, or in one of the psalms, and what we think we understand based on current associations may be misleading. Be aware of what *is* said in the very specific words of the text one is studying, and also what is assumed or otherwise left *unsaid*.

On first impression Luke 14:25-35 strikes us as a rather strange group of sayings, seemingly rather unrelated. Some verses even seem to be at odds with each other. The two examples (of the tower builder and the warring king) appear to counsel prudence and caution, whereas the sayings on discipleship seem radical and uncompromising. The various parts of the passage seem unrelated, if not actually contradictory, and we have to ask ourselves on what logical basis Luke has put them together.

Focusing on specific sayings, we wonder what "hate" means in the injunction to hate family. Does it really mean "hate" as we use the word? Does a disciple have no right to love his or her family, and—even worse—must he or she turn against them? How would this verse be heard by the survivor of abuse within a family? Is it a warrant for hating those at whose hand she suffered? Or what about the child or the spouse of a pastor or of a lay person who is so involved in the work of their church that he or she virtually abandons the family? Or what of the member of a family of someone committed around the clock to crusades for social justice or any moral cause? How would such persons feel about a demand that they see as having robbed them of a parent's or a spouse's time and attention? Or does this saying give warrant to the abandonment of aging parents, while one pursues noble ends? Does a disciple really not value intimate relationships?

How would the *Comadres*—those mothers from El Salvador whose children have "been disappeared"—read such a text? Love of family is one of the impulses that has compelled them to resist and to struggle for justice and basic human rights, which many of them would identify as crucial dimensions of their Christian discipleship. How does one read such a text in the presence of persons like these, who dream that their children and grandchildren will be able to live with dignity, and who are drawn by that dream to share as families in the organized struggle for justice in their land? Or what about the political refugee who has fled homeland and family and who longs to be reunited with them? Do such longings and abiding love and loyalty mean that these people cannot be disciples of Jesus?

Does this text assume that only men—married ones at that—can be disciples, since the list of family that must be hated includes "wife," but does not mention "husband"? We read elsewhere about women following Jesus: Were they not disciples? What about women in the church of Luke's day? Were their roles different from those of men, and, if so, what did being a disciple mean for them? What about unmarried men? By Luke's day had they been excluded from the very positions of leadership for which Paul thought it best that one not be married (1 Cor. 7:32-35)? Had the demands of church leadership changed dramatically in the intervening years? How do we read such sayings in the context of the new groupings of people that consider themselves "families" in today's context? What are the impediments to discipleship today?

How is the requirement to hate "life itself" received by people suffering from depression? Does it become a warrant for suicide? Or can it lead to a life-denying attitude such that God-given talent and life are denied and devalued in the pursuit of discipleship?

What does it mean to "carry the cross"? Crucifixion was a means of execution used by the Romans, but today we often hear it as just a burden to carry (as Radar misquoted on the television show "M*A*S*H": "That's just another bear we all gotta cross!"). If we are not going to trivialize the demand in that way, what does it mean for those of us living in privileged circumstances of wealth and stability? Are people living in the "conflicted zones" of the world the only ones who can be disciples today?

Another detail that would seem not to be critical to the meaning of the text but that evokes our curiosity nevertheless is the idea of building a tower. Why would a person build a tower? Who would build a tower? Is this a project likely to be undertaken by a common citizen, or are we talking about public buildings or part of the estate of a wealthy person? Is the example of the tower-builder just advice to "count the cost" and not over-extend oneself? This seems a trivial follow-up to the saying about carrying the cross! What is going on here besides not making a fool of oneself?

What should be made of the fact that military strategy is invoked uncritically as guidance for "right living"? And what image of peace making does this offer, if seeking peace is simply a strategy of the weaker combattant to avoid defeat? Does this passage in fact portray peace as nothing more than a form of submission to superior power?

Must one really give up all one's possessions in order to be a disciple? Who, then, is truly a disciple? Anyone? Does "all my possessions" even include food and the home that provides shelter? What about the automobile that carries me to work? If my most prized "possession" is my education, which might be put to use for good ends, why should I give that up? What does it mean to give it up? A demand to give up everything as a condition of discipleship sounds unreasonable and hard. And how would such a view of material goods be heard in the ghetto, in the *barrio*, or in a village that has been ravaged by war or other disaster, and that lacks basic necessities? Is their destitution a mark of discipleship, a social tragedy, or even evidence of institutional violence committed against vulnerable peoples and communities? Can the text really be portraying destitution as a positive condition, when the lack of basic necessities is destructive of health and even life for so many of the earth's people? Is *that* what the gospel demands?

The saying about salt is just dropped into the text without explanation, like a proverb that everyone would get right away. What practices or uses of salt underlie that saying? What does it mean that salt is not "fit for the ground"—or "for the manure pile"? One would assume that even salt "fit for the ground" serves some useful function, but here it sounds as though the salt is worse than useless—a kind of toxic waste. The basic meaning seems to be clear enough even if we don't know the details: Be salty—that is, be useful—or be discarded (carefully, where no harm will be done). But the details underlying the meaning may be worth checking, since it still doesn't make a lot of sense in this context. What is the "salty taste" of discipleship that should not be lost? It is clear that we are to be "salty," but what does "being salty" entail?

Similar to this question of saltiness is the notion of discipleship itself. "Disciple" is used frequently in the text. This is also a very common word in our religious vocabulary and therefore very familiar to most of us. It is used more generally in our culture as well. For example, we say that x is a disciple of y, meaning that x follows in the basic school of thought or practice of y. But does the word "disciple" in this text mean the same thing we mean by it?

How does a person who is hearing impaired read the concluding sentence, "Let anyone with ears to hear listen!"?

Remembering Past and Other Experiences with the Text

Often when we meet someone for the first time, our initial impressions are shaped by what we have heard about them ahead of time, or by someone else of whom they remind us. Similarly, when we begin to study a particular text in the Bible, our initial response has usually been shaped by some prior contact, either directly in church or synagogue, or indirectly through the culture. This is true both in Europe and North America, where art, music, literature, and legal systems bear evidence of the influence of the Bible, and also in those parts of the world where missionaries brought the Bible wrapped in that same cultural package.

For that reason, it is important to remember that none of us comes totally fresh to our reading of a biblical text. What we find there is shaped in part by what we expect to find. An important factor in those expectations is what we have learned and experienced from the various communities that have shaped us, and particularly from our religious communities or our communities of faith. For instance, memories of a rote or mechanical use of the Psalms in public worship can lead people to have difficulty recognizing them as texts that might carry any real meaning at all. Conversely, fond memories of the Psalms as bearers of the rhythms and cadences of important and meaningful rituals of the church can make it difficult for a person to recognize dissonances or even the troubling violence of such texts as Ps. 137:9.

The worship life of one's religious community and deeply ingrained attitudes toward other practices and traditions can provide implicit memories of interpretation that affect the readings of biblical texts. Passages presenting the priestly practices of ancient Israel, for example, may collide with a lifetime of experience—embodied memories—of more informal worship, and perhaps even of a negative assessment of "wooden" or "ritualistic" worship. Those same passages might intersect with memories that evoke prejudices against the Roman Catholic Church among some Protestants, or persistent anti-Jewish biases in the unconscious or even the conscious attitudes of some Christians.

The same anti-Jewish memories can affect one's reading of the legal material of the Hebrew Bible, leading to its dismissal as legalistic or as something superseded or even discredited by Paul's version of the gospel. In that case, extra care is needed to help readers be open to positive values carried in many of the laws (support of justice and the defense of vulnerable members of the society, as in Lev. 19:9-17; 25:1-55, for example), as well as to the narrative foundation of Torah and its celebration as a welcome gift from a gracious God.

Memories of the typical casting of legal and liturgical materials as belonging to the Hebrew Bible can make it difficult for readers to recognize that one might well be looking at both types of material in the New Testament as well. Legal material is scattered through the Sermon on the Mount (Matthew 5–7), for example, and abounds in the ethical or "parenetic" sections of the letters. Liturgical materials are found in the doxologies with which most of the letters end, and in hymns found in John 1:1-18 and Phil. 2:5-11, among other places. There are also prayers (Luke 11:2-4 par. Matt. 6:9-13; John 17) and traditions related to the eucharist (1 Cor. 11:17-34; Matt. 26:26-29 par. Mark 14:22-25 par. Luke 22:15-20). In fact, the entire letter to the Hebrews is replete with highly liturgical forms and images.

Readers who have experienced portions of the Bible used against them because of their gender or their sexual identity usually find those memories standing between them and those texts. Particularly problematic is legal material designed to regulate women's behavior (for example, Eph. 5:22-24; Col. 3:18; Lev. 15:19-30) or condemning relations between persons of the same sex (Rom. 1:26-27; 1 Cor. 6:9). Where biblical texts have been used to excuse or justify suffering—such as the household codes being used to explain and permit the continuation of the battering of a woman by her husband, or to warrant the institution of slavery—the memories connected to the text may be so painful and powerful that a person may find it difficult to continue to study that text, particularly in a group context.

In another vein, the parables attributed to Jesus suffer greatly from over-familiarity. Sermons and Sunday school lessons have already told people countless times what a given parable means. Of all of the biblical texts, only the Christmas story in Luke 1–2 may suffer more than the parables from the problem of over-exposure! Identifying those remembered interpretations as specifically as possible is especially important if a parable (or the Christmas story, for that matter) is to receive a fresh reading. Remembered interpretations of parables often cluster under two distinct approaches to parables that have been current in the history of the church and of academic interpretation. One cluster will be allegorical readings, in which each detail of the story is equated with a parallel detail in the real world, and the sum of the details is concluded to reveal the meaning of the parable. The other cluster will come from those whose memories are of the single point, idea, or moral, of which the parable itself is seen as a narrative illustration. In both cases the meaning is usually seen as something in a distinctively religious sphere of life—a bias that tends to obscure the critique of social, economic, or political conditions or assumptions carried in many parables, and to limit questions and insights related to those spheres of life.

Genesis is a book that also taps rich veins of memories. Some are from readings in the religious community, and others have filtered through other cultural routes. For example, the creation stories in Genesis 1–3 are intricately intertwined with cultural attitudes toward gender and gender roles. In fact, it is not always easy to sort out whether the memory is of an interpreter's reading of Genesis, or whether it is a memory of the creation stories being used to interpret the culture. Stories from Genesis 1–11 often evoke memories of debates around the relationship between science and religion, or, more properly, between scientific and religious truth. Many of these memories come into focus through debates about public school curricula related to the origins of the cosmos. They connect also to attitudes about "myths of origin" from other cultures, and their relationship to the biblical stories. In short, these memories often uncover a deep uneasiness about the meaning and nature of truth—scientific, historical, religious, or moral—which is a set of questions close to the heart of the task of interpretation (see the discussion in chapter 11).

In moving through your study of a text, then, after having jotted down your own initial responses to the passage, take a few minutes to identify (in the group or in writing) what you remember having been told about the passage in sermons, in Sunday school, or in other church settings. How has this text been reflected in the popular culture? What have you heard in an academic context? If you have heard the passage connected to a particular theologian or preacher, you might find it worth investigating what that person has said about the text. For example, most Protestant Christians read Paul's treatment of "justification by faith" through the lens of Martin Luther's theology. Similarly, for North American Christians the account of the Exodus has been shaped by the wealth of readings—often communicated to the wider community through the music of spirituals and freedom songs—from the African American church tradition. It can be surprising to realize that such persons or groups, and not the biblical text itself, are the source of what we now assume a passage means.

What has been your response to the interpretations that you have experienced? Have you responded in anger or disgust at what you have been told? Have you found them to be helpful, or supportive, or perhaps a source of guidance? Have you experienced these interpretations as a put down? Or have you been puzzled or perplexed either about how such conclusions could possibly have been drawn, or about what they might mean for your own life? Not only the interpretations themselves, but also your feelings about them will influence your subsequent reading of the text. Remember, however, that these are interpretations to which you are now responding. You will want to test the validity of those interpretations against your own reading of the biblical text.

Remember also that it may not be only an interpretation of *this* particular text that shapes one's reading, but rather sermons or teachings on the same general theme. When we push our mental search button and enter "disciple," our minds will tend to retrieve every memory that contains disciple. This leads to the strong tendency to conflate all teachings on discipleship, to distill common themes, and to read every text on the topic in accordance with those themes. To go through such a process in order to develop a theory of discipleship can be a worthy project. But the development of a general concept cannot substitute for the exploration of the particular meaning the word has in a specific text.

In addition to the multiplicity of texts and interpretations on related subjects that clamor for attention as we begin to work on a particular text, we also take with us into that task a multiplicity of communities that have shaped us. Since at any given moment, as well as during the whole course of our life, we all participate in multiple communities—families; friends; neighborhoods; religious communities; and groups sharing a common culture shaped by gender, race, ethnicity, or set of historical circumstances—we will hear different voices within ourselves telling us what a text means. We must find ways to embrace that multifaceted personal reality just as we assume that such a variety characterizes our multi-cultural world. It is important not to shy away from the different voices both within and without, even when they carry competing messages. Instead, note those differences so that you can sort out where they come from and what values inform them.

We have relatively few memories of explicit references to Luke 14:25-35, and we remember almost no discussion of it in the scholarly literature. On the other hand, several phrases found in this text are common in the life of our churches and in our culture. One such phrase is "bearing the cross," which is frequently cited, and just as frequently trivialized. Putting up with life's irritations is often encouraged with the phrase "that's just my cross to bear." Preachers may equate bearing the cross with undertaking a responsibility (often in support of the institutional church). One wears cross-shaped jewelry, and thus bears the cross as a sign of identity.

Another such phrase is "counting the costs," which is often invoked to urge prudence in undertaking a task. It can be a way to encourage people not to disturb the status quo, for one can never be *absolutely* sure that one has adequately provided for all contingencies that might arise. This and similar texts are even invoked to counsel a person to stay in an abusive or otherwise oppressive setting, since there are always enormous risks and uncertainties entailed in any attempt to move into a new situation.

One part of the passage that we do remember hearing explained is the troubling teaching that talks of "hating family." We remember the explanation that "hating" really means "putting in second place." So we begin our reading of this particular text with that relatively comforting interpretation resonating in our minds. That beginning point, in turn, shapes our reading of the rest of the passage. Since the saying about hating family members is literally the beginning of the passage, the assurance that "hating" means "putting in second place" blunts the sharp points of the other sayings about discipleship as well. Even the calculated pragmatism of the illustrations (vv. 28-32) appears consistent. Such a reading can be very tempting, and we are in serious danger of letting that comforting possibility govern our interpretation of this text.

On the other hand, to read "hate family" as "putting the family in second place" endorses the choices of the person who ranks God's work first (whether in the form of church programs or projects working for charity or social justice), and gives to the family only the time that is left over—if any. What about persons for whom the integrity and survival of their families has been threatened by war, by the official violence of oppression, or by the random violence of the streets? How would this teaching sound to them? Would such readings not seem to trivialize their loss and suffering, and in the process increase their pain? Such interpretations pose serious pastoral problems relative to this text!

Taking Stock of Where We Are

By now a group of people studying together should be buzzing with questions, feelings, and reactions generated by initial time with the text. Or if you are working alone, you should be accompanied by a growing pile of scrap paper with notes of your own reactions and questions, amplified by an imaginative and sympathetic attention to concerns that might be raised by readers whose perspective on life is different. The feeling of both the group and the individual interpreter at this stage is often one of growing confusion rather than emerging clarity, and of having generated more heat than light about the text. That is appropriate, for those questions, feelings, and points of confusion set the stage for a careful examination of the text itself, and then for research into the work of other interpreters.

Chapter 3

A Close Reading of the Biblical Text: Steps in the Process

To resume the metaphor with which we began the previous chapter, when one is getting acquainted with someone, it is important to pay careful attention to how they present themselves, and to their agenda. They must be given space to be themselves, and not merely a projection of one's own assumptions and impressions of them. Once they have spoken and one has attempted to understand them as clearly as possible, one is in a better position to know how to respond to them. Do both parties want the relationship to develop? Is there a meshing of interests and demands? Does each recognize in the other a potential partner or a likely adversary?

The process of getting acquainted with someone includes in the first place attention to what that person is actually saying—the words they use, the structure of their sentences, the images by which they communicate, and so on. These data are amplified by the "context" of the speech in the person's posture, attitude, and appearance. Such factors not only influence our feelings about the person who is addressing us, but they also help us know how to hear the words they say. For example, the statement "I'm hungry!" will be understood differently, depending on whether the person saying it is an infant, a teenager, or an elderly person, or whether he or she is rich or poor. The context of hearing is further specified by information about where the person lives, and what their immediate or longer term life experience has been.

In the case of a person we meet, we have an immediate sensory impression of many of these details. What we don't know and feel we need to know, we can ask. In the unfolding of a relationship, there are actual living beings involved. In the case of developing an acquaintance with a text, however, one of those partners consists of words on a page. Even though those words are far from inert, but rather have the power to address and confront the interpreter, words on a page do not form the same sort of active conversation partner that one finds in a human being. In particular, when one is reading a text, the whole task of attention to the context and assumed meanings of both partners to the conversation rests on the side of the reader. The reader does not, however, engage in the process of coming to know a text as a detached observer. Instead, the process unfolds in a dialogue of question and answer, hypothesis and test, suggestion and correction. It is that process that we are calling "close reading."

Going Forward by Circling Around

One might assume that in a "close reading" the process involves beginning with the first word of a text and proceeding word by word until the end. In fact, what is involved is a much more circular and interactive process. It involves attention to specific vocabulary, and also to grammatical clues to how the passage is organized. Characters, actions, or the logic of arguments draw one back to the notes, questions, and feelings that arose in the initial reading—sometimes refining, enlarging, or even answering them. Details of the passage draw one into passages elsewhere in the Bible or in other literature where similar details are found, and one occurrence begins to interrogate and interpret the other.

One way to put it is that in a close reading, a number of dialogues are taking place at the same time. There is the principal dialogue between readers and text. There are also dialogues among readers in the same immediate community and in distant communities, whose initial responses and questions to the text lead them in different directions. There may also be a dialogue within the text, between the final form of the text and earlier traditions from which it is taken, or the related traditions where similar material is found. Many of the interpretative tasks that a reader undertakes interact with each other, so that a step in one direction may require one to rethink a previous conclusion and review an earlier part of the process from a new perspective. For that reason, it is almost impossible to outline this process in linear fashion. In fact, to do so can be misleading, for it suggests that one builds systematically toward a final, conclusive, and definitive result, instead of toward an ever more richly textured appreciation of and relationship with the text.

On the other hand, the very nature of the print medium is that it is linear: Word follows word, sentence follows sentence, and chapter follows chapter in sequential fashion. As a result, the process outlined here risks appearing much more orderly and mechanical than is actually the case. We will try to indicate some of the places where one may want deliberately to break sequence and to pursue an inquiry that is addressed only later in the process. It is, however, important to be aware that we will also work in such a circular manner ourselves, both deliberately and also unconsciously as we follow the inner logic of the process.

On Text and Reality: Words of Caution and Affirmation

The work of close reading focuses on the text itself and is not built on a compilation of research. On the contrary, the close reading clarifies the questions one subsequently takes to various reference works and into dialogue with the interpretations of the passage by other readers. That does not mean, however, that information about such issues as the social and cultural reality of the communities from which the various biblical books came is irrelevant. On the contrary, the more familiar one is with biblical texts and with the world of biblical studies and commentaries, the more information one will bring to enrich the reading.

However, the same familiarity with the social environment of the texts and greater comfort with methods of interpretation that come with experience in studying the Bible can also be limiting. Familiarity can prevent us from seeing the obvious. For that reason it is important to formulate questions about the text, even if at first the answers seem obvious, rather than to assume that one need only list the answers one has previously heard or read.

One should sit lightly with such previously acquired information, for all information comes from specific social settings (such as the church or a college or seminary classroom). Far from being objective, universal, or value-neutral, that information or analysis is shaped by and for those settings. In that sense, it establishes a specific angle of vision on the biblical world, which is always a foreign world, no matter how familiar it may become. Modern Western readers can never fully and finally comprehend that world because of the distance imposed by time, place, language, and other cultural factors. Access to that world is also limited by the data that were recorded in the media that survive, and by the gaps in available knowledge created by the silent and silenced voices of persons who had no access to those media.

Written texts provide access to only one limited perspective on the past. Especially in the time before education was widely available, writing was a skill included among the privileges of the wealthier classes. Even where public education has made writing a more widely available skill, until fairly recent times literacy has also carried a gender bias, for in all social classes men were given more opportunities than women to learn to read and write. Even more important, women who did write tended to be confined to writing personal letters, accounts, and diaries, for they usually did not have access to the means of producing documents and literature of the public realm. In all ages, the publication and dissemination of such public writings has been a costly enterprise, and thus has been the province of people (mostly men) of means. Not surprisingly, those texts tend to preserve data of interest to, or that serve the interests of, members of those classes.

To supplement this meager and one-sided glimpse of the past provided by written texts, it is important to be attentive to other sources of information. For example, artifacts uncovered by archaeologists often include household goods used by women of all socioeconomic groups and men of the poorer classes, and from them one can begin to get a picture of the contours of daily life in a given period. The arts provide another window into the life of ancient societies. Though the fine arts were usually the province of the wealthy classes, folk art and crafts provide additional insight into the life of the less well-to-do. By filling out the picture we have of the past, this additional information also provides important interpretative clues for reading the literary texts that a society has produced. Again, though, contemporary interpreters are limited by the relatively few non-literary artifacts that have survived, and by the selectivity with which those remains have been made available.

The reading of literary texts must also be informed by as broad a range as possible of the written data that are available. For example, typically the work of Christian scholars has not been informed by a critical reading of the multiple volumes of Jewish literature that could illumine the early centuries of the Common Era (abbreviated C.E., and referring to the time common to the Jewish and Christian witnesses; dates in that period have traditionally been identified by the Christian label A.D.—"Anno Domini" or "Year of the Lord"). Similarly, most Protestant scholars have paid little attention to those texts which their church tradition has assigned to the Apocrypha or to the Pseudepigrapha, and which are therefore not part of the Protestant Bible. These are, however, important texts from the centuries immediately before the Common Era, and thus are important to the understanding of Judaism at the time of the development of the earliest Christian communities. They also offer a distinctive interpretation of the Hebrew Bible. In addition, interpreters of the New Testament may fail to pay attention to the different perspectives on the formative years of the church that are found in documents from that period which were not included in the canon, and which have been recovered only recently.

Another word of caution needs to be added about the limits of what can be learned from written texts. It is often possible on the basis of a written text to sketch fairly detailed contours of the social world that the author assumed to characterize the situation about which that author spoke. Notice the caution and tentativeness in that statement. The text presents the author's view of, for example, an earlier time (in the case of the Gospels and "historical" books), a different place (in the case of Paul's letters written to communities from which he is absent), or a set of ethical or cultic requirements (in the case of the legal material). The author's perception would have been shaped by his or her own context, just as is that of a modern interpreter. The resulting world created by the text may tell as much if not more about the author's context and point of view, as about what is being described. The relationship between the written text and any underlying events becomes even more complex, because the author's perception may also have been filtered through layers of interpretation as the underlying traditions were circulated in various forms before becoming part of the author's text. An important part of the interpreter's task, then, is to become aware of the correction supplied by these various lenses (including, of course, the interpreter's own), in order better to understand the reality at which one is looking.

Despite all of these words of caution about the limits of what can be learned from written texts, each text does create a world of meanings and values. That world is unfolded in the unique and specific details of characters, setting, social institutions and practices, and vocabulary of the texts themselves. The tendency when viewing a distant society is to generalize from one instance or one example to the whole. To do so, however, masks the fact that within any society there are differences affected by the intersection of such factors as geography, economic status, ethnicity, and gender. Rules governing one context. may be irrelevant to another. In fact, a set of rules or laws may represent the norms desired by the writer and by the group or class from which the writer comes, but may not reflect the actual practice of the community at all. Similarly, customs that shape one group or class may not be shared by others. Thus, texts can be appreciated as a collection of artist's sketches that give a number of specific—albeit not unbiased—glimpses into the world the author has created. These specific glimpses should be probed and examined by the interpreter as fully as possible, without falling into the trap of over-generalization or abstract pronouncements of universal truths.

Keeping in mind an appropriate humility about the limited information and certainty about either facts or meaning that a close reading of a text can yield, and a sense of freedom about the sequence of any steps that are outlined, it is possible to identify crucial areas of investigation.

Preparing a Translation of the Text

Translation is already a significant step toward interpretation. That is equally true whether a reader uses a standard translation of the Bible or whether the reader prepares his or her own translation of the original Greek or Hebrew. When we work with a text in translation, we encounter in it the assumptions, values, and language system of the translators as well as those of the author of the text. For example, the KJV presents the biblical texts in the language and style of Elizabethan English, which is not that of contemporary spoken English. The TEV, like similar versions prepared by the United Bible Societies in other languages, presents the same material in a relatively simple and contemporary linguistic form, in order to make it accessible to people whose reading skills are more rudimentary. The NRSV has attempted to reflect changes in English usage to avoid giving pre-eminence to the masculine gender (for example, by avoiding the use of masculine pronouns to refer to a person whose gender has not been identified). In short, all translations reflect their own contexts of origin. None is a precise equivalent of the original. Some try to stay as close as possible to the language of the original, while others are more overtly paraphrases that try to convey meaning (according to the translator's judgment) rather than specific words.

If you have not done so earlier in the process, make notes about differences in several translations of your passage that seem to make a difference in its meaning. If you can work with the original language, prepare your own translation of the passage.

The Greek of this passage is relatively straightforward, and a literal translation of it comes out very close to what is found in such translations as the KJV, RSV, NRSV, NIV, NEB, REB, and NJB. A problem arises, however, in the "Good News Bible" or TEV (and in its equivalents in other modern languages, such as the Spanish *Dios habla hoy*, in which we first discovered the problem). The problem centers on the word "hate." The other translations render it literally from the Greek, and leave the interpreter with the task of figuring out what hating one's family might mean as a requirement of discipleship. The United Bible Societies' versions attempt to resolve the interpreter's problem by translating this verse to reflect the similar one in Matt. 10:37, which warns against loving family members "more than" Jesus. In that translation, Luke 14:26 reads, "Whoever comes to me cannot be my disciple unless he loves me more than he loves [the various family members]." They explain their decision (according to a footnote in the annotated version of the Spanish) as reflecting a "semitic way of speaking" in which a comparison is expressed in terms of an absolute contrast. The evidence of such language usage is not clear, and it seems to us to be premature to resolve the problem of the meaning of the saying by such a translation.

Besides this major problem, the other differences in English translations affect principally how tightly the various sayings seem to be linked together. In TEV, for example, the first two sayings (vv. 26-27) and the two examples (vv. 28-32) seem simply to be strung together. Only v. 33 is identified as a conclusion to the preceding sayings. In contrast, the NRSV uses the conjunction "for" to identify the stories in vv. 28-30 and vv. 31-32 as illustrations or explanations of the first two affirmations (vv. 26-27). The role of v. 33 as a conclusion to the foregoing statements is identified by the word "therefore" instead of by an explicit statement ("concluded Jesus") as in TEV. In all of the translations, as well as in the paragraphing of the United Bible Societies' edition of the Greek New Testament, the sayings about salt (vv. 34-35) are separated from the preceding sayings. Even such a formal indication of separation between parts of the passage must be recognized as an interpretative decision, since the Greek manuscripts themselves contained no such divisions. Instead, clues within a passage (such as introductory words or changes of location or audience) marked breaks between units of the text. Since no such indicators are to be found here, we should treat these verses as connected to what precedes, and we need to investigate the basis on which the author relates them.

Identifying the Shape of the Text

Read the passage again, this time making notes about details of its structure. What holds the passage together? What seems out of place or dissonant? Where are there transitions? If it is a story, who are the characters, what is the situation, and by what steps does the narrative unfold? What is the common cultural ground or social context that the author is counting on the readers or hearers to recognize? Does the author provide any overt commentary on the story, such as a concluding "moral" or a summary statement?

If the passage is part of an argument or theological discussion, what verbal clues does the author give about how the various statements or steps of the argument are related to each other? Which are important thesis statements, and which provide support for or amplify those main points? On what supporting evidence does the author draw? What kinds of evidence are invoked? Is scriptural tradition or a commonly recognized practice cited to support the author's point? Or common-sense arguments? Does the text argue by analogy? What common ground with the hearers or readers does the author presuppose? Are there specific shared experiences that are referred to, or a vocabulary that seems to reflect an earlier conversation or an ongoing discussion? Are there common central beliefs on which the passage builds? What is the conclusion to which the author wants readers to come?

Sometimes it helps to make an outline of major and minor sections of the passage. It can also be useful to identify patterns (such as repetitions, echoes, or contrasts) of words, images, or ideas. For stories such as parables or narratives, dramatic blocking of the movement of the story is one way to trace the development of the action, and consequently of the structure of the passage.

We noted above that Luke 14:25-35 appears on first impression to be a rather disjointed collection of sayings. A closer look, however, reveals unifying features in the text. For example, it begins with the transitional phrase that sets the scene and introduces the speech (v. 25). Following this passage, Luke 15 begins with another introductory sentence that indicates a new scene. The passage also ends with the kind of statement that clues the audience that a speech has ended: "Let anyone with ears to hear listen!" (v. 35b). These details within the text indicate that the author intends the passage to be understood as a unified whole. Our task is to figure out what holds it together.

Following the introductory verse, we find two general statements of exclusion: Whoever does not do what is indicated cannot be a disciple of Jesus (vv. 26 and 27). A similar statement concludes the passage (v. 33, "So therefore"), but with the negative consequence, which here is applied specifically to the hearers ("none of you can become my disciples"), presented before the condition that would exclude them ("if you do not give up all your possessions").

The first two statements and the concluding one are followed by what amount to commonsense or proverbial examples (vv. 28-30, 31-32, 34-35a). The first two are linked explicitly to the initial statements by the introductory word "for" or "because" (v. 28). They are presented as questions that anticipate a negative answer: No one would do such a thing! The proverb about salt is simply placed in a like position after the concluding statement. A schematic picture of the relationships of the parts of the passage might look like this:

Setting and introduction—v. 25

*Negative affirmation #1: third person ("*whoever* comes and does not hate . . . cannot be my disciple")—v. 26

*Negative affirmation #2: third person ("*whoever* does not carry . . . cannot be my disciple")—v. 27

"For,". . .

    Analogy #1 (tower builder)—vv. 28-30

Analogy #2 (king waging war)—vv. 31-32
*Concluding negative affirmation: direct address ("therefore none
    of you can become my disciple if you do not. . . .")— v. 33
Analogy #3 (salt)—vv. 34-35a
Final call to pay attention—v. 35b

The three negative affirmations (marked by asterisks) are the main points of the argument. They assume that being a disciple of Jesus is something that the hearers desire. The appropriateness of the conditions they set forth is defended by the analogies, which the readers will presumably grasp right away. That structure assumes, in turn, that the readers will identify with the projects of the tower builder and the king, and that they have experience with the positive and negative properties of salt.

Comparing with Texts of Similar Material

Another step in establishing and becoming aware of the specific text with which one is working is to see if all or part of the material is also found elsewhere in the Bible. It is not unusual in either Testament to find similar sayings or fragments of poetry in several different settings (for example, Isa. 2:2-4 and Mic. 4:1-3; and Matt. 19:30, 20:16, Mark 10:31, and Luke 13:30), or to find the same or similar stories told in more than one place (for example, stories of the jeopardizing of a matriarch in Gen. 12:10–13:1, 20:1-18, and 26:6-11; the raising of a widow's son by Elijah in 1 Kings 17:17-24, by Elisha in 2 Kings 4:18, and by Jesus in Luke 7:11-17; and Jesus' anointing by a woman in Matt. 26:6-13, Mark 14:3-9, John 12:1-8, and Luke 7:36-50). Differences in detail in these occurrences of similar material can highlight concerns or emphases of the particular authors or editors who chose to use them. These differences are worth noting for consideration as one's work on a passage continues.

Sometimes notes in the margins of a Bible will suggest such cross-references, but each one must be assessed carefully, since editors have different criteria for identifying related passages. In the case of the first three Gospels, a way to identify other occurrences of a passage is to consult a "parallel" edition of the Gospels, in which related passages are set side by side in columns. One can then easily compare them to identify similarities and differences. Another way to find other occurrences of parts or all of the passage would be to look up key words in a concordance, and then to see if the references in fact correspond.

In our sample passage, the saying about family members (v. 26) is paralleled in Matt. 10:37, but in the less harsh form that our memories favor and that has predominated in the interpretations of this passage with which we are familiar. In that parallel text the word "hate" is missing, and instead the issue is that one must love Jesus more than "father or mother" or than "son or daughter." Further, because Matthew lacks Luke's fuller list of family members (including wife, brothers, and sisters), the lack of mention of a wife is not as striking as it is in Luke. Matthew also says nothing about one's stance toward one's own life. Even though the word "disciple" is not found in the saying (at issue is how to be "worthy" of Jesus), in Matthew as in Luke it is usually interpreted as dealing with discipleship, since it is accompanied in Matt. 10:38-39 by both the saying about taking up the cross and the saying on finding and losing life (see also Matt. 16:24-25; Mark 8:34-35; Luke 9:23-24).

The sayings in vv. 26-27 are echoed also in the *Gospel of Thomas*, a collection of 114 sayings and parables allegedly dictated by Jesus to Thomas the Twin. Fragments of the collection were discovered in Egypt near the beginning of the twentieth century, but a complete copy was not discovered until mid-century. The document does not present a narrative of Jesus' ministry and passion, as do the canonical Gospels, and it is not part of the Bible, but many of the teachings or *logia* echo teachings found especially in the Gospels of Luke and Matthew. Recent "study editions" of the Bible or parallel presentations of the first three Gospels often call attention to related portions of the *Gospel of Thomas* in their notes. Concerning our passage in particular, *logion* 55 of that document reads, "Whoever does not hate father and mother will not be able to be my disciple; and whoever does not hate brothers and sisters and does not take up the cross in my way will not be worthy of me." The more fragmentary *logion* 101 reads, "Whoever does not hate father and mother in my way will not be able to be my disciple, for my mother [gave me falsehood?], but [my true mother?] gave me life."

The harshness of Luke's wording, which is found also in the *Gospel of Thomas*, is striking. He seems to be drawing a line in the sand and daring his readers to cross it. That harshness, along with the explicit reference to what disqualifies one from being a disciple, highlights the importance of the sayings for Luke and will need to be examined further. For example, we will need to explore the meaning of "family" in Luke's context, and why that might be considered an obstacle to discipleship.

Sayings on the value of "saltiness" and the futility of trying to restore that quality once it is lost can be found in Matt. 5:13 and Mark 9:50. Matthew elaborates on the worthlessness of unsalty salt, but only Luke hints at its harmfulness (v. 35a). Again Luke's version is striking for its harshness compared with Matthew and Mark. The implications of that quality of saltiness will need to be explored further, as will what Luke's readers would have heard in such a reference to salt.

Refining the Questions

Having sketched the basic structure of the passage, you are in a position to identify key points about which you need further information. Read the passage again with its structure in mind. Add to the list of questions that you have been compiling any new questions that occur to you, or clarifications of earlier ones. Try to be attentive to how your questions might be framed differently or might not even be raised by interpreters whose contexts differ from your own. The questions that are generated at this stage of the process will form the basis for later research into the language and world assumed in the text, and into the interpretations to which the text gives rise in different contexts. Refining and annotating your questions can be one of the most useful steps of interpretation. In fact, well developed questions themselves can be an appropriate end result of one's interpretation.

The introductory verse contrasts with the previous section of the Gospel (14:1-24), which portrays a fairly intimate gathering at a meal in a household. This passage is directed more broadly to the crowds who were following Jesus. Yet these sayings speak of discipleship. Is Luke's point to have Jesus explain to these others why they are not "disciples," or is the challenge held open to them? A question we will need to pursue is how Luke understood the word "disciple"—who can be included on that list, and how is that group related to Jesus? What would Luke see as the importance of these qualifications for discipleship for his readers who were living after Jesus' death and resurrection?

As we noted earlier, the main points of the argument are in the negative: They say who *cannot* be a disciple, not what one must do in order to be a disciple. Does this suggest that a central issue in the passage is to identify reasons for exclusion from the community? That suggestion jars our sensitivities. We would like to think of the conditions of discipleship as being goals which we can strive to achieve: Reach the goal and achieve success. But these sayings do not tell us what it takes to be a disciple. We also note that three disqualifications are listed. So, we ask, why three? Why not just one, for example, or five? And what is there about these three that makes them so important? Is there anything else that keeps one from qualifying as a disciple?

The first disqualification pushes us to focus on the family. When we look at the meaning of the family for Luke's audience, we need to acknowledge the societal definitions of that term which govern our own perspectives. The different realities in which we live lead modern readers from different contexts to bring to the text presuppositions, some of which may be at odds with those of the writers and audiences of the biblical texts. Getting our own assumptions on the table, along with the questions and problems those assumptions introduce, is an important step in preparing the way to uncover the author's perspective, and thus to allow a clearer reading of the text.

For example, the authors of this book would most naturally view "family" through the lenses of the world of the Euro-American middle class, in which at least the ideal still represents the family as the immediate family of parent(s) and children. Both our families of origin and our present family situations (which we discussed in chapter 1) have given us our particular slant even on that reality, for the stable and generally happy families we have been privileged to be a part of do not represent the dominant—and certainly not the universal—experience of the family in our larger social context.

Regardless of the particular configuration that the family takes, or the quality of life it engenders for its members, in our world the family is seen as a private domain from which one goes out into the larger society. Although for members of some communities a long ancestry may not be traceable, the family provides an individual with a heritage in the sense of a specific family tree and (where personal history and geographical proximity allow) some additional relatives. According to the ideal, the family provides affection, love, and emotional security for the individual members, and a locus of social and economic security for dependent members such as the very young and maybe the very old.

On the other hand, personal economic security and independence is the goal of individuals within the family. Even teenagers are encouraged to earn their own money and thereby to seek a certain degree of economic independence. Furthermore, schools, social security systems, and other governmental structures provide the safety nets that are expected to assure individuals of economic and social well-being, whether or not the family is willing or able to do so. Echoing the goal of economic independence is the goal of an independent identity: In our culture everyone wants to be known as a unique individual, and not merely as part of a particular family. What the family offers (at its best) is primarily emotional security and support for members in their individual lives. That is the goal of "successful parenting," and that is the bond of familial relations. Whatever the reality may be, when the notion of family is evoked, its appeal is predominantly emotional, playing on the memory of holiday meals and family picnics, and invoking images of romantic love and parental tenderness. These, and not such public values as economic or social justice are what we usually mean by "family values."

For these reasons, we instinctively read the phrase "hate family" as an emotional response—some blend of dislike, disdain, animosity, and anger—toward family members. We find such a requirement distasteful and puzzling. Doesn't it seem more logical that hating instead of *not* hating should disqualify one from being a disciple? Matthew's alternative reading that avoids the word "hate" in favor of placing the family in second place to one's religious commitment is much more appealing, and we are tempted to direct our response to that instead of to Luke's version of the saying. Matthew seems to allow us the freedom—even to encourage us—to pursue the noble goals of economic, social, or intellectual independence from the family. The fact is, however, that we have to deal with Luke's harsher reading, and our discomfort leaves us noting for further research the question of whether Luke shares our assumptions about families, and why not "hating" them disqualifies one from being a disciple.

The issues shift when the contexts of modern interpreters shift, however. In African American, Hispanic/Latino, Asian or Asian American, and Native American communities, for example, as well as in parts of the two thirds world, families are often more broadly defined to include several generations and persons less immediately or formally related to each other. The family is the fundamental structure by which a person's identity is constructed, and by which one's connection to the community is made possible. The family is also more directly involved in the economic and social security of its members, regardless of the role that public agencies play in those concerns. Independence from one's family is not a value that is prized, and persons who set themselves apart from their families are viewed with puzzlement, and even suspicion.

Similarly, in many cultures and regions of the world, family ties are so essential to the coherence of the social and cultural fabric that when governments desire absolute control over their people, they recognize that they must break down the family structures by any means necessary. Both the structural violence of extreme poverty and random violence of official terrorism (kidnappings, "disappearances," and outright murders) conspire to drive families apart. Strong affirmations of family loyalty, such as the relentless search for "disappeared" family members by the *Comadres* of El Salvador or the Mothers of the Plaza de Mayo in Buenos Aires, Argentina, are consequently viewed as a threat to the public order. In such contexts the saying in v. 26 would be subject to manipulation by those out to destroy the family. In turn, to understand "hating" one's family in a positive way as a mark of a disciple would demand that one see the gospel as so central to life that it would make worthwhile the incredible dislocation and suffering that now are imposed upon them.

In any cultural or social context when physical, emotional, or sexual abuse is experienced within the home, inflicted by or with the collusion of other members of one's family, the saying in v. 26 requires a dramatically different reading. In action if not in words, the context of hate is already present, and the family is the locus of danger, not of security. For persons caught in that web, the saying about "hating" the family might provide the affirmation needed to encourage victims to become survivors by removing themselves from the situation, and by that exodus to acquire the physical, emotional, and spiritual distance necessary for healing to begin. In such a context, "hate" toward the abuser might actually be a first step toward justice, recognized as thoroughly consistent with discipleship.

Another context in which sharp questions arise about the appropriateness of these sayings involves their use by various religious cults. Recruiters cite this and similar passages to convince their victims to reject their families of origin and to surrender all their possessions to the control of the cult. That group will then become the new "family" that will provide for all of the member's needs, security, and identity. The appeal is couched in biblical language, portraying the cult as the true embodiment of what Jesus envisioned. Given that use of this passage, how would it be read by someone who has lost a family member to such a group? How would it be read by persons who themselves have spent time in such a group and subsequently left? How would it be read by those who have stayed in such a group, and recognize in it all of the positive values that were promised?

On the table for our further study, then, is the question of what Luke's context might have led him to understand by "family," and why not hating members of one's family makes one ineligible to be a disciple. This sketch of some contemporary readings, and of the dilemmas and possibilities for understanding that follow from them, serves to uncover some of our individual assumptions, so that we do not impose those assumptions on the point Luke is trying to make about discipleship.

A serious question that must be considered is whether Luke's teachings in this passage provide appropriate insights about discipleship in every reader's context. For instance, while the passage may provide a helpful challenge to us once we have made the necessary translations into our different context, there may be social contexts—of poverty, war, or other type of social crisis—where the teachings do not fit. In circumstances where one's family and one's few meager possessions are essential to survival, holding this text as a standard might literally be a death sentence. A question that always needs to be on our agenda as interpreters is how we are going to deal with a text whose consequences are harmful.

The question of discipleship—what it means, and why these particular failures should prevent one from being a disciple—pushes us to additional reflections. Again, we should be cautious about assuming too quickly that we understand the familiar language. "Disciple" is such a common word in the vocabulary of Christians that we often ignore the differences in the ways people use it. For example, governed by the individualism of Euro-American culture, we tend to hear such sayings as having a private, individual reference. To be a disciple has to do with a personal posture—to believe correctly, for example, or to behave properly. In contexts where people understand themselves principally not as individuals, but as participants in communities or groups (such as families, villages, or tribes), to become a disciple might be understood to mean becoming a member of a new community, or even participating in a new family. In other words, to become a disciple would be to find a new locus of identity, or to derive one's fundamental security from a different source.

The latter case might help to clarify the dynamic of the statement in v. 26, explaining why one cannot be a disciple if one does not "hate family." Where one's identity is understood to be "communal" rather than individual, it is simply not possible for two *separate* communities—both one's own family and the community or "family" of Jesus—to define one's identity at the same time. Even though the social clue of communal identity provides a hint about the logic of Luke's saying, however, we need still to explore why the family itself would be seen as necessarily separate from (and thus not consistent with) the community of Jesus' followers. Are the many churches that today see the family as the principal building block of the church missing something in Luke's saying? Or is the key to the meaning of discipleship assumed in this saying thoroughly entangled in Luke's understanding of the word "family"?

In the above discussion we have tried to imagine how considering different cultural worlds might affect our understanding of the role of family, and consequently also the meaning of discipleship. This line of inquiry leads us naturally to wonder about the social world of Luke's own community. What can we learn about the concept of family that would have governed the hearing of this text within that community? What can we learn of Luke's understanding of discipleship? While in actual practice one might at this point want to pursue these issues immediately, we will discuss that process at a later stage of the study (chapter 4). The collection of notes that we will take into our subsequent research on these topics is forming an intricate web indeed!

The second of the negative affirmations—"whoever does not carry the cross and follow" Jesus cannot be his disciple—also invites our assumption that we understand what Luke means. We already noted some of the popular understandings. In this text carrying the cross is connected to following Jesus. Clearly for Luke this is a way to speak about the Christian life. But we have to ask if more is not intended. Would Luke's community still have recognized the cross as an instrument of execution that they might expect to face because they follow Jesus? What is it—in Luke's context and in our own—that if one fails to do it, one cannot be a disciple?

The text itself provides a hint of a possible meaning for Luke's community of the reference to carrying the cross. Both of the analogies presented in vv. 28-32 refer to the negative consequences of starting a project one is not prepared to complete. Similarly, Luke seems to be saying, a disciple must be prepared to follow Jesus even to the bitter end of crucifixion. Could this saying be a warning to those who tend to abandon their faith or the commitments it entails whenever the going gets rough? Everyone knows people who fit that description, and if we are honest, we may recognize one of them when we look into a mirror. But in different contexts, the obstacles to persevering in the faith differ widely. We might think of the press of time and other responsibilities that distract us. In other parts of the world, following Jesus can actually lead to persecution, not only of the follower himself or herself, but also of beloved members of their family. Where on such a continuum of obstacles to completing one's task of discipleship do people in Luke's community fall? Do we get any additional clues to the identity of the "fair weather Christians" Luke may be addressing?

The specific characters and occasions in the analogies of the tower builder and the king may provide such clues. We will need to look into the building of towers: Who did it, where, and why? What historical reference, if any, might underlie the reference to the king going to war? The structure of the passage, which makes these analogies the self-evident examples that prove the previous statements, means that Luke's readers are expected to identify with both the characters and the situations contained in the analogies. Both of the examples appear to be developed around themes dealing with issues of security and of honor, and thus around characters who have prestige, power, or property that is worth defending. Other people who also have status and possessions (and an image to protect) can be expected to empathize with the need to defend one's turf, and also to get the point that it is disastrous to risk public embarrassment. On the other hand, people who have no prestige or honor, and little if any property to defend, would find the predicaments humorous, and just the comeuppance the characters deserved. For such persons, the analogies would not be convincing arguments for the legitimacy of the initial statements. In this way we may get a clue that Luke is directing this passage to prestigious members of his community. What remains, then, is to investigate further who they might be.

The fact that the two analogies turn on issues of honor and

security and presuppose the interests of persons of relatively high social standing may shed further light on the two initial statements (vv. 26-27). Those statements too may well identify the protection of honor and security as a major obstacle to discipleship. How might that work? The case of carrying the cross is fairly obvious. People with a stake in the status quo of their societies are hardly eager to get involved with groups or activities that would open them to charges of capital offenses. A possibility that we will need to test in our research is that for such people in particular, families also were keys to honor and prestige. If that proves to be the case, then, the statement in v. 26 would mean that unless one is prepared to surrender one's claim to such privilege ("hating" or rejecting one's family and relying instead on one's identity as a follower of Jesus), one cannot be a disciple. Being a disciple would then involve willingness to take on a new identity that is not guaranteed by the social status of one's family, and in particular an identity that does not afford the society's traditional guarantees of security and prestige.

The concluding affirmation seems to follow closely on such an understanding of the role of the family. In most societies, "possessions" or wealth—if there is enough of it—function as arbiters of prestige and provide at least the appearance of security. In this concluding statement the indirect, third-person form of the first two statements gives way to a challenge addressed directly to the audience (both the crowds that Luke mentions in v. 25 and the church to which he writes). The progression of thought in the passage continues in the negative affirmation that none *of you* who cannot relinquish possessions can be a disciple.

The requirement to dispose of "all that one has" raises questions about women's legal rights to own property of various sorts. Could women of Luke's day hold title to real estate, for example? Did they have the right to dispose of property on their own, or was the authorization of a father, husband, son, brother, or other male relative or guardian necessary? Did this requirement for discipleship, like that to leave one's family, implicitly exclude or at least ignore women?

Insofar as those addressed are people for whom possessions do mediate prestige and security, this saying seems to fit with the rest of the passage. People who are very poor, on the other hand, find no more prestige or security in their possessions than in the social standing of their family. For them, the few possessions—perhaps a few cooking utensils, a minimal amount of clothing, blankets to protect them from the cold and some shelter or covering to keep off the rain—are the difference between staying alive and dying of hunger or exposure. It is hard to imagine such a saying addressed to them! Yet how are people in such circumstances, who want to be "disciples," to understand this saying?

The existence of so obvious an exception to the "rule" posited by the saying, plus the contrast between the saying in v. 33 and the two analogies in vv. 28-32 (which seem to counsel a prudent use of one's possessions by not becoming over-extended and by remembering to "count the cost" lest one begin a project that one cannot complete), provide a tremendous temptation to those of us to whom the full challenge of v. 33 would be directed. Because we do lodge our sense of security in our possessions, and because we keep trying not to relinquish them but to accumulate more (since we can never be absolutely sure that we have enough to be secure), we try to convince ourselves that the saying could not possibly mean what it says. We try to read it as an ideal that we are not expected to follow completely, or as a rule only for those in the early church who expected the world to end any day anyway, and not a demand that continues to be valid. Or we read it as urging us to have a particular attitude toward our possessions—to use them wisely or generously, and not to be overly preoccupied with them—and not actually to give them up.

The saying about salt (vv. 34-35a) seems deliberately planted to trip up such attempts to negotiate a more palatable reading of this entire passage. The first part of the saying is so obvious that it seems almost a throw-away line: You can't salt salt! The second part moves beyond the obvious, to point to the poisonous quality of salt that can no longer serve its appropriate uses. It is tempting to get lost in an inquiry into how people in Luke's audience might have used salt, and to understand what value it would have held for them. While that might be interesting, in terms of this passage, the text itself makes the crucial point: Salt is either valuable for its saltiness, or it is toxic. There is no halfway point.

The three statements in vv. 26, 27, and 33 identify things that, so to speak, make a disciple lose his or her "discipleness." The sayings about salt suggest that that is not a mere lapse from the ideal, but a fatal loss. Instead of being useful or even essential (just as salt is necessary for preserving as well as flavoring food), the one who does not do the things Luke identifies has become a contaminant or a danger. Such either/or language is troubling: What happened to grace or forgiveness of our human weakness? What if we really want to follow the difficult path, but just can't quite succeed? According to this passage, Luke cuts no slack for human weakness in the matter of discipleship. The lines are sharply drawn for those to whom the teachings are directed: Any who fit that category had better pay attention!

Taking Stock of Where We Are

The close study of the passage has resulted in clarity about how the passage is structured so that the author can lead the readers or hearers to the desired conclusion. Questions that were evoked in the initial response to the passage have been amplified, clarified, or answered. Some of those that remain unresolved can focus the reading and research on the passage that will form the next phase of the process, which leads us into questions of "context." Other questions that continue to claim our attention pose the crucial theological and ethical concerns that face us as readers when the passage intersects our own reality, and the realities of other individuals and communities that are part of our global context.

Chapter 4

Reading Contextually:
Finding the Passage in Its Place

Up to this point the discussion has been focused on the passage itself, examining the clues within the text itself that help readers understand the passage, and allowing questions to emerge. No biblical passage exists by itself, however, like a collection of words on a file card to be picked out and read or listened to in isolation. Instead, each passage is part of several larger "contexts." The first of these is the "literary context." That refers to the place and function of the passage in the biblical book in which it is found. The common practice of looking at individual passages—or even individual verses—as the focus of study and preaching masks the fact that these parts always contribute to a larger whole, which, in turn also informs the meaning of the individual unit.

The "social context" of a passage refers principally to the life circumstances of the readers to whom the larger work in which the passage is found was initially addressed. The author's own assumptions about culture, economics, politics, religion, and society, and those held by the community being addressed, provide the vocabulary, images, and social situations through which the point the author wants to make is conveyed. Sometimes—such as in the cases of the "historical books" of the Hebrew Bible and the Gospels and Acts of the New Testament—it is possible also to identify clues to such earlier social contexts or life circumstances as those of the period about which the book speaks, or those of other communities that told a particular story before it was incorporated into the larger work. Those earlier embedded contexts are always more difficult to recognize, since they are covered over by the assumptions of the author's own world.

Finally, the social context is related also to the "theological context" of a passage. The specific passage—and the questions, beliefs, concerns, and affirmations to which it points—both add to what the author is saying about a particular theological agenda, and, in turn, are shaped by other things the author says about the same theme. The particular author's theological voice also has a place in the larger context of the Bible, where that voice may find both echoes and dissonances.

Part of the task of contextual interpretation can be carried out on the basis of each reader's own familiarity with the Bible, or his or her previous study of the biblical book in which a passage is found. For other aspects of the investigation of the social context of a particular text, however, it will be necessary to do some research into reference works such as Bible dictionaries, introductions to both Testaments, and commentaries (see chapter 12 for a discussion of some types of reference works that might prove helpful). It has already become clear in the initial work on the passage how the life circumstances of different groups of interpreters shape what they can see in the passage, and that is true also of the work of the so-called experts. All readers—scholars included—have their own social and theological contexts that are relevant to the task of interpretation, and in this portion of the study, it will be important to explore the role of those contexts as well as the contexts of the biblical passage itself.

Considering the Literary Context

The first question to be answered in identifying the literary context of a particular passage is in what type of work it is found. Sometimes the answer is obvious from the title supplied in the Bible—for example, Psalms, the Gospel of John, Chronicles, the Letter or "Epistle" to the Romans. Sometimes the titles, which usually have been supplied by the tradition and are not part of the actual works themselves, tell more about the subject matter than the genre (for example, Exodus, Judges, or Acts). In other cases the titles are actually misleading. The books entitled "Chronicles," for example, are not the carefully researched factual data a modern reader might anticipate from that label, and the "Letter to the Hebrews" is really more like a sermon in letter form than an actual communication to a specific group of addressees. The question of genre is important, because we all read different types of texts in different ways. We expect a different sort of truth in poetry than in a news report, and words are used differently in a letter to a loved one than in a legal brief.

We know such things instinctively when we approach the written material of our familiar world, but the literary types of the ancient world may not be as obvious. For example, we cannot assume modern standards of accuracy when we read such "historical" books as 1 and 2 Kings or the book of Acts, because ancient historical writing tended to be overtly moral—that is, it intended to teach attitudes and values to the audience, and not principally to provide information about the past. (The fact that modern historical writing is also value-laden and written as much to persuade as to inform is another issue. The difference in alleged intent and in methods is still significant in affecting what one comes to expect from the works.) To cite another example, the biblical Gospels are all accounts of the ministry, death, and resurrection of Jesus, but the extent to which any of them can be read as providing biographical information about Jesus of Nazareth is a subject of hot debate among scholars and church leaders.

Perhaps even more important, all of these books have been gathered in the Bible. Different parts of the Christian church (as well, of course, as the Jewish community) include different books in their "canon" or official list of "scriptures." Other religious communities might respect the Bible as religious literature, without granting it revelatory, holy, or authoritative status. Different communities also attribute different kinds of authority to the Bible, and they bring different methods and criteria of interpretation to the task of reading that material. People who view the Bible as having come directly from God may have difficulty seeing the connection between a writer's social context and the resulting text. If "the Bible" is practically a synonym for "solemn," readers may not allow themselves to recognize and respond to humor within these texts. If all "scripture" is assumed to be "literally true" on all levels, an interpreter may not recognize the metaphorical truth of poetry, parables, or symbols. If the Bible is equated with ethical authority or norms, it may be hard to ask who benefits from a particular passage, and even more difficult to recognize that people can be harmed by particular mandates or values that the Bible embodies.

Make notes or discuss in your study group your preliminary conclusions about the nature of the book in which the passage you are studying is located. What does that conclusion lead you to expect about it? What are your assumptions about the Bible itself? What expectations do you have about the kind of "truth" found in a biblical text? What view of biblical authority do you hold? If you are working in a group, be aware of the ways differences in your views on these matters might affect the work you are able to do together.

The next phase of the study involves locating the specific passage you are studying in the book as a whole, then moving (as with a zoom lens on a camera) to an ever closer focus on how the passage fits in the author's literary design. It is possible to do this work on the basis of your own knowledge of the specific book. In the case of a short book (like Micah or Galatians, for example), you could read through the whole book and outline it, making written or oral notes about where your passage fits in. For most of us, and especially when we are dealing with one of the longer books, it would be easier to locate a specific passage with the help of an outline of the structure and contents of the book, such as one might find at the beginning of a commentary. Keep in mind that different readers might well see the overall organization of a book a bit differently, though, and use such outlines only to get the most general perspective. (Questions of literary context must be approached differently in books like Psalms, Proverbs, or some of the prophets, where the overall coherence of the book is less evident. See the discussion of such issues in chapters 7 and 8.)

Having identified the general location—beginning, middle, or end—or major block of the book within which your passage is found, look for clues to how that section is developed. (Keep in mind that chapter and verse divisions have been provided by later copyists and editors, for the sake of convenient reference. They do not necessarily reflect natural breaks either around or within a given passage, and they may or may not coincide with the structural units you have identified.) Where does your passage occur in the larger section of the book? Does it introduce, summarize, or conclude a sub-section?

Often it will be helpful to identify the "genre" of the passage itself. For example, is it a psalm or other poetry, a prophetic pronouncement or "oracle" (many of which are also poetic in form), a parable, part of a saga, the greeting of a letter, a story that focuses on a saying of Jesus, part of a liturgy, a prayer, or a section of legal material? Does its form give you any clues about the role it may have played in the community to which it was addressed? Is the passage you are studying complete in itself (a psalm, a folk tale, or a parable), or is it part of an extended discussion (such as a cycle of stories about one of the patriarchs, or a longer argument in one of Paul's letters)? What clues in the text lead you to this conclusion? If your passage is part of a narrative, what is the general story being told, and how are the stages in the story marked off from one another? What clues is the author giving about characters, setting, and action? If the passage is part of a logical argument, how is the argument put together, and where does your passage fit in? If it is a piece of teaching or legal material, what principle seems to be holding together the section in which it is found? The closer your "zoom lens" brings you to the passage itself, the more you should be testing your hunches—and those of other members of your study group or those in reference works—by a careful reading of the text itself.

Having drawn some preliminary conclusions about the literary context of the passage, refine those conclusions from two perspectives. First, explore how the literary setting affects your reading of the passage. How does the surrounding material influence what you see as the author's principal emphases or concerns in the passage you are studying? Has the author tried to prepare you to respond to or evaluate aspects of the passage in a particular way by what has preceded it? Second, make notes of the specific accents or concerns your passage adds to the general agenda of the section of the book in which it is found. Is a particular piece of an overall argument developed here? Does the teaching sharpen or soften a point made before or after it? Does an example expand or limit the group who would hear themselves addressed by the passage? Is something new revealed about an important character in an ongoing narrative? What would be lost if your passage were not a part of this section of the book?

The sample text for this study is part of Luke's Gospel. His own preface to the Gospel (1:1-3) states his claim to join others who have provided "an orderly account of the events that have been fulfilled among us," about which his addressee Theophilus has been "instructed." At this point we do not know who Theophilus was (though his name will prove important to the question of Luke's social context in the next phase of our study), or on what basis Luke was "ordering" his account. These introductory comments, plus the fact that we have already found portions of this passage occurring in different contexts in other Gospels, suggest that Luke has chosen his order deliberately. We have to set aside our modern assumption that "orderly" must mean "biographically accurate," and recognize that really all Luke has told us is that he has put the Gospel together as he has on purpose.

The specific passage we are considering is part of the large section of the Gospel that tells of Jesus' journey to Jerusalem (9:51–19:44). The actual travelogue occupies little of Luke's attention. Instead, the journey is a very spare framework on which Luke has hung many sayings and teachings on a variety of themes. Not long before this passage (13:22) has come Luke's first reminder of the destination of the journey since its beginning (9:51). That reminder introduces dire warnings about how difficult it is—particularly for those who see themselves as having an inside track to God's favor (13:30)—to participate in the salvation that Jesus is proclaiming (13:23-30), and to share in the banquet of God's reign (13:29). The chapter ends with ominous words about Jerusalem—the report of a threat from Herod, and the picture of a city that metes out death to the prophets (13:31-35). That threat, in turn, echoes in the passage we are examining, particularly in the saying about "carrying the cross" in 14:27.

The set of teachings in 14:1-24 recall the banquet reference in 13:29, both by their setting at a banquet in the home of a Pharisee and by the banquet theme of the parable in vv. 16-24. Again, these teachings all point to unexpected terms of access to or participation in God's reign, and they provide some instructions about what one must do to participate in the new order. In that sense they seem to develop the saying of 13:30 about "firsts" and "lasts." Throughout chap. 14 the teachings and parable feature the radical exclusion of persons who appear to be the privileged ones (14:7-11, 12, 24) and the radical inclusion of persons on the margins (14:13, 21, 23). These teachings, directed to the select audience of guests at the banquet, thus echo the earlier set directed to an anonymous traveler (13:23-30).

The pattern of contrasting groups of winners and losers that characterizes both the earlier part of chap. 14 and 13:23-30 is broken in our focus passage. Instead of stating that values and priorities are reversed in the coming reign, our passage identifies specific actions that exclude one from being a disciple. The three negative statements—things that prevent one from being a disciple—seem to align the passage as a whole with the fate of the privileged people in the

94

parable of 14:16-24, who turn out to be excluded from the banquet, or, by extension, who cannot be Jesus' disciples. Like 13:23-30, the sayings in 14:26-35 are directed to people in the crowd traveling with Jesus, and not to an obviously select group like those in the Pharisee's house.

The common voice of the three sets of teachings is thus striking, for it sounds as though Luke is identifying the followers in general (perhaps thus also his church in general) with people who assume that they are in positions of privileged access to God's blessings because of some factor in their current social status. If that is the case, then our earlier hunch that the three negative statements target especially people who find a measure of honor and security in the institutions of their society seems to be confirmed. That hunch will need to be explored further in our probing of the social context of the passage and of Luke's Gospel as a whole. On the matter of Luke's theological concerns, furthermore, the literary context seems to support the hunch that for Luke being a disciple of Jesus involves stepping outside of the system that allocates identity and security on the basis of one's inherited or acquired status in the surrounding society.

The subsequent section of the Gospel (15:1-32) connects again to the good news/bad news pattern of 13:23-30 and 14:1-24. The joy over the "losts" that are found is itself lost on persons who prefer that such outsiders as tax collectors and sinners remain missing from the community. Thus, the grumbling of the religious leaders over the company Jesus keeps is echoed by the behavior of the older brother in the last of the trio of parables about "losts" and "founds." At issue is not the required *action* of discipleship, but rather the *fact* of the value system of the new reign present in Jesus, when all the rules are changed. As the parable of 14:16-24 makes explicit, the dramatic inclusiveness of the new order excludes or offends those who cannot bring themselves to give up the old rules. The material gathered in chap. 15 thus echoes the pattern of negative affirmation ("whoever does not . . . cannot be my disciple") of our passage.

Locating the Social Context

If we recognize that the principal purpose of the biblical authors was to communicate to their audiences their perspectives on God and on the blessings and the responsibilities of humankind's relationship to God and to the rest of creation, then it is important to spend some time getting to know that particular community of ancestors-in-the-faith who were the originating audience of the book one is studying. In what historical circumstances did they live? What events marked their larger world and (insofar as we can figure that out) their immediate community? Did they live in generally good times or bad? Were the times good for some and bad for others, and if so, what facts of life made the crucial difference?

Are there any clues in the passage about the daily life of the people to whom the book was written? How did people earn a living? What was housing like? How was family life structured? What was life like for people who did not have families in the usual sense? How did the society provide for persons kept on the margins due to their economic, social, ethnic, or religious status, or because of illness or physical disability? How were young people taught the stories, values, and behavior that were thought to shape their identity? Was the content of that education different for girls than for boys, or for rich people than for poor people? What can we know about the rituals and institutions of religious life? How did people's experiences of their religion differ in different social classes, or for men and women? To what life-issues do the larger work and the passage in particular speak? What questions about life does the passage seem to answer? What seem to be the ethical values of the community at that point in its life?

It is important to bear in mind the fact that formal literature like the texts of the Bible represents principally the points of view of elite sectors of their societies. For example, texts that speak of servants tend to portray their lives from the perspective of those they serve, and women's lives are portrayed as the male authors (and the largely male leadership of the early church and of the religious institutions of Judaism) saw them, for those are the groups that would have done the writing. Often texts that seem to be *describing* what is, are in fact *prescribing* what those in charge think should be the practice in their communities. Similarly, theological views presented in a positive light represent those that eventually prevailed in the church. They may not represent the dominant views in the author's own community. One ought, therefore, to be cautious about drawing descriptive conclusions about the authors' communities on the basis of the evidence of the texts, whether or not one extends the same skepticism to the values and principles the texts espouse.

Make some notes (oral or written) about clues you find in the passage to the author's theological concerns. What does the author seem to see as the burning issues or questions, and what seems to lie at the heart of the author's faith confession? How does the text make those points or present those issues? To what extent does the author seem to be arguing for a perspective that the audience may not hold, and to what extent is the author building on a network of shared assumptions? What social circumstances, religious activities, and theological affirmations seem to be assumed or advocated? What is the presumed worldview, "conventional wisdom," or *cosmovisión* within which the text is operating? What seem to be the theological issues raised by the passage for its original audience? What are the *sociological* or *political* implications of those *theological* issues? Is the author's primary purpose to make a point about God, about the will of God, about the human condition, about ethics, about a faith community, or (if it is a New Testament passage) about Christ? Are you aware of other places in Scripture where different points are made about such issues?

One's initial acquaintance with and impressions of the author and the author's communities is through the text being studied. That knowledge, however, is not limited by the reader's own experiences, but rather it can be supplemented or even corrected by the interpretations of others. Important insights will come from other persons in one's own community, both those who may have information because of their previous study and those whose own life experience gives them insight into crucial questions and possible references in the text. Other sources of help in examining social context are such written sources as books, articles, study materials, and various non-print media that may be available to you.

You will want intentionally to engage diverse conversation partners as a part of this process. This will not happen automatically, and not always easily. Most of the commentaries in libraries and other collections in North America are still written by Euro-American males, though that is now changing. More and more libraries are working to acquire a more diverse collection, and more and more perspectives are now finding expression in the written literature. Some of these are coming from historically marginalized racial or ethnic communities, and from women of all communities, in North America. Others are being published in Africa, Asia, and Latin America, where until recently libraries have been captive to patterns of publishing in Europe and North America. Even where new voices are finding their way into print, however, it is important to remember that the authors of such formal resources share the common social location and ideology of universities and related academic institutions. The rules and methodologies as well as the values and interests of academic research cannot help but exclude some aspects of meaning in a text, even as they are helpful in opening up others. Thus, one will want to seek interpreters from outside the academic arena as well. In addition to such traditional resources as books and journals, many libraries are also systematically collecting resources in other media, including resources from oral cultures or segments of society.

Basic reference works or introductions to both Testaments (see the discussion of resources in chapter 12) will provide brief essays on each biblical book, and they will usually discuss the general historical background in which the book was written. Commentaries will normally provide more detailed discussions of such issues. Begin with that preliminary reading, noting details that seem relevant or surprising to you. If you are working in a study group, divide up the work with resources as people are able to use them, and come together to share information. Do not be surprised if most general reference works and even commentaries give you little if any information about the specific social context of the community. Many interpreters have been content to paint a general picture of the major historical events and religious or philosophical movements that characterize the time and region of the world from which a biblical book came. Until recently, few have investigated the economic structures and systems, social organization, patterns of family life, or other types of information that would inform them and their readers about daily life or social characteristics of the community to which a book was directed. Those are relatively recently discovered questions in the world of biblical study, and you will need to be fairly resourceful in order to pursue them. You can, for example, supplement the information found in reference works about the general background of the period with information from other sources about the social, political, economic and religious context of the appropriate period of history, or by what you know or can learn about analogous communities today. Keep in mind the fact that ancient societies were diverse, just as are modern societies, and avoid the temptation to make hasty generalizations that obscure specific details. It is important to understand the issues of a particular community as it lives within the larger context and interacts with various elements of the surrounding culture.

You may find that a specific aspect of this community stirs your imagination, particularly as it affects your reading of the text. There are shelves full of books that can help you in your research. (Again, see chapter 12 for some suggestions.) However, you may find that the issue which piques your interest is nowhere addressed in those books or articles. It may be something that the scholarly community did not deem significant or preferred to ignore. It may be something that the scholarly community did not even notice. Or you may find that your initial observations about issues that are important or about the meaning or implications of details are at odds with the judgments of the experts. There is no need immediately to dismiss the experts, but neither is there any reason to distrust your own observations about what questions are important, or what issues the passage appears to address. Even the most seasoned interpreters can be startled into new readings of a text by someone's tentative question that begins, "I don't know if this makes any sense, but do you suppose . . . ?"

Authors of commentaries will probably answer some of the questions about grammar, vocabulary, and perhaps historical and social context. Each will give you *one* perspective on the significance of the passage: *None* is totally unbiased. For that reason it is important to consult resources from a variety of perspectives—by women as well as by men, by Jewish as well as by Christian interpreters, and by persons from a variety of racial, ethnic, and geographical backgrounds. These various social locations will lead the authors to emphasize different sets of questions related to the texts, and to uncover fresh responses to the questions many scholars take for granted. In addition to the author's social context or perspective, her or his theological orientation and chosen method of interpretation will influence what questions are deemed important. Once again, the greater the variety of commentaries and other resources that you consult, the greater the likelihood that one of the methods will focus on your questions. Even if your questions—such as those related to the social context assumed in the text—are not addressed in any of the resources available to you, do not forget those questions. Note them carefully, for such questions might well give shape and focus to the next generation of scholarship on your passage. Of course it is always possible that you yourself might eventually decide that a particular question was really not that important or interesting, but defer any such conclusion until the end of your study. Meanwhile, keep probing.

There are a number of tools that will help you pursue some aspects of your questions on your own. For example, if there are particular words you think are important, you can begin your investigation into those words with an "analytical concordance" to the biblical translation you are using, in order to identify other passages where the precise word in your passage is to be found. (See the discussion of concordances in chapter 12.) Focus on those occurrences in the same biblical book in order to grasp the theological context out of which the author is working and to get a better feel for the field of meaning of key words and phrases. Use a concordance cautiously, though, remembering that different authors may well use the word with different nuances of meaning, and that even a single author may use a word in different ways in different contexts or for different audiences.

If you find a word that seems particularly crucial or freighted with theological significance, you might want to consult a biblical or theological dictionary (not your desk copy of Webster's!). The essays in such dictionaries can make available in brief form the results of years of research. Remember, though, that the authors' and editors' biases will be reflected in how they have gone about their research and in what aspects of the word's meaning are deemed important. (Again, you will find some of the recently published dictionaries discussed in chapter 12.)

Hold yourself, others who are reading with you, and the various resources you consult, accountable to the best data, and to the fullest reading of available data, that you can acquire. Do not settle for assumptions and conclusions that subsequent research has shown to be inadequate or inaccurate. New information is being discovered all the time by archaeologists and others, and scholars are learning to interpret data in new ways. For example, recent studies that focus on questions of gender have encouraged scholars to examine artifacts related to women's spheres of activity that in earlier days were deemed not worth studying. Thus, for years archaeologists working in the Middle East identified a class of objects found in many digs as "small toys." When people began to pay attention to the lives of contemporary women living in the region, they found similar objects still in use: Those "toys" were really whorls used in the spinning of thread, an activity essential to the domestic economy! Sensitivity to issues of gender has also led Jewish historians studying the lives of women in formative periods of their community's history to uncover evidence of considerable variety in women's lives in the early part of the first century, depending on a family's economic status, geographical location, and relationship to the Jerusalem temple. The assumption widely held by earlier generations of scholars that all women's lives were circumscribed by rigorous adherence to the laws found in Leviticus concerning ritual purity has been shown to be invalid for many if not most women in Palestine.

Scholars often publish their newest work in journal articles, prior to completing enough research to produce a whole book. Sometimes the question that intrigues you will turn out to be on the cutting edge of someone's work, and not something irrelevant at all! In particular, the work of newer scholars, who include many more women and members of historically excluded racial and ethnic groups than were present among earlier generations of scholars, is often found only in journal articles, and it is there that questions of particular relevance to such communities will be discussed. The number of scholarly journals is growing rapidly, and if you have the time and library resources to pursue your study through journal articles, it is important to become familiar with the various indexes of periodical literature, as well as with *Old Testament Abstracts* and *New Testament Abstracts*. These specialized "abstracts" or summaries of journal articles will give you an idea whether a particular article will be helpful to your specific question, and they will guide you to the precise location of the full text of the article. All of these printed research tools are being supplemented (and may soon be replaced in places where the technology is available) by computerized research tools such as databases, networks, and a growing variety of software programs through which to retrieve and analyze resources.

It is important to remember that one engages all of these resources, not to get "right" answers, and not simply to collect information or other people's opinions about the passage, but to find conversation partners in the common task of interpreting your passage. This principle is especially hard to keep in mind since the authors of those resources can claim the authority of experts. Consult commentaries, articles, books, and other resources with your mind open to the interpreters' insights, but stay focused on the passage itself. The notes and questions which you have been recording, based on your reading of and reflection on the text, should allow you to enter into dialogue with those other interpreters around the text which is your common focus.

———

Luke's audience

General introductions assign the Gospel of Luke, and its companion book, Acts, to an urban center of the Roman Empire, somewhere outside of Palestine. The specific location is debated, with candidates being suggested everywhere from Greece to Egypt. Dates between 75 and 85 C.E. are proposed as the time of composition. (Though such proposals may sound vague to modern readers accustomed to precise bibliographical information, they often have to suffice in dealing with ancient literature.) The urban setting itself implies several factors about the social structure of Luke's community. Foremost among them is the function of "honor" and "shame" in providing the framework for social status. Within urban societies of the empire there was considerable clarity about how people's worth was assessed, depending on the combination of such factors as wealth, legal status (freeborn, slave, or freed person), social position, gender, and age.

Honor could be inherent in the very data of one's existence, or it could be attributed by specific acts and signs of deference from other persons. Those of lower status were expected to honor a person of higher status. If the proper honor were not accorded, the status of the more prominent party would be diminished. Those with greater honor would be expected to receive and not to show deference, so if the reverse occurred, the person so honored would be elevated in status. People of lower status were expected to exhibit proper "shame"—that is, behavior appropriate to their status—and to be properly deferential to their superiors: To have appropriate shame meant to know one's place.

The resulting strictly stratified and competitive environment would mark the general context to which Luke was directing his Gospel. For a number of decades, scholars suggested that the prominence Luke gives to poor and marginalized people and to women—all categories of persons with relatively low status—meant that Luke saw the gospel as contradicting the values represented in that competitive environment. Instead, the gospel would represent "good news" especially to such groups. More recent studies suggest that Luke wrote *about* the impact of the gospel for such groups, but *to* persons of higher status, whose world might be threatened by the "good news" attributed to Jesus. The degree to which Luke was actually calling into question the stratified world of his day is now much debated. Most scholars recognize that Luke is not calling for an immediate and dramatic overthrow of that world. Some conclude that he is in fact supporting it, while trying only to mitigate some of its harshest aspects.

A clue that supports these more recent suggestions can be found in the name of the person to whom Luke has addressed his work. In Greek the name "Theophilus" means "friend of God" or "one who loves God." Such names that carry meaning were not in themselves uncommon (much like names such as Prudence or Patience among the Pilgrim settlers in the North American colonies). In this case, though, Theophilus might not be someone's actual name, but rather a symbolic reference to a group of people who may have formed a major portion of Luke's church. That group is Gentile "God-fearers," who were deeply attracted to Judaism—and in particular to its ethical principles—but who for various reasons did not wish to become full converts to that religion. Christianity, which at least since the time of Paul had been welcoming Gentiles as well as Jews, without requiring the former to undergo circumcision and take on the whole law (in other words, to become converts to Judaism), provided a religious home for many of these people. The God-fearers generally tended to represent the merchant classes or people of even higher status in their society. In fact, some scholars suggest that their reluctance to convert to Judaism reflected a reluctance to jeopardize their elevated social position. Luke's address to "most excellent Theophilus" is deeply respectful, and it may well indicate that "he" (or those he represents) would be worthy of such honor.

In light of the hints in Luke's own preface that at least some in Luke's community enjoyed a fairly high social status, the significance of the first part of 14:26 becomes clearer. Once one recognizes that "hate" refers not to the deep emotions we hear in that word, but rather ignoring, rejecting, or not acknowledging these family members (Deut. 33:9), it is clear that those being addressed were being warned that being a disciple involves a willingness to give up the social position that depends on the status inherited in one's family. To do so would be a particular challenge to those who benefitted most from that relationship.

The saying in 14:26 is not the only place where Luke's Gospel links discipleship with the call to leave behind the security of a stable home and family. A similar note is sounded in 9:57-62, in the replies to three people who want to follow Jesus. The first is challenged to face homelessness (9:58), and the other two are forbidden to meet even the basic obligations of burying one's father (9:59-60) and saying good-by to one's family (9:61-62). More than haste or the urgency of the mission is at issue. Familial piety—to honor one's father and mother (Exod. 20:12; Deut. 5:16)—is at the heart of the life of faithful observers of Torah and of the ethical core of Jewish religion to which God-fearers were attracted. Being a disciple of Jesus thus becomes a challenge not only to the biological and social identity one has by virtue of membership in a family, but also to one's identity as a child (literally, a "son") of the covenant, and to the religious security that identity brings with it.

It is important to note also that both the issue of religious identity and secular trading in honor would have pertained principally (if not only) to males in Luke's society. For men to leave behind both their families of birth (from which they would receive their status) and the families of which they themselves were the head (and for which honor demanded that they be responsible) as part of a religious commitment would be a serious challenge (Deut. 33:8-11). On the other hand, inclusion in a family would also have been crucial to a woman, who otherwise would lose her proper way of interfacing with the public society outside the household. It is clear from the witness of all of the Gospels that there were women among Jesus' followers, and no one seriously suggests that there were no women in the early churches, Luke's included. So what are we to make of the fact that only wives and not husbands are included on Luke's list of those to be left behind?

For women in Luke's day, discipleship apparently did not involve the same rejection of the status and privilege accorded by being part of a family. That difference in requirements can be read in at least two ways. On the one hand, a woman outside the structures of a family or household would be vulnerable on several levels. Since families were the principal units of economic production, such a woman would be economically at risk unless she happened to have considerable private resources at her disposal (which she was legally able to possess according to the Roman law in effect in the Gospel writers' communities). A woman's reputation would also be in jeopardy, for abandoning her family in this way would entail abandoning her proper status or "shame." According to Luke a woman's discipleship seems not to include that demand.

On the other hand, the different requirements of discipleship for men and women might not have been totally benign or designed for women's protection. Instead, they might reflect a double standard. The social revolution and challenge to the status quo that the Gospel entailed for men seems to be in contrast to social conservatism around questions of gender. The discipleship of men thus means that women risk abandonment by husbands, brothers, and fathers committed to their new vocation as disciples of Jesus. In contrast, women in this Gospel (and also in Acts, despite the witness in Paul's letters to women's active public ministry in the early church) play very traditional roles still focused within the family. Women bear children (Luke 1 and 2), they serve at table (4:39; 10:38-42), and they tend the dead (24:1). Even the student Mary remains at home. She listens without interacting with Jesus as the male disciples do, and without receiving a subsequent commission to go out and pass along what she has learned (10:38-42).

The requirement that one carry the cross (14:27) and be prepared to relinquish one's own life (14:26b) suggests a context in which being a follower of Jesus entailed some risk. It is not clear to what extent that actually involved for Luke's community the threat of a political execution like that which Jesus suffered. It may be that this is one point at which the context of the Gospel writer and that of the story being told are quite different. In 9:23—part of a set of teachings drawing parallels between the fate of the disciples and that of Jesus (9:23-27)—Luke seems to use the disciples' "daily" cross-bearing as a metaphor for general struggle and burden over the long term, rather than as a reference to the political threat which each person could encounter fully only once. Similarly, Luke's version of the prayer that God grant them "each day's" bread (11:3) suggests that his community was considering how to prepare for long term faithfulness, rather than for an immediate crisis. Such a lifestyle of always being ready to face danger or to bear burdens would be more familiar to the more marginalized members of Luke's community. For those of higher status, both facing danger and bearing burdens might well have been sufficiently unfamiliar conditions that the distinction between them blurred into a general risk to well-being that seemed life-threatening.

A similar mood is struck in 14:33. What one must be prepared to relinquish is literally "all that one has," not just the material "possessions" suggested in the NRSV. Everything is set aside in the name of this new vocation as a disciple: Family, status, security, safety, and the material goods often perceived as the basis of all of those comforts. Again, such a requirement is significant only for those who have something to lose, and particularly for those who have accepted the notion that such wealth is evidence of God's blessing. The three negative affirmations about being a disciple thus converge on members of Luke's community with a stake in the status quo. They involve a willingness to place oneself at risk, and so to identify oneself directly with persons of less honor and lower status.

The implications of these requirements represent a costly discipleship, but one that is still a positive choice for those who can recognize their new security and identity in the project Jesus represents and in the company around him. That positive component is not mentioned in this passage, but it forms a striking conclusion to another discussion of discipleship in 18:18-30. In that account, a ruler seeking eternal life balks at surrendering all that he has (in this case, specifically to give it to the poor). His response leads to a comment and a proverb about how hard it is for those who have wealth to participate in God's reign (18:24-25). Peter's observation that he and the other followers have done precisely that evokes a concluding assurance from Jesus that, for any who have "left house or wife or brothers or parents or children" for the sake of God's reign, much more will be restored to them "in this age, and in the age to come, eternal life" (18:29). The list of persons left behind—including the striking reference to a wife, with no mention of a husband—is so closely parallel to the one in 14:26 that, in the larger context of the Gospel, one might hear the implicit promise in this passage as well.

The initial costliness of the step that appears to be at hand for the crowd leads to a more explicit warning in 14:28-32. The two examples—introduced in a way to evoke the quick response that, of course, no one would be so foolish—both depict the hazards of costly projects undertaken without prudent planning. In a rural setting such as that of Jesus' own ministry, a "tower" would probably have been assumed to be a farm building. Such a structure would have served both as a watch tower that would allow a farmer or vineyard owner to protect the property from thieves or animals, and as a temporary shelter or storage shed in fields distant from their homes in the town. Urban readers such as Luke's audience would likely not envision such a simple structure, but rather an elaborate building palatial in size and luxury, like those built by various representatives of the Roman administration. Only wealthy people would identify with someone planning such a structure, recognizing the dramatic loss of honor that would be entailed if one were to design and begin to build a more lavish structure than one could afford to complete. Poor people among the audience, however, would likely identify negatively with the example, for generally such projects were carried out by their own hard labor, and, in the case of public structures, by taxes exacted from their hard-earned income.

The example of the king pressed to sue for peace because of being confronted by a stronger enemy does not appear to have any specific historic event behind it, but rather it is a dilemma that would carry meaning for persons of a sufficiently high social station to have had to take on such public responsibilities. Both examples thus develop their point by reference to the world of social elites. The message of both examples is thus clear: Don't start what you are not able to finish. In the context of the statements about those who cannot be Jesus' disciples, the warning seems to be that the hearers (the "crowd") not jump into this relationship with enthusiasm that has not reckoned with the costliness of the commitment—costliness precisely in those arenas of life that the hearers hold most dear. Know from the beginning, Luke says, that those costs will be exacted.

The apprehensive tone of the passage—warnings to count the cost before you start, and dire challenges to accustomed well-being—is echoed in the warning of the concluding proverb about salt. Forms of the proverb are found also in Mark 9:50 and Matt. 5:13, but Luke presents the most elaborate form. This part of the passage seems not to be directed to a specific social class, for salt was a substance common throughout the society. It was used as a seasoning and a preservative in the diets of the poor as well as the rich. (One is reminded of how basic it is to life by the diet of tortillas and salt that even today sustains the poorest of Central America's many poor people.) In addition to such culinary uses, salt has medicinal properties, and it is an irritant. Although it is an essential ingredient in the chemistry of the human body, too much salt is toxic, and "salted land" can be symbolic of total destruction, not only of a land's past, but also of its future potential. In fact, the famines that devastate northern Africa and parts of Asia can be traced in part to the unfertile land that is a consequence of excessive irrigation with salty water—a consequence that is then compounded by the injustices that characterize systems of global distribution of the food surpluses produced elsewhere.

At least two of those qualities of salt—its use as a seasoning and its destructiveness—figure in the extended proverb. "Salt" can lose its saltiness when the salt itself is more soluble than a mineral with which it is mixed. When the mixture is exposed to moisture, the salt leeches away, leaving a (usually) tasteless residue that is good for nothing, and that can make soil or manure with which it is mixed a medium toxic to the plants that one might try to grow in it. What has begun as something good has lost its essential property and become a hazard.

Luke is not clear about the nature of the disciples' "zing," or about how they might lose it, or in what sense they might then become toxic. Probably one should not get lost in speculating about whether the "salt" of the disciples refers to their healing powers, their role in the preservation of values, or the "flavor" they add to the life of the larger society. In fact, none of these specific aspects seems to figure in the saying. Instead the emphasis is on the polluting power of disciples who have lost their unique identity. In the immediate context of these sayings, as well as in the larger context of Luke's teachings on discipleship, it appears that one key facet of that identity is the followers' readiness to leave behind the value system of their dominant culture. By implication, then, a follower of Jesus who returns to those values, and to the systems that support them, is the one against whom Luke is warning most vehemently.

Taking Stock of Where We Are

Work on the literary and social contexts of a passage has provided answers to many of the specific questions that have arisen from the text. The passage has emerged as a part of a larger whole that the author is addressing to a specific community. In addition to some general ideas about who these people were, what their lives were like, and what affirmations and questions made them tick, you have a number of specific details related to the particular passage under study. You may have information about the social class of the audience (or of that part being addressed most directly in the passage), and about aspects of their lives that were of particular importance. The ethical or theological concerns that the passage develops have moved from abstraction into some specific connections to the life circumstances of the audience.

This part of the study has tended to address specific questions about details rather than providing a framework for understanding the concerns of the passage as a whole. In that process, however, unifying themes may emerge. The information gained or the structural insights derived may reinforce earlier observations, or they may contradict earlier hunches. Whatever the findings have been to this point, integrative questions now need to be developed that will begin to pull together the scattered notes and comments those questions have generated, and to re-connect them to the readers' lives.

Chapter 5

Engaging the Text, Other Readers, and Our Communities

Engaging the Text

The time has come for the particular questions, impressions, and bits of information arising from reflection and research on the text to steep together into an emerging picture of the agenda and implications of the passage as a whole. In order to take this next step, read the passage again, naming aloud or in notes your responses to the passage at this stage of your work. How do they differ from your initial responses? What strike you at this point as the principal issues or concerns it raised for the author's audience? What have you learned about the role these issues played for that community? Are they important issues for you or for your church? If so, how have they been reformulated in your context or vocabulary? If they no longer seem important, why do you think they have faded into the background? Is it because of the different social context? Have other issues moved into the center of people's concerns, hopes, and longings? If the passage you have been studying is a story, are there characters or situations that particularly attract you or put you off now that you have come to understand them better? Are there situations in the story or points in the discussion with which you simply cannot identify? If the passage contains ethical teachings or rules, do you experience them as helpful, irrelevant, or harmful in your context? If they seem irrelevant or harmful, what options do you have for dealing with their presence in the Bible? What conclusion does the author seem to want you to reach by the end of the passage? Are you able to understand how that conclusion would have functioned for the author's audience? Can you both understand that conclusion and accept it as life-affirming in the initial context? In your own context? If not, why not? What do you see as the implications for you and for your community of the fact that this message is in the Bible?

Being as honest with yourself (and with the other people in your study group) as you can be, note what clues these observations give you about your own concerns, cares, biases, life story, theological assumptions, or social, historical, economic, and cultural context. Are there aspects of your life situation or your confessional assumptions that seem to be preventing you from responding to the text, or do your experience and context suggest concerns or perspectives that are invisible to the author? For instance, has a male author glossed over or given a slanted reading to something in women's experience? Does the author's world view lead to the neglect of questions to which you would like answers, such as what *really* happened in the plagues of Exodus or in the Gospel healing stories? Has the focus of an author on the experience of the Israelites led to less information than you would like about the roles and circumstances of Cushites or other African peoples, or about the tribal peoples resident in Canaan, who appear in narratives of the Hebrew Bible? Does the Jewish or Gentile identity of the author of a New Testament text result in a caricature of the other perspective within early Christianity, or do you detect a Christian bias against Judaism? If so, how do you hear anti-Jewish language today, in a world that has seen the Holocaust?

Clearly Luke 14:25-35 is about being a disciple or follower of Jesus. More specifically, it makes some harsh statements about what keeps a person from being a disciple. It gives no positive guidelines about what one has to do to be a disciple. That is frustrating, because being a disciple must involve more than not making certain mistakes!

The tone of the passage is negative, warning, and restrictive, especially in contrast to the open invitations to the banquet in the parable that precedes it. Luke seems to be concerned that people might rush to Jesus without thinking through the seriousness of their commitment. The passage seems especially to have been aimed at persons who were fairly well established in their society, and who depended for their security and identity on the status that came with their family's position and the things (material and otherwise) they possessed. Unless they were willing to give up those things, and accept certain burdens—the generalized "daily" cross (9:23)—they could not be Jesus' disciples.

In our Euro-American middle class culture, status and security (for an adult, at least) are based more on a person's own achievement in acquiring power or wealth than on one's family name or on family connections. For that reason it is hard to hear the first of these sayings in the same way that Luke's audience would have. For us, hating one's family entails emotional feelings rather than social or economic risk-taking, and it is hard to see how such hatred could relate to being a disciple. But if we recognize that the challenge to the well-to-do folks of Luke's community is to surrender the props to their identity and security, these sayings get uncomfortably close to home.

This passage appears to address the negative side of a radical change of identity and a letting go of old sources of security for one's life. For us, "all that we have" (14:33) encompasses comfortable homes, job titles, tenure, retirement plans, credit ratings, and the respect that goes with our profession. Those things establish our (elevated) place in our society, and allow us to sleep more or less soundly at night. Two obvious questions strike us: Why is it necessary to give these up in order to be disciples? And how could we ever do it?

There is something important that this passage is not addressing, and for which we have to look elsewhere in Luke, namely the affirmation that being a disciple is not intended to leave anyone destitute and isolated, but rather that one has a new basis for security and identity. The promise of 18:29-30 is that people who do take such radical steps will "get back very much more in this age" as well as eternal life in the age to come. Similarly, Jesus himself is said to claim as his own family "those who hear the word of God and do it" (8:21), thus following the path he himself has taken—being his disciples.

Where Luke seems to be going, then, is to interpret discipleship as emphasizing not what the church often emphasizes, namely the personal experience of a "call" from Jesus, followed by our response as a matter of living up to standards of personal achievement. Instead, Luke seems to be trying to get his community to recognize that discipleship entails a new social grounding, a change in the basis of one's security and identity from such socially sanctioned institutions as the family, to the new community of the church. For wealthier and more "honored" members of his community, the negative affirmations of the passage entail a risk to their place in the old order. For all of the members of the community, however, rich and poor alike, the passage affirms that being a disciple is not really risky for the rich, and it is truly a word of good news to those who are poor, since it results in a new identity and security in the new community of disciples.

Such observations take us back to the example cited in chapter 1, of the seminary student who feels caught between a call to the specific vocation of church leadership, and mounting indebtedness and family stress as she or he attempts to respond to that call by obtaining the necessary education. Perhaps the key factor in the discomfort felt by an individual in such circumstances is the lack of an alternative structure, either in the seminary or in the church, that can provide the necessary material and emotional support. Living out one's discipleship in such a new community might feel just as risky at the moment of transition, when one must leave old sources of security and support. Such a move would quickly become an experience of good news, however, as discipleship comes to be seen not as the hero's quest, but as the community's commitment together.

What *is* entailed in discipleship can be talked about in stark terms of life and death (the cross), and in harsh language of hating family and giving up all one has, because it entails an absolute shift from the old identity to the new. It is not possible to hedge one's bets on such a matter, holding on to the old while trying on the new for size, for that means that one is still living in the old order and "cannot be [Jesus'] disciple." To try to do so makes one both useless as a disciple and contaminating to the community (14:34-35a).

There is an irony, then, in the two examples (14:28-32) that seem clearly to counsel prudence and forethought, because what seems like the most imprudent move possible for the privileged members of that society turns out to be the most prudent. In doing a cost analysis, the cost that one needs to count is forsaking old forms of security. The benefit to be realized is discovering that this new family rather than the old is where true identity, security, and indeed life itself are lodged.

Of course that assumes that the new family of disciples has in fact become a social reality in Luke's community. Perhaps that is what allows the members of a disciple's family to be left behind ("hated") without their being abandoned. They are simply left in the safety and care of the new family. Luke does not tell us much about how this new family is organized, or how its life is managed from day to day, but the restricted roles played by women in the Gospel as a whole

114

cause us to suspect that it still has many of the attributes of patriarchy that characterize the old social and familial order that Luke is otherwise rejecting. (In a similar vein, the fact that the example of the king waging war [14:31-32] reduces pursuing peace to a strategy of weakness suggests that Luke has not dealt critically with the prevailing ideology that glorifies might and raw power.)

Even if the disciples of Luke's community did successfully become the new, reliable source of identity and security for one another and for dependent family members, it is clear to us that that has not happened in the churches with which we are most familiar. Discipleship is viewed not as creating a new social matrix, but as presenting criteria for individual behavior and religious experience. When we consider the parents and children who depend on each of us and recognize that there is not an alternative community that can be relied upon to care for them, we find ourselves rejecting the demands of this passage in our context. Of course that excuse colludes with our less laudable reluctance to abandon the benefits we enjoy, so we need to be suspicious even of its apparent legitimacy. In our best moments, we find ourselves asking what would need to happen for the community of believers to become such a place of uncompromising security that would free persons to respond to the Gospel without putting those family members who depend on them in jeopardy. And we ponder what it would mean to use our resources—including the intangible but, for us, foundational resources of our education—and our relative privilege to give flesh to that vision. But that is only in our best moments. Usually we find enough details with which to quibble, so that we are able to flee from the discomfort the passage creates in us.

Entering into Dialogue with Other Readers

One of the greatest obstacles to creative and vital biblical interpretation is the temptation to read a text simply to reinforce one's prior conclusions about a problem or theme. That trap is most dangerously available when one works alone or in a study group made up of people whose life contexts and experiences are similar to one's own. A crucial step, especially at the point of responding to the text, is deliberately to expand one's circle of conversation partners. One way to do that, if such resources are available, is through commentaries, articles, and other published resources, or through resources in such other media as films or other artwork and audio- or videotapes of lectures or other presentations. The process of dialogue with other interpreters has already begun in the research focused on specific questions about context or vocabulary. There it became clear that not every interpreter has asked the same questions about a passage. What is deemed important reflects aspects of the various interpreters' identities, contexts, and ideological and methodological commitments.

It is now time to go back to the commentaries and articles to learn what the various authors conclude about the passage as a whole. What does each see as its principal concerns or themes? What point do they think the author is trying to get across? How do they see the passage contributing to the larger project of the biblical author? Again, try to locate resources from different historical periods, from women as well as men, and from persons of different racial or ethnic backgrounds or from different parts of the world. Look for works by writers from different religious or theological perspectives as well as from writers who claim no religious perspective at all. It is important to seek out Jewish as well as Christian resources, and to be attentive to voices representing the great variety of communities and perspectives within each of those over-arching categories. Sometimes you can find helpful insights from resources that are not specifically biblical, such as books on African American religious history and theology.

If you are working in a group, it might help to distribute the available resources and share summaries of them. If you are working alone, make a few notes about each work so that you can distinguish among the various voices. Remember that you are not looking for the one magic book that will deliver the right answer, nor should you assume that an accumulation of data will add up to the whole truth. Instead, you are trying to be as sensitive as you can to the variety of ways people have interpreted and responded to your text. When you have listened as carefully as you can to the various voices, see if you can figure out how the writers' contexts have shaped their readings—not in order to dismiss them for their bias, but in order to appreciate the integrity of each unique voice, and what it does and does not contribute to an opening up of the passage.

Especially if you have been working largely by yourself, it is crucial at this point also to engage in dialogue with other "live" interpreters in addition to those encountered through your reading and library study. Just as you worked to find a diverse collection of printed resources and other media, look for other persons whose life contexts and experiences differ from your own or from that of your study group. Share what you have learned and engage one another in a discussion of some of your tentative conclusions. With as much honesty and grace as possible, try to help one another understand the effect of your various contexts and theological assumptions on your reading of the passage. Talk together about your conclusions concerning the importance of the passage for your beliefs and moral practice, and for the life of your church. What insights does this passage give you about cultural, social, political, and economic structures? About gender relationships? About racial or ethnic relationships? What do you learn from the passage about the nature of God, Christ, faith, the gospel, the church, or what it means to be a human being—a child of God? Note that both Testaments can enrich our understanding of such Christian concerns as Christ, the gospel, or the church. The Hebrew Bible does so not by predicting or foreshadowing the New Testament, but by enabling us to deepen and broaden our experience of God and of the relationship between God and humankind as they come to expression in the literature of our earlier ancestors.

We include this section of our study with some misgivings. In no way are we suggesting that we have engaged in all of the conversations that could illumine this text. We also do not want to speak for the others from whom we have learned so much. However, we want to keep faith with the process in which we ask you to engage, and so we are sharing with you some of our findings. Please use these notes just to get you started, so that you can experience for yourselves the excitement of participating in such conversations.

Studies of this text in commentaries tend to focus on a comparison of this to other passages on the theme of discipleship, or to other references to the family in the Gospels, without attention to its pastoral or theological implications. The only other written treatment of it that we were able to uncover was Dietrich Bonhoeffer's classic study in *The Cost of Discipleship*. He emphasizes Jesus' call to discipleship that makes people "individuals," requiring each to break away from such "natural" ties as those to the family, which lead to an attempt to escape or to protect oneself from one's call. His study clearly reflects its roots in existentialist philosophy, in neo-orthodox theology, and in the emerging crisis in Europe prior to World War II. The church as the community of the cross becomes for him the new ground of security as an alternative to the seductive institutions of the society that he views as threatening to dissolve individual responsibility and integrity into mass conformity that contradicts the gospel.

Conversations with contemporary interpreters reveal how much the context has shifted since Bonhoeffer's writing. The reference to hating the family first grabs most people's attention, with varied results. In seminary classes and local church groups, North American readers of both European and African ancestry tended to take refuge in the alternative reading in Matt. 10:37, where the harsh "hate" is rendered instead "love less," as representing the real meaning of this passage. Some readers found support for this suggestion in notes in their Bibles that said that the Hebrew word really did not mean hate after all. Others simply asserted that Jesus could not have required people to hate their families, because Jesus supported "family values." One African American reader cited her community's confidence that "the Lord will make a way" as indeed making even the survival of one's family a matter of secondary importance: With or without a family, as they have learned through the centuries, God alone can be counted on and will suffice.

This general reading was nuanced in several ways. Many women noted the absence of husbands on the list of family members to be hated, and dismissed that as reflecting cultural circumstances that would not have allowed women to strike out on their own. Today, however, they found themselves equally challenged by the pull to stay in the relative security of their families, instead of responding to a call to serve God. Women who had experienced violence in their family of origin expressed two different responses to the passage. Some spoke of its importance as a biblical text giving them permission to break from their families, in contrast to the overwhelming use of biblical mandates to keep them in those contexts that were threatening their lives and their emotional health. On the other hand, the strong theme of sacrifice in the passage was all too familiar. As one put it, "The price is too great, because I've already paid so many prices and lost so much of value. This doesn't give credit to non-chosen sacrifice, and it doesn't affirm the courage and integrity of survivors who have moved mountains just to survive." Several spoke of how this passage requires "hero's work," and does not speak to the importance of the strength that comes from community. On the other hand, many resonated with the wisdom of the parables about "counting the cost," which is a lesson survivors have to learn and relearn, over and over.

Another nuanced reading within the otherwise dominant culture came from persons who had experienced family members being "taken" by religious cults. Particularly when such groups had a veneer of Christian language in their recruiting programs, they often drew on this passage to compel young adults to turn on their families in favor of the cult, and to turn over all the monetary resources to which they could get access—"all that they have." For persons who speak of having "lost" children or siblings to such movements, this passage evokes painful connections.

When we moved into other cultural or national groups, the responses to the passage took even more turns. A woman from one of the Indigenous nations of North America, for example, said that "hating family" in the sense of utterly rejecting them made no sense in her community. A person simply cannot do that, because one's family is who one is, and without it, there is no meaningful entity that can be called a person. On the other hand, giving "all that one has" makes perfect sense to her. "We've been doing that for years," she said, "in the potlatch or give-away" by which members of her community mark significant moments or events in life.

Members of a Korean immigrant community and several African Christians spoke with pain and anger about the use of this passage by missionaries from Europe and North America who had brought Christianity to their peoples. This passage was often used to convince new Christians that they must turn on their non-Christian families and reject the veneration of their ancestors that is so central to their cultures. Instead of challenging them to reject human institutions of status and security, the passage was experienced as threatening cultural integrity and survival.

While we have been working on this passage, Sharon has found herself thinking often of a conversation with a Korean friend during a time of political repression when Christian leaders who advocated for human rights were often in jeopardy. The woman was debating whether to respond to her sense of call to more visible leadership in the ordained ministry of her church. She said, "I do not hate my family. I *cannot* hate my family. I love them. But my children are old enough that they could survive on their own if I were taken. So I think maybe now I have to be ordained, for their sakes and for the gospel."

That voice is echoed by many in countries under political tyranny.

In such circumstances, identification with one's family is not a means of security in competition with one's discipleship, but rather a means of expressing it. *"No es justo"*—"It's not right"—is the response to this passage by many in Central America who risk their lives each day to find members of their families who have been disappeared. They are echoed by women in Chile who stitch into *arpilleras* (fabric pictures crafted in appliqué and embroidery) their stories of suffering and hope, their love of their families, and their sense of commitment to Christ and to their people. In both cases, their commitment to *"el proyecto de Dios"*—"the project of God"—in the reign of justice and peace that is at the heart of discipleship is fueled, not by a sense of freedom from family ties, but by their love for their families and their dream that children and grandchildren will live in a better world. While none of these groups holds poverty as an ideal or "giving up all that one has" as a requirement, the circumstances of their lives make that a descriptive rather than a prescriptive aspect of their Christianity.

A discussion of the passage in a middle class, suburban congregation led to the recognition that the congregation itself might have a role in supporting members who might feel called to a radical expression of their discipleship in a short- or long-term mission project. That possibility was quickly set aside, however, with the observation, "Our world is just not set up for that." This aborted discussion reminded Fred of the Quaker tradition of the "released friend." In this practice, someone feeling such a call would share in a process of discernment with the "meeting" or congregation. If the person was "released," others in the congregation would take responsibility for his or her family until the work was completed. (John Woolman's "release" to work on the anti-slavery issue is probably the best-known example from Quaker history.) Fred noted, however, that the practice is becoming rare in this country, due to the enculturation of the Quaker movement in the dominant stratum of North American society.

Taking Stock of Where We Are

The point of this step in the process is not to apply your conclusion about the meaning of a passage to your life situation. Rather, this is a time to pull together your reflections into a response that in turn becomes part of your ongoing interaction with the text. Who you are as interpreters—demographic data, information about your social and cultural context, experiences that have shaped you, and ongoing commitments that define you as individuals or as a group—shapes your reading of a text, and your response to a text changes who you are. Because of that change, in turn, your next reading of the same text may well be quite different. The process is like a spiral of ever deepening reading, reflection, response, and action, which in turn calls you back into a reading of the text.

It is important to reaffirm that one's response is always part of a dialogue with the text, and not necessarily assent to it. One may not always agree with what one has understood to be the point being made by the author to the author's own community. In such a case, one's response may well be a challenge to discern imaginative alternatives to the conclusion apparently reached in the text. One's response may also lead one to pay special attention to the absent or silenced voices one has come to recognize, rather than simply accepting the agenda of the author.

The response to the passage ought to be recorded in some medium, and not simply held in each reader's own heart and head. We are all, after all, embodied creatures, and our responses too need a chance to take on flesh. When you are studying in a group, the discussion in which you share often suffices to record your response: Being "heard into speech" (as the late theologian Nelle Morton used to say), when others receive and acknowledge your thoughts and feelings, is a powerful affirmation of one's value as a human being. Sometimes, though, the response will be even more concrete. One might be led to shape a case study as one's experience with the biblical text intersects with one's work or one's life. The response might also find expression in a sermon or as part of an academic exegesis paper. A group might move from biblical reflection to action on a particular problem or task. An individual interpreter or a group working together might give expression to their response in a spoken or a written prayer, or in music, dance, poetry, a video, or in some form of graphic art.

We have included our own reflections at this point, even though we have not done so following the "taking stock" sections of other chapters. We offer them not as a definitive conclusion, but as a way of bringing closure to the process in which you have been accompanying us through this study.

As we talked through our response to this passage in light of the various conversations and dialogues with others in which we engaged, we found ourselves fighting a constant temptation to get lost in details. Usually they were details that had an impact on others' responses, but that were not directly part of our own. For example, we talked often about the structure and role of families in various racial or ethnic groups or in other parts of the world. We contrasted the language of "hating" one's family with the courageous affirmation of family we encounter among the mothers of the disappeared in Central America that surely marks a life of discipleship. We talked about the way survivors of various expressions of violence in their families of origin or in intimate relationships have spoken of the impact of the passage. We talked about the experiences of gay men and lesbians who have had to reckon with losing contact with their families and putting their jobs in jeopardy as the price of coming out, or of making open commitments to the persons they love, or of working for justice for their communities—positions often taken in response to their sense of Christian commitment and vocation. And we talked about the twisted messages of self-denial, self-sacrifice, and self-deprecation often heard by gay men and lesbians, by women of all classes and circumstances, and by members of marginalized racial or ethnic groups in the statements about hating "even life itself" and carrying the cross (14:26b-27).

Those were not our own experiences, though. What was hardest was to translate the challenges underlying the passage for Luke's community into our own context. The principal challenge had to do with the relationship between being a disciple and relinquishing systems of security on which we rely. Related to that challenge is the warning to "count the cost."

We focused on the issue of security instead of talking specifically about families, because we recognized that for us other aspects of our lives—our professions and our efforts to establish a level of financial security—played the social role that families played in Luke's context. In fact, our own commitments to family members who depend on us are often factors in our reluctance to jeopardize other types of security, because in our contexts there are no real alternatives—no "new family" in the church or elsewhere in the community, to whose care we can confidently entrust them.

Our conversation about what it would mean to risk our professional situations in order to be "disciples" moved from the easy to the threatening. We recognized that some people in our position could be in jeopardy because of even as gentle a challenge to the traditional methods of biblical interpretation found in the academy and in the church as that represented in this book. Our own seminaries, however, and many in the professional society of our discipline are very supportive of the growing diversity of voices and methods in biblical interpretation. Even though our work on this model of interpretation has grown out of a sense of its importance in supporting the health and wholeness that is at the heart of the gospel, we cannot kid ourselves into thinking that by doing this work we are proving that we have not flunked discipleship!

Our security in our professions is bound up in our life as tenured members of seminary faculties. From that vantage point, we can commit our time and energy to work for greater inclusiveness in our student bodies, in the courses we teach, and in the composition of our faculties. All of these may well be commendable ways to use our privileged positions, and they may tempt us to say that the point is not to give all that up (14:33), but rather to use it on behalf of the gospel agenda of justice. But there is a big difference between being committed to inclusiveness, for example, when we are considering hiring persons to fill vacant positions, and being equally committed if we should be looking at changing the occupants of the chairs we now hold. When Fred came up with that observation, we looked at each other, laughed, and said, "Yeah, right. Don't say that around the people who balance the budgets!" Perhaps what we most need is a structure of accountability to keep us from fooling ourselves.

We had been thinking of the seminary as part of the family that, according to Luke's paradigm of discipleship, might need to be left behind. But we pondered what it would mean for our institutions to become the sort of alternative family envisioned by Luke for his community, which would care and provide for dependent family members if someone on the faculty or staff were to leave the institution, even for a limited period of time, to live out their ministry in an urban *barrio* or a rural area of our own country, or in some part of the two-thirds world. Could those left behind be convinced to pool resources and pull together to make such a ministry possible, both for the person's own family and in the ongoing life and responsibilities of the school? What might be the process by which we as a community would discern the call to such a vision for ministry? Could we use our positions on the faculty to encourage such a shift in orientation and re-direction of resources? What if we might not be among those left to manage things in the new "family," but instead those who need to strike out toward other places? Our eyes lit up as we felt the pull back to Africa and Central America. Then we talked about why this is not yet the time, but perhaps when our families no longer depend on us, or when we are closer to retirement, or when the church or the seminary becomes the new "family" on which we can rely (maybe we could work on developing that instead?), or when . . .

It is that persistent risk of fooling ourselves about the honesty of our commitment that pulls us back to the warning carried in the two examples of the need to count the cost. In a real sense the cost of discipleship cannot be calculated ahead of time, and there is no way to be sure you really know what you are getting into. We shared stories of experiences of tiny steps taken that suddenly left us continents away from home, in places and situations we had never envisioned when we started out. Any work for justice—any ministry or discipleship—seems to risk that. The risk of not being able to follow through to the end—becoming unsalty and maybe poisonous salt (14:34-35a)—is real.

Our response to this passage is finally unresolved. We began our work thinking it might be helpful to do some work on the puzzling language of 14:26 and the extreme demand of 14:33. We have come to the end of this turn through the spiral of interpretation no longer able to take advantage of the escape hatches of such labels as "puzzling" and "extreme," in order to get away from the discomfort that the passage causes us. Its word about the things that prevent discipleship is all too clear, and it is intimately connected to our lives. And so the challenge of the implied question remains: "Whoever comes to me and does not . . . cannot be my disciple."

A Final Word

Responding to a biblical passage can feel risky. After all, we have been told what these passages are supposed to mean! But often in the process of careful reading and analysis, questioning and research, reflection and dialogue, different voices are heard. The temptation is to become defensive of what we have always thought to be true, and to be afraid of what is new. Underlying such anxious self-protectiveness is a host of personal issues unique to each of us. But the sense of risk comes also from a host of faith questions common to all of us:

- whether we dare to trust that to love God requires the fullness of our intellect as well as of our energy and adoration;

- whether we dare to trust that God is active in our own particular histories—personal, social, and cultural; and

- whether we dare to imagine that our own questions and insights can be received as a revelation from God—part of God's self-disclosure—and a gift to the people of faith.

PART 2

Additional Sample Texts

Introductory Note to Part 2

In this section of the book we invite you to continue our journey as we engage five additional biblical texts, representing different types of literature from both Testaments. Following the interpretative process outlined in chapter 1, we discuss our selection of each text as a part of "locating the readers and the reading context." Since the basic method has already been presented, in the following chapters we move directly to our work with the biblical texts, with each chapter devoted to a separate text. We have, however, woven into the interpretative process itself our discussion of modifications or adaptations of the roadmap which emerge from our work with each of these texts. Since we cannot deal with every type of literature and cannot anticipate all issues and questions that interpreters might bring to texts, our intent here, as always, is to offer guidelines. By illustrating some modifications of the process, we invite you to make your own adaptations of this roadmap as you follow it on your journey with these and other texts.

Since we have attempted to be as brief as possible, while still moving through the various stages of the process, our interpretations are not presented here as completed work. This is especially significant in the final section, "Engaging the Text, Other Readers, and Our Communities." We report some of the issues that engage us and our communities, but we have not fully developed that process. Likewise, we suggest other readers whose perspectives have informed our work, but we have not attempted to record their contributions. We also do not limit our engagement with other readers to those mentioned here. Our intent is not to minimize the importance of this step in the process. Rather it is simply to provide a basic orientation. We invite you, as the readers of these texts with us, to continue in that process of engagement with these texts, other readers, and your communities.

Chapter 6

Numbers 10:11–12:16

Locating the Readers and the Reading Context

Selecting the Biblical Text

The first additional text on which we have chosen to focus is a narrative from the Pentateuch, the first five books of the Bible. We have selected a rather lengthy text, one which includes several discrete units or sub-plots: the process of setting out from Sinai (including being led by the ark of the covenant), complaints about the food, appointment of the elders, and a challenge to Moses' position as leader. Viewed as a whole, however, the unit narrates a single episode within the account of Israel's wandering in the wilderness. The unit opens with a statement that the Israelites set out by stages from the wilderness of Sinai en route to Paran (10:12), and it concludes with the report that the Israelites "camped in the wilderness of Paran" (12:16). The narrator has thus clearly situated these incidents within that journey from the wilderness of Sinai to the wilderness of Paran.

The larger narrative of Israel's wanderings in the wilderness, which begins at Exod. 13:17 and continues through the end of Deuteronomy, provides the literary context for this text. Because of the importance of that literary context for understanding the specific unit being studied, the interpreter may find it important to read at least some of that larger narrative—especially the portion that tells of the movement from Egypt to the wilderness of Sinai (Exod. 13:7–19:6), which is in many ways parallel to the account in our passage—earlier in the interpretative process than is suggested by the roadmap. This serves as a good reminder that the steps outlined in the roadmap are offered as guides, not as a rigid formula, and they should be adapted as necessary for various kinds of biblical texts.

Beginning the Journey at Home

Since this text belongs to the narrative of Israel's wandering in the wilderness, our assumptions and attitudes about wilderness and about the wilderness story as a whole affect our readings. On the one hand, we view the wilderness as a place of relaxation and retreat. It conjures memories of camping trips and vacation homes or cabins, with beautiful scenery, quietness, and serenity—escape from the noise and the frantic pace of urban life. On the other hand, there is the deeply ingrained national story of the settling of the frontier, the taming of the wilderness. In that story the wilderness is not something to be enjoyed, but rather it is frightening and wild, something to be feared and conquered. Closely related to these ambivalent feelings are attitudes about nature and civilization as, on the one hand, polar opposites or even enemies, and, on the other hand, interdependent contextual components of human life. Our religious heritage itself is similarly ambivalent about the wilderness. On the positive side is the wilderness sought by the desert mystics, for whom it was a place of union with God. On the negative side, the wilderness is seen as a place where wild beasts and demons take refuge, and where Satan lies in wait to test Jesus (Matt. 4:1-11; Luke 4:1-13).

Prominent in the text on which we are focusing, as well as in the larger narrative, is the "murmuring" or complaining of Israel. Here we face immediately a cultural norm echoing in our minds: One should not complain. We are encouraged to light up the room with a happy face at all times, and the doodle of a smiling face has become a universally recognized symbol of pleasure or even success on everything from bumper stickers to computer screens. To murmur, on the other hand, is to be negative—to have a bad attitude—and to complain admits failure.

Experiences with food will inform our reading of this text. Our situation of economic and social privilege means that we are reasonably certain that food in great variety will be on the table at meal times, and too readily available between meals. We can remember "murmuring" about the boring food of a school dormitory (and an allusion to this in our classrooms almost always elicits a knowing chuckle from students). But even that memory must be set in the context where it was possible to go home for the holidays or to eat out for a change of pace, and even in the dorm one normally has some choice of foods. Thus it is rather easy for us to trivialize the plight of the Israelites, and we can speak confidently—even smugly—about their lack of trust in God. We find ourselves wondering, however, how Israel's complaints and the stories of God's provision of food would be heard by persons in today's world who live with the reality of malnutrition, or with the constant threat of famine. For example, how might a peasant in Guatemala or the homeless in our cities and rural areas, whose strength is dried up due to the lack of a balanced diet, read such a text? Doubtless some would find the whining of the Israelites about the lack of variety in their food supply unnecessary. After all, they did have food to eat. But who determines the legitimacy of a community's craving for food?

Central to this text is the struggle with and about leadership roles. As persons who live in the societal context of elected leadership and in the religious atmosphere of the Protestant tradition, we feel a certain affinity with those who mounted a challenge to Moses as the unique voice of God. On the other hand, both of us are ordained ministers, with the power and privilege of that position. We have both had the "hood" of professorial authority placed around our shoulders, and Fred has even served in the dean's office. In these capacities, we can see ourselves mirrored in Moses, as persons entrusted with the authority and responsibility of leadership. We both can identify with Moses' frustration and weariness from attempting to meet seemingly impossible demands, but Sharon also finds her identity with Miriam, experiencing in various ways the impact of sexism on issues of leadership. We would like to think that men and women have equal access to positions of leadership, and that they are held equally responsible and, when necessary, equally culpable. Yet we know that cultural values and systemic structures convey other messages and create a different reality: If women in corporate hierarchies bump their heads on "glass ceilings," women in the church find their vocational lives interrupted by "stained-glass ceilings" that are equally effective at blocking access to places and roles. Women are often severely punished for errors for which men would receive a less harsh reprimand, and women as a group tend to be blamed for any woman's mistakes. We are also aware that biases of gender and of race, culture, and ethnicity are part even of such supposedly objective criteria as the "aptitude" or "achievement" tests used to determine admission to schools, allocation of financial aid, or eligibility for employment, and the norms by which papers and exams are graded.

Encountering the Biblical Text: Read, Feel, Question, React

First Impressions

One is struck immediately by the account of the orderly procedures by which the Israelites set out from Sinai. The image created is quite a contrast to that of the flight from Egypt and the movement through the wilderness prior to the encampment at Sinai. This assembly of escaped slaves is now forming into an organized army, with each company marching under its own standard, and with the ark of the covenant marching before them to scatter the enemy. This image of the congregation marching forth from Sinai, the mountain of God, evokes on one level shivers of excitement. The image turns out to be double edged, however, as this victory parade is revealed as an army of invaders marching toward the land they intend to conquer in the name of their God. How does this text feel to Indigenous peoples of the Americas, against whom invading armies, with their religious leaders in their midst, have marched—following the banner of God—to seize the land that has been the Indigenous peoples' ancestral home? How is this text read now in southern Africa, after centuries of the use of the Exodus-to-the-Promised-Land saga to legitimate White rule, at the same time that it held out a vision of freedom for Blacks denied authority over their own lives? How have those readings changed since the end of apartheid?

Closely related to this image of a people that is now well organized—even regimented—are the questions that emerge about how roles of leadership are allocated and practiced. The first of the stories that make up the unit we are studying—the appointment of the elders and the response to the men who prophesy—reflects a sharing of leadership responsibilities that strikes us as a positive and commendable practice. On the other hand, the elders receive their power when God takes some of the spirit from Moses and puts it on them. This would seem to suggest that, in distinction to God's power (11:23), human power exists in a limited quantity. If one person is to receive more power, it must be taken away from someone else, making the allocation of power a zero-sum game in which there must always be competition for the scarce commodity—losers as well as winners. Also related to the issue of power is the suggestion of this story that the authority of subordinate leaders is derivative, coming from the authority of the superior. Is the power of the elders only a power subordinate to that of the chief?

What is the significance of the interweaving of the story about the appointment of the elders with that about the craving for food? Is Moses simply being given reinforcements to control the unrest—security forces, as it were? Or is this the beginning of an administrative structure to address the social needs of this people with its own emerging identity and common life?

The story of the people's craving for food also introduces several questions about the nature and behavior of God. This is an instance in which God responds in anger to the people's complaint, which supports the common idea that the murmuring of the Israelites is wrong, and that it betrays a lack of trust in God. The response attributed to God also offers a rather interesting and even puzzling image of God's behavior, for God appears to say, "You want meat to eat; I'll give you meat to eat—so much that you'll get sick!" It's as if—in a fit of irritation—God turns spiteful!

The Israelites' memory of their time in Egypt (11:4-6) seems to be a classic instance of nostalgia for the "good old days" that were not very good at all. Was slavery in Egypt really one big feast? Was the boredom of a steady diet of manna really that horrible a price to pay for freedom? The passage might be almost comical, were it not so easily misread to confirm the false notion that slaves (or other categories of oppressed people) are really not that bad off after all, even that these people prefer the "security" of their familiar lives to the demands of freedom. Such logic echoes through the history of the defense of slavery in the United States, as well as in contemporary rhetoric about persons who receive public assistance.

A more compassionate reading of the Israelites' murmuring comes, in our experience, from women who have fled from a situation of abuse. The physical and emotional battering of the past is often described as enslavement, especially when the woman saw no alternatives that would not put her and her dependent children in further jeopardy. Once she leaves that situation, she can look back on the move as one toward freedom or liberation, but the "wilderness" to which she has come is a place where death threatens too, in the form of homelessness, poverty, hunger, rejection by friends and family, and a host of other threats and attacks. Her old life, as bad as it was, at least usually included a roof over her head and food for the children: Maybe she should go back, and learn to duck better!

African American readers also bring insights into the wilderness traditions from their history. Despite the centrality of the Exodus from Egypt as a paradigm of freedom in African American theology, stories of their own journey since the Emancipation Proclamation resonate with the physical hunger and the political struggles that mark the account of Israel's long journey. By comparison, forty years seems like a short time in the wilderness!

On another subject, what is the significance of the Cushite woman whom Moses married (chap. 12)? Who were the Cushites, and what was their relationship to Moses' people? Why did Miriam object to this marriage? Is there any connection between the two challenges against Moses—that concerning his wife (12:1) and that concerning the right to be the sole mediator of the word of God (12:2)? Why is only Miriam punished (12:15), when both Miriam and Aaron have spoken against Moses (12:1)?

Remembering Past and Other Experiences with the Text

We hold almost no memories from our church involvement of discussions of or sermons on Numbers 10–12, and relatively few memories of references to the wilderness story as a whole. Instead, the story we heard most often moved directly from slavery in Egypt into the Promised Land—a saga mirrored in our ancestors' flight from political, religious, or economic oppression in Europe, to successful establishment in the United States! When we heard the wilderness narrative recounted, it was almost always with the intent to demonstrate Israel's lack of faith in God, evidenced by their constant murmuring. Murmuring is also a favorite motif, evoked without its narrative context, whenever the "rabble" within a group grumble about initiatives which the leadership wants to take.

We both encountered Miriam in our Sunday school and church

experience (and, generally, in our own seminary educations as well) only on lists of "women of the Bible," and we recall nothing being said about her other than that she was a "prophetess." She was vaguely connected to a story about singing and dancing—a cheerleader for the star player, Moses. The gender dynamic of the narrative was generally not included in discussions about it. More recently, concern about the gender dynamic of the narrative of Numbers 12 has brought this text into the center of discussion in seminary classes on the Hebrew Bible or on women and the Bible, and also into focus in a number of scholarly articles as well as more general studies of the Pentateuch. Similarly, reflections on the narrative role of the Cushite woman have contributed to recent examinations of the African geographical, social, and historical references in the Bible, and of relationships between the Israelites and the Cushites and other African as well as Canaanite peoples.

A Close Reading of the Biblical Text: Steps in the Process

Preparing a Translation of the Text

In this narrative there are relatively few variations among the translations, and most of those reflect only slight differences in nuance or differences in editorial policy concerning gender-inclusive language. In the latter category, for example, translations such as JPS and JB describe Moses as more humble than any *other man*, while the NRSV, TEV, and NIV more closely reflect the gender inclusive nature of the Hebrew text by describing him as more humble than *anyone else*. The Christian audience of the NIV clearly has shaped the decision of its editors to capitalize "Spirit" in 11:17, 25, 26-29, evoking an association with the Holy Spirit, the third person of the Christian Trinity.

Four issues of translation raise possibilities of substantively different meanings in the text. First, in 11:2-3 both NRSV and JPS read that God "burned against them," while TEV, NIV, and JB read "among them." The latter softens the sense that God is directly attacking the people. Second, TEV identifies the complainers who crave meat (11:4) as "foreigners traveling with the Israelites," rather than the "rabble" (NRSV, NIV, JB) or "riffraff" (JPS) among the people themselves. The reading in TEV clearly sets up a different dynamic from that intended

137

by the text, where the issue is dissension among the Israelites. Third, TEV concludes Moses' complaint to God in 11:15 by attributing blame to God for his discomfort ("so that I won't have to endure your cruelty"), rather than simply by Moses' longing for his suffering to end ("and do not let me see my misery"), as in the NRSV (see also JPS, JB, NIV). Finally, while the principal English versions all identify the wife of Moses as a Cushite, the Latin American Spanish translation of 12:1 obscures this issue by referring to her as simply *la mujer extranjera*—"the foreign woman"—thus obscuring the issue of her African identity.

Considering the Literary Context

The passage on which this study is focused needs to be understood as part of the canonical form of the narrative that takes Israel from its long time of slavery in Egypt to the crucial events of revelation and giving of the law at Sinai, and from Sinai to the banks of the Jordan River. Because of the importance of this literary frame in shaping the meaning of the passage, it is important to examine that literary context earlier in the process of study than one would do with most texts.

That larger narrative begins with the relatively brief account of Israel's movement from Egypt to Sinai (Exod. 13:17–19:6). That account is overshadowed, in both its length and the theological significance attributed to it, by the long report of the people's sojourn at Sinai (Exod. 19:7–Num. 10:10, including the entire book of Leviticus). The Sinai episode centers on the revelation of the laws that will shape Israel's life as a people in covenant with God, and it includes also narratives of some of the activities of the Israelites and their various leaders, such as the familiar story of their making and worshiping the golden calf. In the portion of the Sinai story told in Numbers, we get the report of the census that was taken in preparation for the Israelites' departure from Sinai, which leads up to our text. The rest of the book of Numbers (10:11–36:13) takes the Israelites to their next resting place—namely, the border of the land they understand to have been promised to them. There the book of Deuteronomy reviews the journey from Egypt—a story that stands as Moses' final legacy to the people before his death, and before they cross the Jordan River under a new generation of leaders.

There are a number of parallels between the pre-Sinai and the post-Sinai journeys (Exod. 13:17–19:6 and Num. 10:11–36:13). The motif of the Israelites' murmuring is found several times in both stages of their journey. There are the crises when the people lack water (Exod. 15:22-27 and Exodus 17 pre-Sinai, and Numbers 20 post-Sinai) and concerns about their supply of food (Exodus 16 pre-Sinai, and Numbers 11 post-Sinai). The concern for shared leadership also arises both before and after Sinai (Exodus 18 and Numbers 11).

These latter two issues—leadership and the clamor for food—take different forms and meanings before and after Sinai. Before Sinai the two issues are separate. The people's clamoring for food in Exodus 16 is motivated by concern about the people's survival, and Moses's authority is not challenged. After the time at Sinai, however, the people's complaints about food become an occasion to raise and address issues of leadership responsibilities. The appointment of the seventy elders, the men who prophesy, and the challenge of Miriam and Aaron are not simply stories of survival in the desert. Rather, these are stories that reflect the tensions within a community that is seeking to develop structures and norms of leadership.

Similar issues continue through the stories that follow our text. The account of the spies sets Joshua and Caleb against the captain to be elected to lead the assembly back to Egypt (Numbers 13–14). Issues of priestly relationships and responsibilities are woven into the story of the confrontation between Moses and Korah and his followers (Numbers 16), and into the instruction concerning the Aaronic priests and Levites (Numbers 18). The account of the lack of water results in the pronouncement that Moses and Aaron will not enter the Promised Land, which leads to issues of the transition from the "exodus" generation to those who will lead the "conquest," or occupation of the land (Num. 20:1-13).

Identifying the Shape of the Text

As noted above, the specific text on which we are focusing (Num. 10:11–12:16) opens with a description of the companies of Israelites, each marching under its own banner and all following the lead of the ark of the covenant of the Lord. That image of the ark (Num. 11:35-36) and the language of the cloud (Num. 10:11-12, 34) convey the notion

139

of divine guidance and leadership and offer assurance that the promise will be fulfilled, that the journey will lead to the Promised Land. Tension is created, however, by crises within the community, each of which raises issues about leadership.

The first unit (11:1-3) reports a complaint of the people, God's angry response, and the successful intercession of Moses. Here leadership manifested through intercession for the people establishes the leader's solidarity with the community. The second unit (11:4-34) interweaves two issues. The first issue is the craving of the "rabble" for meat, but within that context and in response to the weeping of these people, Moses expresses his frustration with the burden of leadership (11:11-15). God responds both to the craving for food and to the leadership crisis. In the latter case God instructs Moses in the appointment of elders to assist him. In response to the former, God promises meat—enough meat to make them sick. At that point Moses again raises a concern about his role as leader: How will he find food in such abundance to give the people on God's behalf? The story then reports the implementation of both parts of God's strategy. Although the initial issue is that of food, concerns about the frustrations of leadership are woven into the fabric of the text in such a way that the two issues are inextricably linked. This text clearly places issues of leadership within the context of concerns about the availability and distribution of resources within and for the sake of the community.

Although the specific language of murmuring or complaint is not used, in Num. 11:4-35 there are two (or possibly even three) instances of complaining. The first is the "rabble's" craving for food, to which God responds in anger. The second is Moses' complaint to God about the burdens of leadership, in response to which God does not show anger. (A third might be the question about the two men who were prophesying.) According to the narrative, to raise one's voice in complaint is not necessarily wrong, and complaining itself is not portrayed as evidence of a lack of faith, as we so often assume in our reading of these stories. What is equally clear, though, is that specific complaints can be judged to be inappropriate. At issue is the criteria by which this judgment is made, and who determines the criteria.

In this episode Moses himself raises two issues related to the burden of leadership, in which the common concern is about self-sufficiency. First, Moses is not able to bear the burden of leadership by himself.

140

Second, he questions the adequacy of his own resources to provide the quantity of food that God has said will be delivered to the Israelites. In response to the latter concern God poses the rhetorical question: Is the power of God limited? Moses' power of leadership is not derived from himself alone; it is granted by God. Moses' leadership depends neither on his own power to provide nor on his own resources. The available resources come from God, whose power is not limited. The response to the first concern, that of Moses' frustration with the burden of leadership, however, does suggest that his own abilities and power are limited. God responds by relieving Moses of sole responsibility for the leadership of the people, giving the new leaders—still a select and limited group—some of Moses' power (spirit). Within the text itself, however, is another perspective on the distribution of power and leadership. When the two men who remain in the camp begin to prophesy and a protest is voiced to Moses, he responds by wishing that such prophetic power were shared by all the people (Num. 11:29). Instead of the view of power as a scarce commodity to be carefully doled out to a select group, this little parenthesis envisions an abundance of power sufficient for everyone to share.

The debate about who has access to power is given a particular expression in the narrative of Miriam's and Aaron's challenge to Moses (Numbers 12). They object first to Moses' marriage with a Cushite woman, but that objection serves only as the occasion for the second: "Has the LORD spoken only through Moses?" (Num. 12:2). It is this second question that the text addresses by establishing the unique role of Moses. Considerations of leadership are set in the context of social dynamics and assumptions about societal patterns and privileges.

Several issues can be noted here. First, this text creates its own tension with the earlier provision of a shared leadership and the desire that the spirit rest upon all (Numbers 11). Having just enlarged the circle of leadership, the text focuses again on the unique role of Moses. Second, the text notes Miriam's objection against Moses' marriage with the Cushite woman, but Miriam's subsequent punishment is specifically linked to her challenge to Moses' leadership. The text is not clear about whether that punishment also condemns her objection to Moses' marriage to a foreigner. Third, the text states that Miriam and Aaron both challenge Moses, but only Miriam is punished. The text thus participates in and reinforces a cultural pattern in which the woman is

141

blamed and punished for actions committed by both men and women (a pattern often reflected in readings of the Adam and Eve story of Genesis 3). A rationale frequently offered for the lack of punishment of Aaron was the narrator's need to protect the priestly purity of Aaron, which would be viewed as blemished by leprosy. That explanation identifies a social interest of the text itself and reminds us that the narrative arises out of and serves the specific social context of its own community of origin.

Comparing with Texts of Similar Material

In the earlier discussion of literary context we talked about the parallel texts within the wilderness narrative, with echoes of the stories about the need for food, lack of water, and appointment of elders. One might also look more generally at stories of the people's murmuring or complaining about a variety of circumstances in their individual and communal lives.

In addition to these parallels within the wilderness narrative itself, there are other instances in which the wilderness wanderings are recounted in the Bible, such as Deut. 9:7-29; Pss. 78:15-31; 105:39-42; 106:7-33: Jer. 2:2-3; and Ezek. 20:9-26. These texts, which tend either to condemn Israel for their rebellious and sinful acts of murmuring or to praise God for acts of mercy and guidance, have played a powerful role in shaping our responses to the narrative of the wilderness wanderings, and specifically to the murmurings.

The motif of God's provision of food in the wilderness also finds connection with the stories in the Gospels of the feeding of the multitudes (Matt. 14:13-21; 15:32-39; Mark 6:30-44; 8:1-10; Luke 9:10-17; John 6:1-14). Specific connection to our text is made, for example, in Matt. 15:33, in which the disciples ask Jesus: "Where are we to get enough bread in the desert to feed so great a crowd?" (see Moses' question in Num. 11:23). Another connection can be seen between the story of Joshua's complaint brought to Moses about the two men in the camp who prophesy (Num. 11:26-30) and the Gospel accounts of the concern voiced to Jesus that persons who are not explicitly Jesus' followers are healing in his name (Mark 9:38-41; Luke 9:49-50).

Reading Contextually:
Finding the Passage in Its Place

Considering the Literary Context

You will recall that the literary context of this passage was discussed earlier in the "close reading" section (p. 138) because of the importance of that larger context for this passage. You may wish to review that discussion at this time, to see if new questions have been raised by your intervening work.

Locating the Social Context

It is important to be clear that when we talk here about the social context, we are not speaking of the world described by the narrative—the context of the wilderness wanderings themselves. What we seek to determine, to the extent that we can do so, is the setting within which and for which the narrative was shaped and written. That narrative, in the form in which we now read it, clearly draws on many early traditions about the wilderness, and even on previous versions of a wilderness narrative. Our interest here, however, is not to reconstruct those traditions and their settings—a task emphasized in many commentaries. It is essential to recognize that different questions are addressed by those earlier sources than are addressed in the final form of the text on which this study focuses. The fact that the final text builds on those earlier sources contributes to the complexity of that final narrative, for embedded within that narrative are layers of tradition, each with its own perspective. These layers do not always fit together in total harmony. They are, however, joined into a single coherent narrative that is given shape and social and theological content by those persons responsible for this final form of the narrative.

The general historical context in which that final shaping took place is the aftermath of the exile, when those returning from exile were seeking a new sense of identity and purpose. While it is still difficult to reconstruct with any assurance the social dynamics of exilic and post-exilic Israel, some observations can be made. One thing that is clear is that Israel was not monolithic, as some efforts to establish the general historical context of texts from that period might lead one

143

to believe. A variety of communities struggled, each in its own way, to understand and to respond to the crises and opportunities of the exile.

Both during and after the exile, there were competing visions and a variety of efforts to establish new patterns of social organization and leadership. For example, there were those who found hope in the anticipation of the day when the Davidic throne would be reestablished, and others who centered their vision on a theocracy under priestly control. An alternative vision seems to underlie our text, however. The emphasis on Moses' appointment of the elders, in obedience to God's direction, would lend support to those who would try to establish a similar structure of authority in the new social reality of post-exilic Israel. Within this particular community, though the priests played an important role, neither they nor the royal household constituted the basic governing unit. This is consistent with the portrait of Aaron, representative of the priests, in our text. Insofar as he shares with Miriam in the challenge against Moses, he is on the "wrong" side of that dispute about leadership. On the other hand, he does occupy a privileged status, and because of that, he is not punished as Miriam is, but rather he intercedes on her behalf. Although our text has frequently been placed in the social context of the priestly circles, that conclusion does not appear to be fully supported by the narrative itself.

Engaging the Text, Other Readers, and Our Communities

The issues of leadership that have emerged as a motif running through this narrative engage us in a consideration of perspectives on power. Encountering this text as persons who have various leadership responsibilities, we resonate with the frustration voiced by Moses over his burden of responsibility. We find some comfort in the nature of God's response of appointing elders to share that burden. By implication, this text encourages us to share the burden with God, and subsequently with the other people given by God to help carry it. The passage thus offers a double challenge to persons in power, first, to recognize and voice feelings of limitation, and, second, to be open to sharing leadership with others. The offer of colleagues to share the power can be a gift, and it can also be perceived as a threat. The text thus challenges any need we may feel to be able to do it all and to control everything by ourselves.

That challenge, however, is still shaped by a narrative that tends to assume that power is defined hierarchically, that it belongs to those in positions of authority, and that it is a limited commodity. Power is still passed from superior to inferior—from Moses to the elders—and it is granted only to a select group. Power is also presented in this narrative as a scarce commodity, which some win only when others lose, and thus as something to be obtained and to be guarded jealously by those who have it. (As we observed above, however, there is within the narrative a hint of an alternative view, in which power is not limited and not to be jealously protected. That is suggested, however, in a side comment overshadowed by the principal perspective of the narrative.)

This story focuses on the role of individual persons, particularly that of the hero Moses. Such a narrative plays easily into the individualism of the dominant culture, where power and the spirit are understood in terms of a person's ability to control and direct. In cultures that are more communal in orientation, however, power is understood to reside within the community and to be manifest in the process of communal interaction. We would want to engage in conversation with persons from such contexts in order to learn how their assumptions, which are so different from our own, shape their reading of this text.

We also resonate with Moses' concern about the apparent insufficiency of resources to accomplish the task that God has put before us. In the face of overwhelming need caused by the lack of food, potable water, shelter, or other needed resources, we typically are paralyzed by the disparity between overwhelming needs and limited resources. Yet we are also aware of groups that have been led to recognize such needs within their communities, and that set out boldly to respond to those needs, trusting that the power of God is not limited. The vision of this text and of such groups challenges our practical management orientation that would assume that we must have within our control and purview all the necessary resources before we begin to act.

This text confronts persons with responsibility for the welfare of others with a different angle of vision on the availability and distribution of resources. We wonder, for example, how this text would be read by persons who have assumed roles of leadership in a refugee camp in Rwanda. How is it read by persons bearing responsibility for sheltering the homeless in our cities and towns? How is it read by pastors and lay leaders in congregations who are struggling to respond to demands of justice and human need on their scarce resources—God's call in their specific circumstances?

But there is another side to the story. How would this story be understood by the masses of persons huddled together in that refugee camp, or those who have sought protection from the elements in a shelter, or the community that gathers for worship—in other words, those not in positions of leadership? The other side of the dilemmas of the leaders is the experience and perspective of the community. In this text, when the "rabble" protests about the food provided, that complaint evokes a negative response. This raises the question of who gets to determine the legitimacy of an expressed need. Does the community speak for itself, and so become the subject of its own life? Or do those in positions of power determine what needs are legitimate or real, making the "rabble" the object of the leaders' beneficence or condemnation? We recognize within ourselves how easy it is to sit in judgment about the expressed dissatisfaction of others. When an unemployed person expresses the need for a car to get to work, we can easily point to the nearest bus route! In this narrative, in which God and Moses alike disapprove of the people's craving for food, those in positions of power and leadership get to determine the legitimacy of the need. The community's own perception is dismissed, and the voice of a community struggling to give expression to its own future is denied recognition. Clearly not every expressed need is necessarily legitimate or of equal value, but one has to raise the question of who gets to make that determination.

We also wonder how this text is read in contexts where God has not provided food and water in the context of a "wilderness." In refugee camps where people die every day for lack of food and water, shelter and medication, what is the meaning of a narrative in which God provides for the people's needs, and which affirms that God's power is not limited? Similarly, how is this narrative read where budget deficits result in cuts even to minimal social services, and where nutrition and health care programs are terminated? How do people read a story like this when God appears not to provide the needed help?

The narrative of Numbers 12 about the challenge of Miriam and Aaron to the actions and authority of Moses confronts us with complex dynamics of gender and ethnicity that affect social relationships and norms for authority. We are uncomfortable with the fact that only Miriam is punished, even though she and Aaron acted together. The text thus both assumes and perpetuates a gender bias. Intertwined with that bias, however, is another issue raised by Miriam's and Aaron's objection to Moses' marriage to a Cushite woman. Though the text never addresses this objection directly, and Miriam is explicitly said to be punished for challenging Moses' leadership and not his choice of a spouse, the fact that she is punished may imply a critique of the latter objection as well. If so, we have a text that affirms ethnic and racial inclusivity, while leaving its gender bias in place.

Especially in the early years of the feminist movement among Euro-American biblical scholars, interpreters often reversed that dynamic. They raised our sensitivity to gender issues, while remaining silent on dynamics of ethnicity. African American interpreters, on the other hand, have focused attention on the specific significance of the "Cushite" woman, which raises the issue of the intermarriage of an Israelite and not just any foreigner, but specifically an African. This mention of the Cushite woman is just one example of the close interface of the biblical world with the ancient world of Africa—a connection that has not informed the work of biblical scholarship from the dominant culture. The interpretive and historical work of African American and African scholars has raised new questions, not only about the reading of this text, but about the very horizons of biblical scholarship.

A similar pattern of both attention and neglect can be observed in the anti-Judaism that has been identified in some Christian feminist interpretations. In addressing important and legitimate concerns relative to gender issues, these interpreters have ignored the bias in their own religious assumptions. Or in doing gender and ethnic analysis, interpreters have ignored the dynamics of economic class. What we can recognize in this text is the complex of interacting dynamics that shape who we are, making everyone multi-cultural and multi-contextual. Furthermore, the elements that define a person's social context are always shifting, being formed by the particular configuration of factors operative at a given time and in a given situation.

In dealing with a narrative such as this, it is important to remember that a function of narrative is usually to resolve the tension that the narrative itself creates or identifies. That resolution serves the needs of the community that gives shape to the narrative. In our reading of this text we find some of our struggles mirrored in the challenges presented by the text, but the resolution offered by this narrative introduces additional struggles and concerns when it is intersected by the data and values of our context (around issues of gender, for example). The narrative presents a single resolution, but we are left wondering about others that might be possible. To put it another way, does God speak to such struggles only with this voice?

Chapter 7

Jeremiah 22:24–23:8

Locating the Readers and the Reading Context

Selecting the Biblical Text

We wanted to work with a text from the prophetic books for several reasons. First, prophetic texts from the Hebrew Bible that are read as foretelling the coming of the Messiah have played an important role in the life of the Christian church. Second, the prophets have often been assumed to be predictors of the future, and their literary legacy continues to be plumbed for foreshadowings of events in our own day or for clues to what is yet to happen in the world. Finally, and on a related point, this literature raises in a striking manner such theological issues as God's "intervention" in events in human history, or, more generally, the continuing relationship of the divine to the created order.

The particular text selected, Jeremiah 22:24–23:8, is usually treated by interpreters as having three separate parts only loosely strung together: 22:24-30, composed of pronouncements of judgment against King Coniah; 23:1-4, containing sayings about the "shepherds"; and 23:5-8, the promise of the "righteous Branch" and other events of the coming days. In contrast to that approach, this study will look at the passage in its canonical form as an integral unit. The unit is held together by the issue of the future of David's throne (22:30 and 23:5), and by the brackets evident in the initial oath of God, "As I live" (22:24) and the concluding confessions that begin "As the LORD lives. . . ." (23:7-8). The unit thus begins with words of judgment concerning the political order (focused on the king, Coniah or Jehoiachin), but it concludes with a vision of restoration. In that way, the unit as a whole places before the reader the juxtaposition of judgment and hope. Within the vision of restoration is a text often cited in the Christian tradition as a foretelling of Jesus, the anticipated "righteous Branch," the wise and just ruler from the line of David.

Beginning the Journey at Home

Any time we engage a prophetic text, we bring to that process all of our assumptions about prophets and prophecy. As noted above, the prophets have held a particularly important place in Christian tradition. On the one hand, many of these texts have been read as foretelling the birth, life, death, and resurrection of Jesus. On the other hand, the prophets themselves have served as prominent models for the religious life. Particularly within Protestant Christianity, the prophets have been seen as inspired individuals who stand against the formalism and legalism of institutional religion and who stand outside the stifling ritualism of communal liturgy. From a slightly different perspective, the prophets have been studied as independent voices speaking for social justice. Such ideas fit easily within a culture of individualism and a religion of personal piety. They support the image of the solitary hero who fights for justice against an evil social order.

In our experience, it is the latter view of prophets as champions of social justice that was formative, though the messianic readings have always been present. In our earliest memories and in our current worship settings, messianic texts (principally from Isaiah) have been read during the Advent and Christmas seasons, and the "suffering servant" and other similar texts have figured in the church's preparation for Easter. But our formative years in seminary were at a time (the 1960s, as described in chapter 1) and in contexts where a common teaching was that "The prophets are not foretellers but forthtellers"—that is, not predictors but social critics. Prophets often came to be understood as shrewd analysts of the political scene, good students of the *Times* and of religious tradition. The freshness of that image and the importance of its vision in the context of social movements for civil rights and demonstrations against the war in Vietnam left a strong imprint on our assumptions about the prophets.

Closely related to the notion that the prophets are social critics is the notion that the authentic word of the prophet is the oracle of judgment. Texts of hope or of restoration are frequently identified by scholars as later additions. That identification is not simply descriptive, but rather allows those texts to be ignored, or even trivialized. The additional fact that this word of judgment was intended to reform the present world order led to clear separation between the prophetic books and apocalyptic literature such as Daniel or Revelation. The former were thought to be concerned with this world and its reform, and the latter only with a future life or world. Apocalyptic literature was often dismissed as escapist, whereas prophetic speech was seen to engage the realities of this world and to call for radical acts of justice within the social order.

A central concern of Jeremiah 22:24–23:8 is the shattering word of an exile from which the king will not return, so experiences of and attitudes toward exile become an important aspect of the social location of the reader of such texts. The dislocation of exile is not something we have experienced. However distant in culture and geography, our travels outside the country have always been with a return ticket in hand or assured. We do have some second-hand awareness of the experience of exile, as that experience has been shared with us by groups and individuals living in exile in this country or other countries outside their homeland, or in "internal exile" as displaced persons in their own countries torn apart by years of war. We have also heard the sorrow of families who experience separations because loved ones are in exile, whether for political or for economic reasons.

Reflecting on these experiences, we are reminded that there are many different reasons for exile and varied responses to exile in our own context. For example, despite such common factors as loss of the familiar and the pain of separation, exile is not the same for wealthy landowners or business or professional people as it is for peasants and urban poor people. The former have resources of their own, contacts with friends and former colleagues, and often previous experiences of living or at least traveling in other cultures, to help them cope in their new circumstances, none of which forms of assistance cushion the experience of the latter. Other factors will also shape people's experiences of exile. For example, there is a difference between involuntary exile, in which one has been removed from one's home by the action of another, and voluntary relocation or emigration. Even that distinction blurs, however, when the "voluntary" exile was in response to such circumstances as war, political persecution, or economic devastation. The experience of exile also differs according to the memories and present conditions in the place of origin. A peaceful land filled with happy memories is a place to which emigrants often long to return. On the other hand, persons who have seen their families murdered or disappeared, their villages destroyed, their land ravaged, and the economic and social infrastructures destroyed have no sense of a home to which they can return. In such circumstances thoughts of the homeland may well evoke feelings of pain and horror, rather than of possibility and hope. It is important, therefore, to be attentive to each person's or group's interpretation of this phenomenon called "exile."

It is also important to remember that what may appear from the outside to be similar experiences of living in exile from one's homeland represent different composite experiences, each of which is particular to its own context. For example, Korean Americans describe the differences between the experiences of first-generation immigrants to the United States and those of the second generation who were born in that country. The first generation tends to find support and identity in their culture of origin. The second generation, however, does not share that same sense of connection to Korea, and references by the older generations to "home" carry little or no meaning for the younger generation, even though many in the dominant culture still look upon them as foreigners. On the other hand the experience of second-generation Korean Americans appears similar to that of other cultural or ethnic groups. For example, the contradiction between what they know to be true (that this is their home) and the way they are often treated (as foreigners who don't belong here) echoes in many respects the experience of Puerto Ricans and Chicanos. For many in these latter two groups the United States is their ancestral home and the place where they were born. Nevertheless, they are kept on the distant margins by the dominant culture and are made to feel like aliens in their own land. Although the dynamics are similar, they are experienced differently because of differences in culture and social location. It is important to realize that groups in this latter category may not consider themselves to be in exile at all.

The idea of exile sometimes functions in a metaphorical way. Persons who no longer feel at home in the changing culture that has emerged around them will sometimes describe themselves as being in exile. The assumption, of course, is that they can expect to return to that old culture at some future point—for example, once the country returns to its senses and moral sensibilities. Today mainline churches will sometimes describe their situation as one of exile, sensing that they are no longer at home in the culture, and that they no longer play a central role in public life. Again, the metaphor conveys the hope for return to a remembered status that is both familiar and more comfortable. Exile is not only an image of exclusion or alienation; it also carries the sense of the memory and lure of a homeland from which one is separated and to which one hopes to return.

A final set of concerns related to this text touches on the oracles concerning the shepherds. That language, coupled with the later reference to the "righteous Branch" (which immediately evokes christological connections) sparks the connection to Christian references to Jesus as the "good Shepherd" (John 10:1-18). That implicit connection then evokes the contrast between that good shepherd and those whose failure to do their job is indicted in 23:1-4. Read in the context of the legacy of Christian anti-Semitism, this passage risks being added to the arsenal of texts twisted into the support of that agenda.

Encountering the Biblical Text:
Read, Feel, Question, React

First Impressions

This text seems to focus on the leadership of the country as the primary problem: It is the king (22:24-30) and the shepherds (23:1-3) who stand under judgment. Restoration will come with the establishment of good shepherds (23:4) and the enthronement of a righteous ruler (23:5-6). Does this suggest that hope resides only in the leadership of the people? Is the destiny of the people determined by the top—then trickling down to the people? If so, what is the meaning of such a text in the context of a liberation movement of the people? On the one hand, it does offer the hope for a cessation of violence and an end to the separations of exile. On the other hand, it does not give the people ("the sheep") an active role in that new order. Is there any room here for a theology that approaches its task from "the base"— from the bottom up? In a context that is suspicious about any political solutions that might be concocted by persons in power, how is such a text to be read?

This text is a proclamation of God's actions in history, both of judgment and of restoration. It is God who delivers the king into exile and who will deal with the shepherds. It is God who will raise up new shepherds and the righteous Branch. Does this mean that any exile is God's judgment, or that all exiles are acts of punishment? If so, whose sins are being punished? In this text the leaders are judged and the leaders are sent into exile. But what about those contexts in which the people flee (and in that sense are in exile) in order to escape torture and other forms of persecution at the hand of the leaders? On the other hand, is every return to a previous place of status a fulfillment of God's promise? Is the return of exiled wealthy landowners and merchants to Nicaragua, for example, to be understood as God's act of restoration? How do we recognize and understand the relationship between events in history and God's word?

Remembering Past and Other Experiences with the Text

We find in our memory banks no references to this specific text, though certainly we connect the image of the righteous Branch who will execute justice to Advent texts and hymns.

A Close Reading of the Biblical Text: Steps in the Process

Preparing a Translation of the Text

Several differences in translation can be detected, although most are not of major significance. Some translations of v. 26 (NIV, JB, TEV, JPS) make clear that neither Coniah nor his mother was born in the land to which they will be hurled, and neither will return. The lack of a distinction between the singular and plural "you" in English obscures the fact that in Hebrew the reference is clearly plural. NIV uses the more common name for the king, Jehoiachin, rather than Coniah. That translation also renders v. 22:28b in the future tense rather than the present (as in the NRSV), making it predictive, rather than a statement of fact. It also says of Jehoiachin, in v. 30a, that he will be recorded "as if childless," rather than "as childless." This eliminates any potential confusion for the reader from the fact that Jehoiachin does have offspring, a fact noted in v. 28. At issue is the failure of his heirs to succeed to the throne, which is made clear in the last half of v. 30. TEV speaks of the king "losing" his children, probably also in an effort to make the circumstances clear. But such renderings weaken the meaning of the Hebrew text, which describes the political loss of succession in the stark language of the king's being childless.

In the JPS and JB the verbs of v. 23:1 become permissive ("let" and "allow," respectively) rather than active ("destroy and scatter"). At issue is whether these leaders or elites are being indicted for passive neglect of their duties, or for active malfeasance. The distinction turns on one's reading of the Hebrew verb form, and it becomes significant for one's understanding of the underlying historical circumstances being addressed.

JB speaks of the gathered sheep by saying, "not one shall be lost." This phraseology may be intended to pick up the image of the "lost sheep" from the Gospels, such as Matthew 18:12-14 and Luke 15:3-6, and the reference to Jesus' not losing any of those entrusted to him (John 17:12).

In 23:5-6 translators of all major English versions except the JPS write "branch" with a capital letter, thereby making clear that they understand it as a messianic title. Another dimension of the messianic reading is raised by Spanish translations of the name by which this new Davidic ruler will be called (23:6). English translations agree in the use of the word "righteousness" in that sentence-name. The personal or even moralistic tone of that word is transformed in the use of the word *justicia* ("justice") in the *Reina Valera* and Latin American versions. This language picks up the sense of social integrity carried by the Hebrew word. Yet another issue is raised by the *Versión Popular*, which builds on a less common meaning of the underlying Hebrew word— namely, "defender"—in its use of *victoria* ("victory"). This, however, introduces a triumphalistic connotation, particularly given the frequent christological use of this passage.

Identifying the Shape of the Text

Instead of dividing this passage into separate segments, and attributing each to a specific context of origin and historical and theological agenda (as has been the approach of many commentators), we are exploring the meaning carried by the shape of this passage in its entirety. The text opens with Yahweh declaring an oath of judgment against King Coniah (King Jehoiachin). No reason is given here for the judgment, but it is to take the harsh form of an exile that is definitive and final (22:24-30). The intensity of the experience of exile is underscored when the place of exile is described as a different country from his place of birth—a place he does not know—and the homeland is described as the land for which they long. The extent of devastation of this experience of exile is intensified by the statement that none of Coniah's offspring shall sit on his throne, the throne of David. This twofold pronouncement reinforces the definitive nature of the judgment: Not only is there no hope for the present and past, represented by the king and his mother, but there is no hope for future generations. In contrast, however, the passage ends with the promise of a new king for David, one who will rule with justice and righteousness (23:5-8). The drama created in these two sections is found in the tension between the word of definitive end and the promise of a new beginning.

The middle section (23:1-4) parallels the movement of the first and last taken together, with its proclamation of woe and its word of promise, but the precise relationship of the middle unit to the others is not clear. In that middle section there is an accusation against those "shepherds" who have scattered God's flock. Are the "shepherds who scatter" the kings of Judah, specifically here King Coniah? And are the "shepherds" that God will raise up the same as the righteous king of v. 5? If so, why shepherds (plural) and king (singular)? Do the plural shepherds refer to a coming succession of kings? Or do the shepherds refer to other types of leaders, instead of or in addition to the king?

This middle section also introduces another dimension, namely concern for the "flock" or the people. The reason for the pronouncement of woe is the shepherds' failure to tend the flock. The restoration will result in the well-being of the remnant of the people, a remnant which will be gathered by God, returned by God to the fold, and tended by shepherds raised up by God. Yet that remnant is passive in the text, always the object of the actions of others, and never what liberation theologians call "historical subjects"—active agents in their own lives.

Finally the concluding section of the unit (23:7-8) proclaims the new declaration by which God will be known. No longer is that declaration shaped by the experience of the exodus from Egypt, but by the exile and return to the land.

The unit as a whole exhibits the following structure:

A. DAVIDIC KING: judgment—definitive end . . . . (22:24-30)

B. SHEPHERDS: judgment . . . . (23:1-2)
   1. Woe . . . . (23:1)
   2. Judgment proper. . . . . (23:2)
      a. accusation. . . . . (23:2a)
        (twofold consequence for the people:
        scattered my flock, not *attended* them)
      b. punishment (I will *attend* to you) . . . . (23:2b)

C. PEOPLE: promise of restoration. . . . . (23:3)
   1. God's action (twofold) . . . . (23:3a)
      a. gather the remnant
      b. bring them back
   2. Result for people (fruitful, multiply). . . . . (23:3b)

B'. SHEPHERDS: promise of new leadership . . . . (23:4)
   1. God's action . . . . (23:4a)
   2. Result for people (twofold). . . . . (23:4b)
      a. not fear or be dismayed
      b. none missing

A'. DAVIDIC KING: promise of "righteous Branch" . . . . . . (23:5-6)
   1. God's action . . . . (23:5)
   2. Result for nation(s) . . . . (23:6a)
   3. Name of *righteous* Branch (king). . . . . (23:6b)
      ("The LORD is our *righteousness*")

CONCLUSION: Change of "confession of faith" . . . . . . (23:7-8)
      a. No longer exodus, but restoration from exile .(23:7-8a)
      b. Then they shall live in their own land. . . . . . . (23:8b)

The passage thus portrays the repeating pattern of exile and restoration, rather like concentric circles. Although the framing sections that focus on the king (A and A') do not offer reasons for the exile, the central section dealing with the other leaders and the people (B, C, and B') does: The leadership has failed the people. That explanation is stated in the initial accusation in 23:1 and is amplified in 23:2, where the punishment is directly related to that failure. The language of the NRSV makes this clear. The shepherds have not *attended* to the flocks; therefore, God will *attend* to those shepherds. God's action is not arbitrary or capricious, but is in direct response to actions—or failure to act—of these supposed leaders. There is also an interesting ambiguity in the text regarding the exile of the people themselves. Verse 2 clearly states that it is the shepherds who have driven the flock away, but in v. 3 God claims to have driven the people into these foreign lands. This text thus does not resolve the ambiguity of human responsibility for history and God's active role in shaping history.

The promise of restoration in vv. 3-4 focuses on the well-being of the people themselves. In the promise of a righteous Branch for David, however, the language shifts, and in v. 5 the result of the promised restoration refers to the nations of Judah and Israel. There is a shift from a portrayal of God's concern for the people themselves, to God's concern for the nation(s) as political entities. That shift to language of national restoration, coupled with concern for the future of the Davidic monarchy, changes the emphasis from the well-being of persons to that of institutions. In fact, by framing the unit with references to the monarchy (22:24-30; 23:5-6), and by introducing references to the nations, the central focus on the people (23:3-4) is co-opted into the agenda of monarchical ideology.

The conclusion reinforces that shift of emphasis, giving it theological weight in the proclamation of a new confessional statement. On the one hand, this shift does acknowledge the continuing action of God on behalf of the people: We do not simply confess God's actions on our behalf in a distant past, but celebrate God's new action of restoration. On the other hand, by celebrating God not for the exodus but for bringing about the return from exile, this new confession marks a different view of the focus of divine concern. The exodus is the narrative of God's action on behalf of the poor, the enslaved, the marginalized. As such, it is a narrative that stands as a critique of monarchy. To recall that event in the language of the confession of faith is to acknowledge a God who acts on behalf of the poor. The language of restoration from exile in this new confession, however, is different. That language does recall the return of an exiled people, and as such offers a word of hope. Note, however, what is accomplished in that restoration: The monarchy is restored and the nation reestablished. (The close intersection of restoration of the monarchy and the language of the new confession of faith is signaled by the common language introducing the two texts, which both begin with the formula, "The days are surely coming, says the LORD.") Yes, it is to be a monarchy of justice, but it is the restoration of monarchy just the same. The focus is no longer on the consequences for the most vulnerable sectors of the society, but for those in authority. Theologically, one must ask: For whom is such a word good news?

Comparing Texts of Similar Material

There is one section in this unit that has a parallel in the book of Jeremiah: The promise of 23:5-6 is closely paralleled in 33:14-16. The language of the "branch" also figures in other prophetic books. The most familiar of these references is probably Isaiah 11, the text about the "shoot from the stump of Jesse," though the specific language by which the metaphor is expressed here is different. The same language as that found in Jeremiah also occurs in Zech. 3:8 and 6:12, where it is associated with the program of groups returning from exile to rebuild the temple. In general, references to "the righteous branch" are found, with slightly different implications, in various prophetic texts that are considered by many interpreters to be messianic, and the metaphor itself is treated as a messianic title.

The imagery of sheep and shepherds that is so ambiguous in its referents in this passage becomes focal imagery in such texts as Psalm 23, Matt. 18:12-14, Luke 15:3-7, and John 10:1-18.

Reading Contextually: Finding the Passage in Its Place

Considering the Literary Context

The passage on which we have focused occurs near the end of a major section of the book of Jeremiah (chaps. 1–25) that pronounces judgments against Judah and Jerusalem. Our passage comes at the end of a series of speeches against the kings of Judah, which begins at 21:1. Following our passage is an oracle concerning the prophets, the vision of good and bad figs, and a concluding sermon that draws together the material in chaps. 1–25. That immediate context reinforces the sense that the focus here is Jerusalem and the royal house of Israel.

Interspersed within the larger section are specific accusations of the kings' failure to execute justice for the poor and the oppressed (21:12; 22:13-17). Those accusations provide a framework within which to understand the pronouncements against King Coniah and his house and form the counterpart to the promise of a righteous Branch for the house of David. They also provide a larger context for understanding the relationship of the oracles about the shepherds (23:1–4), both to the judgment against Coniah and to the subsequent promise. The literary context of the passage thus introduces the criterion of justice as the measure for the king's action and affirms the well-being of the people—including the poor—as the norm by which a society and its leadership are judged.

Chapter 24 amplifies another motif that we have discovered in our text. According to that chapter, the future is vested with people who will return from exile. In the vision of the good and bad figs, the future belongs to those among the exiles who will be like the good figs (24:5-7). Even though there is to be new righteousness and a new heart, it is the returned exiles who will shape the future. Since those sent into exile are predominantly the leaders of Jerusalem and Judah, we must ask what meaning this text holds for those persons who were left in Jerusalem and Judah, persons who may have found in the exile of the leadership an opportunity to create their own future in the land.

Locating the Social Context

We are seeking here to examine the social context from which our text itself has come, not the social context reflected by any specific oracle within that text. Commentaries will frequently isolate a particular unit, such as the judgment against the house of Coniah (or even sections within it), and seek to date that portion in relation to the historical person known as Jeremiah, or in terms of the history of the development of the various traditions contained in the book as a whole. The process of study is similar to that engaged in by interpreters of the Synoptic Gospels, who attempt to identify contexts in the life of Jesus, in the life of the church prior to the writing of a particular Gospel, and in the Gospel writer's own community. Just as in the case of a Gospel text, one must focus first of all on the "top layer" of the structure (the Gospel writer's own context), since it is the one that has shaped the final form and function of a particular story or teaching, so with this prophetic passage one must focus on the context in which it took on its final form. In this case that context is the post-exilic era, when some groups have returned from Babylon and have to deal with the social dynamics created by that return. There were tensions between the returning exiles and those who had never left, and the two groups appear to have held different visions for the future. The concluding section of the passage, which promotes the confession of faith in the God of the returned exiles, clearly locates this text within the community of returnees, who anticipate the reestablishment of the monarchy, and who envision a righteous ruler of the house of David.

In considering the social context of any of the prophets or of the tradition that develops around a prophet, we must recognize that the prophet does not function in a social vacuum. In the first place, a society must acknowledge a phenomenon such as prophecy, or no one would listen to the peculiar prophetic blend of social critique, theological confession, and warning or promise about the future. Without such acknowledgment in general, as well as the recognition of the authority of a particular prophet, the prophet's words would be dismissed, never to be remembered or recorded. Furthermore, prophets whose works have been preserved would have found at least some within the society who heard their word in a positive way—as a "word from God," for instance—and who cared enough to preserve their words. Tempting as it may be to take the affirmation of the prophet's words as words of God dropped directly from the heavens, it is important to recall that both the prophet and those who kept the words alive did so in particular contexts and for specific reasons. Often, however, the social locations of these important preservers of portions of the tradition, like that of the original prophet, are nearly impossible to recover.

Engaging the Text, Other Readers, and Our Communities

This text, particularly when seen in its larger literary context, offers an important prophetic word of judgment against those in power or in positions of leadership in any society who ignore their proper mandate. The text proclaims justice for the poor and oppressed as the norm by which any society and its leadership will be judged. It articulates clearly that "the shepherds"—by whatever institutional titles these protectors and caretakers of the society are known—are there to protect the well-being of the sheep. Such a word of judgment

161

against the abuse of power and of wealth is appropriately addressed to persons who have both wealth and power.

It also offers the assuring affirmation that God is active in history, both to scatter and to gather. Such a word is powerful and healing in a time of distress, such as exile or severe social dislocation. In making that affirmation, however, this text suggests a particular understanding or vision of God's action in history. This vision does not provide a blueprint for an alternative social construct or for a wholly new society. It points to a society *re*formed, not *trans*formed. It offers a vision of return and restoration, not of revolution. It focuses on a change of leaders, but not on a transformation of the social structures.

In the context of dominant society these words from the tradition of Jeremiah are both disturbing and comfortable. They are troubling in their judgments against practices of injustice within the social order, and they are comfortable in their acceptance of the basic social order as something to be reformed and restored. We cannot escape the word of judgment in this text, but note what voices are not speaking here. Although there is an expression of concern on behalf of the poor, where are the voices of the poor themselves? We who are part of our society's elite—albeit committed to justice—risk ignoring the "sounds of silence" and the silenced voices in this text, usurping for ourselves the right to speak in their behalf.

We must also ask how this text might be read by persons who experience social dislocation as a result of various movements for change within contemporary society. Is the vision of hope to be found in a strong leader who would reestablish the family and the moral order? The larger context of this text does offer some guidance on this matter, in the language that condemns oppression and violence against the poor. But there is also a limitation: The grammar and perspective of the condemnation can too easily lead to a discussion *about* the poor and oppressed rather than a conversation *with* them.

Through whose eyes do we come to perceive God acting in history? For example, how does one read this text in the context of the political, military, and economic history of Nicaragua in the twentieth century? Does this text suggest that the Sandinista era was the period of exile (which indeed it was for the elites associated with the earlier regime of Somosa)—an exile from which those elites find hope in the prospect of return? Is the new order to be one in which only the excesses of the

Somosa regime will be eliminated? Where are the voices of those peasants, groups of hungry and homeless urban people, and Afro-Caribbean and Indigenous communities who have been excluded from both social orders, and for whom no return to or reform of the old suggests a locus of hope or comfort? Our own experiences have led us to focus our reflections in this section on Latin America, but the ambiguities of exile are experienced by many of the world's people. It would be important to broaden the dialogue to include, for example, the situation of Hutus living outside the borders of Rwanda, fearful of the Tutsi leaders whom they so recently oppressed and massacred. Ethnic strife in the Balkan and Baltic states of Eastern Europe has also given rise to many stories of exile, return, resettlement, and the resulting pain and chaos in people's lives. Similarly, the decades-long division of the Korean peninsula has left families permanently separated from their ancestral homes and family members, and the resulting political situation has led many to seek refuge in other parts of the world.

We have noted above that a primary association of this text in the Christian church has been with the collection of "messianic" prophecies. This association raises a problem: If this text and others like it are read as part of our effort to understand the meaning of the life of Jesus, what christological meaning does it engender? What image of the Christ is evoked? The most obvious one is the image of Christ the King who reigns with justice and tends to the needs of those who are poor. What, then, is the relationship between that image and the narratives of Jesus creating a community *of* the poor? Do such prophecies within the image-system of a hierarchical (though benevolent) social order cloud our vision and obscure the possibility of God's reign—God's *new* world—beginning with those who have never had a home to which to return?

Chapter 8

Psalm 77

Locating the Readers and the Reading Context

Selecting the Biblical Text

One consideration in the selection of a psalm was our desire to follow the roadmap with a poetic text. Another factor was our interest in exploring texts related to the cultic sphere of life in ancient Israel. Protestant churches of the dominant culture have traditionally shown less interest in issues of liturgy than in those of ethics, but the Psalms move us directly into the realm of liturgy. Rather than exhorting the moral life, many of the Psalms lift their voices in praise or lament. And though hymns of praise are regularly sung in our worship services, the lament or complaint is rarely voiced. Thus we have selected Psalm 77, which is a lament or complaint, in order to join persons of the dominant culture on a journey into that foreign territory.

Beginning the Journey at Home

The context for our encounter with some texts will include our past experiences with other examples of that type of literature. For example, our journey into an apocalyptic text will be shaped by our experience of such biblical books as Daniel or Revelation. In engaging any psalm, past experiences with the Psalms in general (or lack of such experiences!) form a significant dimension of the reading context. Some interpreters may have shared in the liturgical practice of praying through the Psalms. Others, particularly those worshipping in a "free church" tradition, will likely have a less rich exposure to the Psalms. Our own memory includes "responsive readings" as a part of the order of worship, but with little awareness that these were often selections from the biblical psalms. They seemed to have no relationship to the rest of the service, nor were they texts for preaching. Otherwise scant attention was given to the Psalms, except for the requirement to

165

memorize Psalm 23. On the other hand, we own copies of the New Testament and Psalms bound together as a single volume. There is some association between the Psalms and our pastoral ministry with the sick and the grieving. In recent years, with more Protestant churches adopting the practice of lectionary readings, we do hear psalms (or sections from psalms) read more frequently in worship. These, however, are selected more on the basis of their content association with the other scriptures than for their function within the liturgy or as texts for preaching in their own right.

Psalm 77 is, as noted, a lament or complaint psalm. Thus we must consider experiences not only with the general category of psalms, but with this particular form. What feelings, words, actions do you and your community associate with "complaining"? How do you hear the word "lament"? How do these associations connect with your religious life? Do you have any experience with expressions of lament in the context of worship?

We do not remember the complaint as a part of our own primary worship experience. Nor do we remember the lament psalms as a topic for sermons. Quite the opposite: The complaint is normally excluded, denied, or excused. We quickly pass over Good Friday, with Jesus' words from the cross, "My God, my God, why have you forsaken me?" (the first lines of Psalm 22—another lament psalm), to get to Easter Sunday. Expressions of pain are discouraged, both in churches of the dominant culture and in society in general. Children are taught to "play through the pain." Expressions of anger are even more taboo, especially if that anger is directed at God. On the other hand, emerging literature on grief and anger is having an impact on such attitudes and should compel us to seek theological language and liturgical expressions that are commensurate with our psychological understandings. But old attitudes persist: Sharon recalls crying quietly in a corner of the sacristy prior to entering the church to conduct the funeral of a friend, when the senior pastor shouted at her to "grow up and be professional" or stay in her office!

We are aware, however, that some communities have incorporated the power of the lament as an expression of the community's life. The music of African American traditions intones the lament in gospel songs, spirituals, and the blues. Vivid in our memories is the cry of communities in Latin America grieving for family members and friends killed or disappeared—a lament that, once voiced, allows the community to face the future. Fred recalls participating in wakes in Africa, where wailing is a part of the ritual process. Each group and each individual will want to reflect carefully on their assumptions about and experiences of lament. The very power of the lament and the poignancy of those occasions that give rise to the cry—or of those forces that deny the cry—are too strong to ignore.

Are members of the group, or is the group itself, experiencing reasons to lament or complain? Has there been recent loss or illness? Is someone dealing with a newly diagnosed life-threatening disease, the loss of a job, or the end of a relationship? Are there events within the community, nation, or world—violence in cities, hunger, homelessness, generations lost to drugs and guns—that evoke cries of pain and anger, deep feelings of frustration? Our own immediate world is relatively stable and secure, as earlier descriptions of our social, economic, and familial contexts would suggest. On the other hand, the memories of devastation, poverty, and health issues in Africa, Asia, and Latin America are never far from our thoughts, nor can we forget the economic crisis and related violence in our cities and in many rural areas. And we have lost friends and family to the ravages of cancer and AIDS.

When it appears to us that the church has abandoned the city for the suburbs, that seminaries have turned away from enabling ministry by and among the poor and toward a focus on revenue producing programs, that commitments to inclusiveness are trivialized, and that revolutionary movements for justice have been turned back, we sometimes wonder if God's promises are at an end for all time. While we may grouse and feel faint of spirit, seldom do we give expression to this despair in personal prayers of lament. Even less frequently do we find vehicles for communal expressions of this pain and distress. Typically, we simply try to keep going—to play through the pain—tending to the demands of the system, and doing what we can.

Encountering the Biblical Text: Read, Feel, Question, React

First Impressions

Since the Psalms belong to the sphere of cultic life, it is important to include in your study an effort to pray the psalm. Even if you are studying by yourself, read the psalm aloud or sign it. If you are working in groups, read the psalm in different ways, for example, antiphonally or responsively. How does it feel to pray the psalm, either privately or corporately? Can you pray it? Or does it feel awkward, even irreverent? What theological issues are being surfaced in these feelings?

Reading poetry is a different experience from reading prose. Poetry plays with words, images, phrases, and symbol systems. It employs sounds and rhythms to evoke emotions. Its form is often more cyclical than linear, as words, images, and sounds repeat themselves, drawing connections that are often subconscious. Poetry evokes much with few words. Therefore, readers will want to be attentive to words, phrases, and images that are especially vivid. Listen carefully for the sounds and rhythms. If you are able to watch a signed interpretation of the psalm, pay attention to what feelings are expressed or evoked by the movements and the signs themselves.

In reading Psalm 77, one immediately encounters the sudden shift from the tone of despair in the first ten verses to the confidence of the concluding ten verses. What allows for that abrupt change? In the managed reality of dominant Euro-American culture, a person is either sad or glad, depressed or optimistic, and thus the assumption is that something must have happened to cause the shift. But we also think of music such as the spirituals and blues of African American traditions that often interweave grief and joy, shouting and wailing, and we wonder how these psalms are prayed and understood in such contexts.

On the other hand we wonder about the response of persons who have cried to God, who have professed confidence in God, and whose experience is that their confidence has been betrayed—that God has continued to forget or ignore them. What questions and issues might such persons pose in reading this psalm? What feelings does it evoke? Or what about the person who has voiced the complaint and has found no support within the community of faith or has even been rebuked for lack of faith?

We tend to perceive another incongruity between these two halves, in that the cry is expressed in personal categories (expressed grammatically in the first person singular), whereas the wondrous deeds that are remembered recall God's actions on behalf of a people. In this psalm there is no strictly personal word of comfort to an individual sufferer and no example of God's intervention on behalf of a solitary person.

Within our cultural context we puzzle over this tension. Would that contrast be as striking, though, in the perspective on human life that is captured in the expression of African and African American cultures, "I am because we are" or "I am because I belong"? Frequently in the Psalms, as in these contemporary cultures, the line between the individual and the community is fluid. How would the psalm be read by persons within such a world view?

We are uncomfortable with language that accuses God of having changed, that questions whether God's power has changed, and that protests that God's love has ceased. We are inclined to think of God as unchanging, of God's love as constant. If our relationship with God feels broken, we tend to assume that we are at fault, not God.

On the other hand, the line "yet your footprints were unseen" (v. 19b) does seize the imagination. It is easy to read this as a statement of God's constant presence, even if God is invisible to us. This, then, opens the door to a reading of the entire psalm as if the problem were really ours after all. It is not that God has changed, but that we have failed to recognize God's invisible presence. How, then, do these last verses relate to the rest of the psalm?

Remembering Past and Other Experiences with the Text

We carry no clear memories of this particular psalm. We have already mentioned the very minimal associations which we have with the Psalms in general, and the virtual elimination of the laments from our corporate and private religious lives.

A Close Reading of the Biblical Text: Steps in the Process

Preparing a Translation of the Text

Translations vary significantly in their ability to capture the poetic quality of these texts. The special vocabulary drawn upon by poets and the highly symbolic nature of that language opens these texts to ambiguity and ranges of meanings. The translator frequently resorts to conjectures about meaning and dependence on ancient translations, such as Greek or Syriac.

Compare, for example, the first verses of Psalm 77 in the NRSV, JPS, JB, and NIV translations:

<table>
<tr><td>

NRSV

I cry aloud to God,
   aloud to God, that he may
     hear me.
In the day of my trouble I seek
   the LORD;
   in the night my hand is
     stretched out without
     wearying;
   my soul refuses to be
     comforted.
I think of God, and I moan;
   I meditate, and my spirit
     faints. *Selah.*

</td><td>

JPS

I cry aloud to God;
   I cry to God that He may
     give ear to me.
In my time of distress I turn
   to the Lord,
   with my hand [uplifted];
   [my eyes] flow all night
     without respite;
I will not be
     comforted.
I call God to mind, I moan,
   I complain, my spirit
     fails. *Selah.*

</td></tr>
<tr><td>

JB

Loudly I cry to God,
   loudly to God who
     hears me.
When in trouble I sought
   the Lord,
   all night long I stretched out
     my hands,
   my soul refusing to be
     consoled.
I thought of God
   and sighed,
   I pondered and my spirit
     failed me.

</td><td>

NIV

I cried out to God for help;
   I cried out to God
     to hear me.
When I was in distress,
   I sought the Lord;
   at night I stretched out
     untiring hands
   and my soul refused to be
     comforted.
I remembered you, O God,
   and I groaned;
   I mused, and my spirit
     grew faint. *Selah.*

</td></tr>
</table>

One can immediately see the different nuances in the ways the cry has been expressed. A more substantive difference is the JB translation of v. 1*b*, "loudly to God *who hears me*," rather than "that he may hear me." This version expresses a confidence that God does hear, which does not seem consistent with the complaint that follows.

Other differences among these four versions of the psalm are also worth noting. Many of these translation issues are directly related to what is assumed about the meaning of the text and the nature of the complaint. For example, NIV (vv. 1-6) and JB (vv. 2-6) put the first verses in past tense, whereas NRSV uses present, shifting the reference to God's mighty works into the future. The effect of the former translations is to make the cry a past event, rather than the immediate context of the psalm. This carries us quickly beyond the cry to the resolution, whereas the psalm wants to lead us into the turmoil. In v. 6 NRSV and JB follow ancient Greek and Syriac versions, whereas NIV works with the Hebrew, and the concluding phrase is rendered either "I search my spirit" (NRSV) or "my spirit searches" (JPS, NIV, JB). JB tempers the questions of v. 7 by casting them in the conditional form, which causes them to lose some of their poignancy. In the NRSV and JB, v. 10 is the final exclamation of grief, whereas in the NIV it is treated as parallel to v. 11, beginning the recalling of God's deeds. In that same verse JPS refers not to "my grief," but to "my fault," which shifts the focus from a complaint about God to the "fault" of the psalmist. In v. 13, in contrast to the NRSV, the other three versions read "your ways," rather than "your way," leaving the parallel with v. 19 less clear.

Identifying the Shape of the Text

As noted above, there is a fundamental dynamic in the movement of this text from distress (in vv. 1-10) to confidence (in vv. 11-20). That shift is marked not only by the content, but also by such devices as the shift of pronouns from third person in the complaint section (with the exception of a short direct accusation in v. 4a), to second person address in the expression of confidence. On the other hand, a close reading identifies elements of continuity between the two parts. For example, the word "meditate" occurs in vv. 3 and 6 of the first part and in v. 12 of the second half. Likewise there is the juxtaposition of "remembering the days of old" in the complaint (v. 5) and in the expression of hope (v. 11). In the first instance it leads to questions about God, and in the second to images of God's way. Also, this language of the "days of old" is a counterpoint to the "day of my trouble" in v. 2.

Psalm 77 begins by describing the "day of my trouble," a day that begins with a cry to God (v. 1) but ends with the psalmist speechless (v. 4b). No specific event or experience, such as personal illness or national defeat, is named as the cause of this distress. Whatever the occasion of this "day of trouble," the experience is such that the final grief is the loss of God, the God of days of old. In the context of that "day of trouble" the psalmist remembers the "days of old" (vv. 5-6), but that initial memory is not satisfying. It only raises questions that intensify the psalmist's anguish in the contrast between present experience and the memory of God's past graciousness and compassion. In that process questions about God compound (vv. 7-9), each carrying a sense of definitiveness or absoluteness ("forever," "never again," "for all time"), culminating in the statement of grief in v. 10. Memory itself does not resolve the anguish, nor does meditation. The God of memory has changed, and that is the psalmist's grief.

There is, however, a second remembering, which is introduced in vv. 11-12. Now the psalmist recalls the mighty deeds of God. No longer is the memory simply of "days of old," but of God's "wonders of old." The psalmist no longer simply meditates (vv. 3, 6), but instead muses on God's mighty deeds (v. 12). What occasions the shift? Some act in the liturgy? Some change in the situation? There is no evidence in the text for either. There are, however, textual connections between the two sections, as noted above. In other words, the text itself seems to maintain a tension between the two sections, and to see the two moods existing simultaneously. The psalmist does not link hope to the resolution of the trouble, but to the confidence that the present turmoil is not forever: God does create a "way." Just as the questions provide the content of the searching spirit, so the depictions of the way (vv. 13-18, 19-20) offer content to the meditation on God's mighty deeds. The remembrance of God's holy way does not deny the reality of the present crisis: God's path was *through* the mighty waters. This memory of God's way-making calls to mind a God who creates a way in the midst of chaos—the God who is the Way Maker of African American spirituality. Whatever the power that opposes an individual or the community, God is more powerful: God will make a way where there is no way.

At the beginning of this section we observed in the psalm the two-part organizing principle of cry (vv. 1-10) and confidence (vv. 11-20). But we have just described another dynamic within the text: the anguish of the day of trouble, with its movement from cry to speechlessness (vv. 1-4), and the memory of the days of old (vv. 5-20). That memory, in turn, consists of two distinct sections (vv. 5-10 and

vv. 11-20). The interplay of these two structuring principles—anguish/confidence on the one hand, and day of trouble/days of old on the other—reveals something of the interplay of anguish and confidence.

The image of unseen footprints (v. 19) can have a powerful effect on the meaning of this psalm. Readers may be led to assume that God was always present. The internal anguish of the psalmist was intensified by a failure to recognize that presence. But that phrase must be seen in the context of the picture of a God whose might was displayed among the peoples (v. 14b), whose appearance caused the waters to tremble (v. 16), and whose manifestations "lit up the world" (vv. 18-19). On the one hand, the psalmist does affirm the quietness of the way through the sea and the wonder of footprints not seen. On the other hand, the psalmist celebrates the noticeable manifestation of God's mighty powers, observed by peoples, perceived by the fearful waters, and witnessed by a trembling earth—manifest power that conquers the forces that trouble. The psalm does not minimize or deny the reality of the anguish, nor does it place the problem at the feet of the psalmist. God's way is that visible, wondrous, liberating power (vv. 13-18), just as God's way is the invisible, mysterious guiding presence (vv. 19-20).

One final dynamic must be examined. We noted above an incongruity between the two parts of this psalm—complaint and confidence—in the language of the personal and the corporate, respectively. The subject of the cry is "I," the first person singular, but the image of God's wondrous acts recalls God's redemption, the political and social liberation of the people. That incongruity might incline the reader to find disparity between the two halves of the psalm, and it might argue for a separation between the two sentiments. But this close reading has detected an interplay within the psalm that maintains the unity of composition, thereby compelling one to hold the two dimensions of personal and communal together. Psalm 77 does not allow one to focus on the plight of the individual as the sole (or even primary) locus of God's activity, nor only on the corporate victory. It does not even allow one to say simply both/and, which would still maintain two separate and discrete spheres of life. Psalm 77 suggests that the boundaries between personal and social are fluid. To raise questions in reference to the one is to raise questions in reference to the other. To speak of one is to address the other. This psalm resonates with the assertion that the personal is political, the political personal: They cannot be disentangled.

Comparing with Texts of Similar Material

Most studies of the Psalms have tended to group similar materials according to their form or type, or according to their common content. Persons working with the method of biblical study known as form criticism have invested considerable effort in identifying and delineating such types of psalms as the hymn; the individual and communal thanksgiving; the individual and communal lament; and royal, wisdom, and enthronement psalms. More recently some scholars have classified psalms according to their function in the lives of individuals or communities—for example, orientation, disorientation, and new orientation. One can find psalms grouped according to such classification systems in introductions and commentaries, and often the footnotes in an annotated Bible give the editor's judgment about the type of psalm. One can then scan the Psalms to find others labeled as the same type, or one can read through other psalms on one's own to identify psalms that share common characteristics.

In comparing psalms of a similar type, one will find similarities and differences that can inform one's reading of them. For example, Psalm 77 shares with other laments the expression of a cry to God. In Psalm 77, however, that cry is not addressed directly to God, as it is in Psalms 13:1*a* and 22:1*a*. That lack of direct address of the lament in Psalm 77 is further supported by the lack of a direct petition in that psalm (again, like that found in Psalms 13:3 or 22:11, 19) or of a specific motivation offered to God (like that found in Psalm 6:5). These differences reinforce the notion that Psalm 77 is more of an internalized (but not privatized) struggle on the day of trouble—reflected in the language of meditating, searching my spirit, and communing with my heart—rather than the externalized cry of lament. But even that internal struggle is given voice in the worship literature of the community, thereby naming the reality of the anguish while also offering hope within the midst of that struggle.

In terms of comparison with literature of a similar content, Psalm 77 contains images found elsewhere. For example, language of the sea occurs frequently in lament psalms, but also in Isaiah 40–55 and in

Exodus 15:1-18, 21. It is interesting to note that the latter song, like the concluding section of Psalm 77, divides into two distinct elements—the episode at the sea and the guidance of Israel. The aggressive language and tone of the strong arm of God in Exodus 15:4-12 is dramatically different from language of the steady hand in 15:13, 17-18. In that song, however, the enemy is specified, and thus hope is found more in the defeat of a particular enemy than in the opening of the way.

Reading Contextually: Finding the Passage in Its Place

Considering the Literary Context

The literary context of those psalms found within the Book of Psalms is simply that of a collection similar to a hymnbook. While one can detect an organizing rubric for the Book for Psalms, such as the present division of the Psalter into five books, meaning is normally not significantly shaped by a psalm's literary context. There are a few instances where psalms that are separated in our Bibles can easily be read as one psalm (like Psalms 9 and 10, for example, which are found as one psalm in Greek translations of the Bible). There are other cases where groups of psalms address a similar mood or theme (like Psalms 146–150, all of which develop the opening refrain "Praise the Lord!"). These cases where literary context seems to be significant, however, are the exceptions.

It is important to note that there are also psalms or songs that occur elsewhere in the Bible, such as Exod. 15:1-18, 21; Judg. 5:2-31b; 1 Sam. 2:1b-10; John 1:1-18; Phil. 2:6-11; and the canticles in Luke 1 and 2. Sometimes a psalm that occurs in the Book of Psalms can also be found in similar form in a narrative context, such as Psalm 18, which is echoed in 2 Sam. 22:2b-51. When interpreting these psalms or hymns, the issue of literary context will function as it does in reading any text.

Locating the Social Context

Determining a particular social location for literature like the Psalms is difficult. As the literature of the cultic life of Israel, the Psalms function in a wide range of social locations. The general institutional context can be identified as the cult, or the worship life of Israel, and some psalms (such as enthronement psalms) can be identified with particular cultic occasions. But that does not locate the Psalms in a social context. On the one hand, the Psalms that are a part of the canonical collection would have emerged in different contexts and functioned in a wide range of social locations. On the other hand, as the literature of the official cultic life of Jerusalem that collection does not reflect the full range of the worship life in Israel. The spoken or sung prayers from the villages were probably not recorded in written documents, and we have little if any material that preserves the daily rhythms of prayer and the cycle of celebrations set in homes. It is quite possible that those religious texts and practices functioned as an expression of opposition to or as an act of resistance against the official theology.

A few psalms (like Psalms 51 and 63) come with a superscription that describes a particular setting or occasion. One should not assume that these superscriptions reflect the occasion for the composition of the psalm, but rather a type of context in which the psalm could be understood.

In one sense the social context of the laments is the common human experience of suffering. Even a lament such as Psalm 69, which includes specific language about rebuilding the cities of Judah, can function in many situations, giving voice to the anguish of any who have felt the pangs of insults. It is that common human experience that enables these psalms to span time and space and to function in the liturgies of diverse communities.

That common experience of suffering, however, does not mean that the social context of that experience is the same for everyone. Each culture, each society, and each group within a culture creates its own context of response to suffering, as to other events and circumstances. Distinctions such as those of economic class will affect such factors as the resources for coping with crises. One's location within the existing order will influence attitudes toward disruptions of that order. One can look, for example, at differing reactions to the uprisings in Los Angeles in the early 1990s. Were they "protests" or "riots"? How close did the fires come to "home"? The fact of human suffering is common and shared, but experiences of that suffering will differ.

Social rituals and practices will also shape the nature of human response to suffering. Thus, the very existence of the lament psalms within the tradition itself constitutes an important part of the social context of the worshiping communities in which they are read. These psalms ritualize a response to suffering, creating the communal context within which and through which grief or pain can be expressed. They also provide language for our private expressions of anguish. The dominant Western culture, for example, whose liturgy is largely lacking in the practice of lament, does not have that resource available to respond to suffering. Without the support of a communal cry to God and against God, and without the liturgical expression of anger and grief, the experience of suffering tends to be privatized and internalized. The primary feelings evoked are those of self-blame and isolation. In such a context, the lament, with its outcry of anger directed to and against God and its questioning or accusations of God, can feel inappropriate. The liturgical context of the lament tradition within Israel created a social context for the people's life experiences. The absence of such a tradition creates a different context.

Engaging the Text, Other Readers, and Our Communities

To engage a lament psalm, then, is not only to encounter a particular text, but also to experience the form and function of lament. Thus we engage this psalm with some ambivalence. It does not fit easily within the primary forms of our religious experience. On the other hand, some contemporary movements and experiences are creating new awareness of and receptivity to the lament. Attention to grief and the grieving process within the fields of psychology and counseling offers new understanding and provides psychological models for assisting individuals in coping with experiences of loss. Encounters (both personal and literary) with communities suffering brutal forms of oppression focus attention on the power of lament in movements for justice. Experiences of rage in the process of consciousness-raising around issues of injustice have made manifest the power of anger. This leads to the recognition that to deny anger and to mute cries for justice internalizes blame, isolates victims, and immobilizes potential for social change. Within this context, we find that the lament psalm provides a model within the biblical tradition that has too long been ignored or dismissed by the dominant culture.

As noted above, Psalm 77 has some tendency toward a more internalized reflection on the "day of trouble," and in that sense feels more comfortable in our context than some of the other lament psalms, but the psalm still creates discomfort. First, there is the expressed cry and the accusation against God. Second, the psalmist does not blame himself or herself: There is no confession of sin or of personal inadequacy. What is being questioned is God's continuing justice and compassion, not the goodness or faithfulness of the psalmist.

This psalmist does not deny the reality of the present "day of trouble" and finds no comfort in seeking God. In fact, God is a tormentor, keeping the psalmist's eyelids open and not permitting even the escape of sleep. The psalmist also refuses to accept the injustice of that present situation or to exclude or excuse God from that reality. The search for God in the context of trouble forces a confrontation between the remembered God of compassion and the pain of present reality. If this situation of anguish defines God, then God has changed. But if the remembered God of compassion were to act within this present trouble, then the situation must change. In the midst of that confrontation the psalmist recalls the mighty deeds of God and proclaims the power of God. The psalmist affirms with confidence that God's liberating justice will be the final word. That affirmation lives, not in response to the resolution of the situation, but as the power of hope within the situation—in the memory that God makes a way, even when there appears to be no way.

The witness of communities in Latin America and the worship life of African American congregations in the heart of our cities proclaims that cries of pain and affirmations of assurance are not mutually exclusive. In doing our close reading of the text we made reference to the African American image of the Way Maker. It would be important to explore further, through both readings and conversations, the ways in which this image has functioned, and how it continues to inform both individual and community life and their understanding of texts like this.

In this psalm the word of hope emerges from within the anguish, not after its resolution. Similarly, a woman in a group discussing this feature of a lament psalm reflected on the experience of childbirth, in which she had simultaneous experiences of pain and expectation. She too could read the two parts and the contrasting emotions as interactive and simultaneous, not necessarily as successive expressions.

We have suggested that interpreters broaden their understanding of Psalm 77 by comparing it to other biblical laments. It is not only in the Bible, however, that comparable expressions can be found. Some of the music that has arisen from African American communities; rituals of mourning that arise at moments of personal, communal, and even national grief; and the poems and prayers of oppressed peoples throughout the world provide rich evidence of the abiding power of laments. These powerful words are met also by such non-verbal expressions of lament as the murals painted on walls in *barrios* and other urban neighborhoods, which give expression in their own idiom to the people's cries for justice and affirmations of hope.

We have also mentioned particular life experiences that may shape one's attitudes toward anger and the complaint. These include participation in consciousness raising groups and experiences of "grief work," aspects of which we have known in our own ways. Our experiences, however, need to be expanded by compassionate attention to experiences of others in similar and different circumstances of grief, crisis, and loss. It would also be important to engage persons who have not been given permission or space to complain. An example of the latter would be the abused wife who could not vocalize her pain because church and society denied its reality, endorsed the pain as "her cross to bear," or blamed her for causing her own suffering or all of the above! And we would want to engage persons or groups who felt betrayed by the lament tradition—persons who cried to God and found no redemption.

We do reflect here on one way in which the social location of the reader provides a grid through which this text is read. It is possible to read this psalm as the voice of frustration of one who remembers the "good old days, when God was in heaven and all was right with the world." But now all that has changed. "The way" is perceived as a way back to God; the path is a return to God's ways. On the one hand, such a reading does remind us that the loss of a comfortable world is a loss, which, like any loss, will be grieved. On the other hand, such a reading does not rest easily with the image of "the way" presented in this psalm.

The way is not a way back, but a way through and beyond. To seek return really denies the loss, assuming that what was lost can be regained. The lament, on the contrary, faces the pain of the loss of the old and looks for God's new creation.

Chapter 9

Mark 3:1-6

Locating the Readers and the Reading Context

Selecting the Biblical Text

We wanted to include a study of one of the healing stories in the Gospels because of the issues raised by the subject matter itself and by the function of such stories in the Gospel traditions. Stories of "miracles" that claim direct causal intervention by God into the lives of individuals or communities collide with the "scientific" world view of modern western culture that assumes a natural cause for every observed effect. In addition to that general cultural or intellectual collision, such stories raise a host of pastoral problems, such as the manipulative agendas of some "faith healers" who claim to mediate God's power in the same way Jesus did, or the pain of people who have prayed for healing that has never come. Stories of Jesus' healing ministry also raise questions about the nature of our belief in Jesus: Does his ability to heal prove he is the Christ, or even that he is God? Sabbath healings like this one also pose questions for Christians about Jesus' relationship to Jewish law, and consequently about the meaning of that religious system for Christian life and spirituality.

Beginning the Journey at Home

Biblical stories about healings or exorcisms are viewed differently in different cultures. Along with such specifically religious questions as their views of the relationship between Jesus and "miracles," people's assumptions about the causes and significance of physical and mental illness, the medical system to which they have access, and their perception of the relationship among physical, emotional, social, and spiritual factors in health and illness all shape the questions such accounts evoke.

For example, as middle class North Americans we share many of the assumptions of Western medicine and a scientific world view, and thus we are curious about diagnosis and treatment: What was the ailment, and how did the treatment resolve it? We bring an instinctive skepticism to stories of a miracle-working God who intervenes in the world and in human lives at apparently arbitrarily chosen moments to contradict what we understand as natural laws of cause and effect. Furthermore, our experiences of the intimate connection of emotions and the human spirit to one's physical condition lead us to reject suggestions that we should dismiss the healings recounted in the Gospels as cases of "hysterical paralysis" and "psychosomatic symptoms," as though that means there was no real illness and no cure. We have also heard both moving testimonies about the power of faith healers or holy places (like Lourdes or the shrine of the Virgin of Guadalupe), and stories of abuses in both cases, so that we bring both wariness and openness to such accounts. The economically stratified access to the formal health care system in the United States, and to Western medicine in the two-thirds world, lead us to recognize the importance of the use of herbs and other folk remedies, especially in primary medical care for people who are poor. Experiences in Africa and Latin America in particular lead both of us also to respect the power of traditional medicine and of the work of people who practice healing arts out of cultural assumptions different from our own.

In addition, for our culture, regulations related to observing the sabbath, or even regular marking of other holy times by ceasing usual activities in favor of special rituals, are foreign notions. (Christmas and Thanksgiving are among the few occasions marked in such ways in the United States, and they are only annual events.) "Blue laws" that restrict business and other activities on Sundays are laughable relics of a former age, and we find ourselves stopping to run errands at the supermarket or shopping mall on the way home from church. Given that in the Protestant churches of the dominant culture religion centers around ethics, and doing good deeds is prized as an appropriate religious activity, the notion that anyone might raise legitimate objections to a good deed at any time, and especially on the sabbath, does not make sense to us. On the other hand, we share in the longings of many in our culture for ways to build into our lives some regular means of spiritual renewal. We long for ways to avoid the burn-out that results from alternating between the extremes of over-work and inertia, for which our culture has invented the labels "workaholic" and "couch potato."

As we attempt to be aware of the sort of questions that might be raised by persons from outside our own immediate community, two specific groups suggest themselves for our attention. First, persons from cultures where traditional or folk medicine is still commonly practiced, and where healers or other shaman figures are well known, would probably ask about the relationship between Jesus' work of healing and such activities in their own cultures. Second, persons from the disabilities community would probably raise questions relative to this and all healing stories about the connection drawn between Jesus' ministry and able-bodiedness. Those questions might follow one of two paths. First, what do the healing stories imply about those persons who are not healed? Why are all not healed, but only a certain few, and what criteria determine which are healed and which are not? More profoundly, why is such a premium placed on able-bodiedness? Why is the "good news" not expressed as a world made accessible to and accepting of persons of all physical, mental, and psychological circumstances, rather than as persons changed to conform to the world's norms?

Encountering the Biblical Text:
Read, Feel, Question, React

First Impressions

The passage in Mark is terse. It is necessary to look back to 2:24 or forward to 3:6 to find out that it is the Pharisees who want to accuse Jesus, and one is left with the picture of these religious leaders forming a procession behind Jesus as they follow him to try to catch him doing something inappropriate. What is entailed in the expectation that Jesus might heal the man? How would Mark's community or Jesus' contemporaries have viewed healers? The text implies that healing on the sabbath is forbidden, but it does not explain what the problem is. Our lack of experience of sabbath rules governing any activity, and especially of such rules governing good deeds, leads us to put down the Pharisees' objections as religious nit-picking. The question follows, therefore, about what laws govern healing on the sabbath. How are those laws related to the question about doing harm or doing good, saving life or killing (3:4)? The bundle of emotions in 3:5 needs to be sorted out: What underlies Jesus' anger and sorrow, and what is meant by their "hardness of heart"? Even more basic is the fact itself of the anger. Not only modern discomfort at anyone's anger (let alone Jesus'!) comes into play, for—as a glance at the parallel stories in Matt. 12:9-14 and Luke 6:6-11 shows—references to Jesus' anger, as well as to the onlookers' "hardness of heart," have already been eliminated by those later biblical writers. The healing itself raises questions of what had been wrong with the man's hand, and how the healing happened. How would onlookers have viewed such an event? What conclusions might they have drawn about the power seen in Jesus' action? Who are the Herodians (3:6), and what underlies their and the Pharisees' desire to destroy Jesus?

Remembering Past and Other Experiences with the Text

We recall hearing this and other healing stories interpreted as illustrations of Jesus' divine power or messianic identity. To what extent were those assumptions shared in the ancient context? What have they meant for the church? The passage has also been read with a decidedly anti-Jewish slant: Legalistic Pharisees are more concerned with fine points of sabbath law than with the healing Jesus is able to perform, and they even respond by plotting against Jesus. What meaning does Mark attribute to those details, and could they have had any place in Jesus' own day? The process of careful reading of the text in terms of its language, its shape, and its various contexts will work to refine and, in some cases, respond to such questions evoked by and through the passage.

A Close Reading of the Biblical Text: Steps in the Process

Preparing a Translation of the Text

Only one translation issue presents itself, and that is the meaning of the phrase "hardness of heart" in 3:5. Many translations follow that literal rendering of the Greek words. The NJB speaks of their being "obstinate," and TEV interprets the metaphor further as "stubborn and wrong." *Dios habla hoy*, the Spanish equivalent of the TEV, softens that interpretation a bit to *"no querían entender"*: they did not want to understand.

The various attempts to interpret the phrase achieve clarity at the expense of losing an important aspect of the role of that phrase in the Hebrew Bible. Meanings such as "obstinate" or "stubborn" suggest that this condition represents a moral fault on the part of the persons involved—in this case the Pharisees. Indeed, in the Hebrew Bible persons are accused of "hardening their hearts" in that moral sense, and of closing themselves off from God's will (see, for example, Exod. 8:15, 32; 9:34; 1 Sam. 6:6, where that description applies to Pharaoh or to the Egyptians; 2 Chron. 36:13, where it applies to Zedekiah; and in a general warning in Ps. 95:8, which is cited in Heb. 3:8, 15; 4:7). More often, however, it is God who is said to harden people's hearts (see, for example, Exod. 4:21; 7:3; 9:12; 10:1, 20, 27; 11:10; 14:4, 8, 17; Josh. 11:20; Isa. 63:17), apparently as part of God's plan for how events are to unfold. If we add to these the cases where the expression is in the passive—"their hearts were hardened"—which is often understood as a "divine passive," with God as the implied cause of the action (for example, Exod. 7:13, 14, 22; 8:19; 9:7, 35), it is clear that in the biblical tradition the moral meaning is not the predominant one. In fact, the passive expression of the metaphor in Mark 6:52 and 8:17 suggests at least the possibility that in Mark 3:5; 10:5; Matt. 19:8 and Eph. 4:18 the description "hardness of heart" should be seen as the consequence of divine action and not human fault. If that is the case, then in 3:5 those who plot against Jesus are being portrayed as fulfilling their appropriate role in the gospel story according to God's plan. This picture of a God who manipulates human hearts to make things turn out according to divine plan, however, raises its own theological problems, but it does mitigate the demonizing of the Pharisees that has so plagued Christian interpretation of the Bible.

Identifying the Shape of the Text

Given that this passage is a narrative or story, one would expect its structure to follow the action being described. Very little actually happens in this passage, however. The substance of the passage is presented by the narrator in comments about intentions (3:2), feelings (3:5), or actions off-stage (3:6). Jesus forms the center point of the passage. He stands between the man whom he summons and instructs to stretch out his hand, and who complies with Jesus' commands, and the Pharisees to whom he addresses a question, and who hover as a silent, hostile presence. The healing itself receives only a mention ("and his hand was restored"), so although that event grabs the attention of most modern readers, it is clearly not the point Mark is stressing in the story.

The question of the shape of this story is related to discussions found in most commentaries about its "form," or "type," or "genre." Most conclude that the story is a hybrid that intertwines a healing story (noting the seriousness of the patient's condition, the encounter between patient and healer, healing words or actions, evidence of the success of the healing, and the response of onlookers) and a pronouncement or conflict story (with an expressed or implied challenge from opponents, a counter question from Jesus, and his concluding declaration). The only part of the conflict story that plays a role in the healing story is the hostile plot against Jesus, which constitutes the crowd's response to the healing. On the other hand, the need for the healing provides the occasion for the implied hostile question, and the healing itself constitutes Jesus' concluding response to his opponents. The healing story could easily have existed without the conflict story, but the conflict story could not have been told without the healing. While the healing thus seems to be the base story, the conflict is the aspect emphasized by Mark's way of telling the story. At issue is the nature of the conflict implied in Jesus' life and for Mark's church.

Comparing with Texts of Similar Material

A comparison of Mark's account with its parallels in Matt. 12:9-14 and Luke 6:6-11 shows both their basic similarity and several key differences. Neither Matthew nor Luke mentions Jesus' anger (Matt. 12:12; Luke 6:10; compare Mark 3:5), for example, and neither refers to the "Herodians"—probably intended to refer to political supporters of Herod Antipas—as co-conspirators with the Pharisees. Otherwise, Luke's version of the story is very similar to Mark's, with only a few differences in detail, such as the heightened gravity of the situation in that it was the "right" hand that was withered—by implication the dominant one. (This theme is found also in the apocryphal Gospel of the Nazareans cited in Jerome's *Commentary on Matthew 12:13*. There the man pleads for help with the words, "I was a mason, earning a living with my hands; I beg you, Jesus, restore my health to me, so that I need not beg for my food in shame.") In addition, in Luke Jesus is portrayed as continuing with the cure even knowing the Pharisees' and the scribes' intentions against him (Luke 6:8). Neither Mark nor Luke discusses Jesus' action in light of specific sabbath regulations, but rather they focus on how Jesus' healing of the man—"doing good"—is consistent with the purposes underlying sabbath laws in both written and oral Torah.

Matthew's version of the story suggests a context where his hearers were being challenged to defend specific behaviors of the community, and their relationship to specific applications of Jewish law. Jesus functions as, in effect, their rabbi who clarifies the law for them. The pattern of argument represented in Matthew's version of this story is echoed in two other sabbath healing stories in Luke 13:10-17 and 14:1-6. The details differ, but in each case Jesus' action is supported by examples of other work that can be done without violating the holiness of the sabbath. In Matthew's version of the story of the man with the withered hand, the Pharisees provoke the confrontation by asking Jesus about the sabbath law concerning healing (Matt. 12:10). Jesus' response cites work that can lawfully be done on the sabbath, namely rescuing an animal whose life is in danger. The conclusion—arguing from what was understood as the lesser (animals) to the greater (humans)—assumes parity between the man's circumstances and the animal in mortal danger (a moot point, since his does not seem to be a life-threatening condition). Matthew's conclusion is an expansion of the law related to work on the sabbath from the obvious specific case—where one would do all that was necessary literally to save any life—to the general conclusion, "So it is lawful to do good on the sabbath." In other words, "doing good" is given equal status with saving a life, as an appropriate way to "remember the sabbath day and keep it holy" (Exod. 20:8), which is the heart of all sabbath law.

Reading Contextually:
Finding the Passage in Its Place

Considering the Literary Context

In Mark this passage concludes a series of five stories that point to increasing tension between Jesus or his followers and the religious authorities (2:1-12, about Jesus' authority to forgive sins; 2:13-17, about Jesus' table community with persons called "sinners"; 2:18-22, about the disciples' failure to fast; 2:23-28, about the disciples' sabbath activity; and 3:1-6, about Jesus' sabbath activity). In each case the collision is over where authority lies concerning these matters, not only in Jesus' own ministry, but especially for his followers in Mark's community. The conclusion to the immediately preceding passage—"so the Human One is sovereign even over the sabbath" (2:28, authors' translation)—is acted out in Jesus' own sabbath activity in the passage under study.

Although the authorities' opposition to Jesus is clear in each of the stories in the series, only the last ends in overt action against him (the death plot), sounding the climactic note to this section of the Gospel. The early occurrence of this threatening note also sets the stage for the prominent role claimed by the events of Jesus' passion and death in Mark's Gospel, and for Mark's emphasis on the suffering and crucified Messiah.

Locating the Social Context

The different concerns of ancient author and modern readers can be seen in the relative interest each finds in the healing of the man's hand. As the close reading of the text showed, the healing is a minor point in the story for Mark. His emphasis is rather on Jesus' authority relative to sabbath law. Modern editors and commentators, however, regularly label this passage "the healing of the man with the withered hand," and they take for granted the challenge to sabbath law as part of Jesus' ministry. The relationship between modern assumptions and the agenda of the text needs to be examined at other points as well. For example, the church's traditional conclusion that such healings demonstrate Jesus' divinity or his identity as messiah must be tested against the views of healing and healers current in the first century hellenistic world.

Clearly neither Jesus nor the Gospel writers shared modern understandings about the cause and treatment of disease. Medical practice in their world was a combination of the use of herbs, diet, sleep, and various physical therapies, and techniques designed to appease harmful powers or enlist the aid and support of benevolent deities on behalf of the suffering person. When healing took place, it was viewed as a victory for the god to whom one had appealed, and as evidence of the power and reliability of the person who invoked that deity's aid. Such assumptions would have been shared by persons from all strata of the society. What was different was the way a person had access to the medical care available.

"Physicians" had the greatest technical skills of all the healers. Insofar as formal education played a part, they were the ones with the greatest knowledge of the human body and of techniques that might be expected to address various conditions. Their services, however, were expensive, and only the wealthy could have access to them. For the rest of the people, there were two other options.

The first was to go to one of the regional healing centers where treatment for "disease" might be available, and where, in the absence of treatment, persons with various "illnesses" could be accommodated. (Following the usage of medical anthropology, "disease" refers to the specific physical malfunction, and "illness" refers to the disease with its social implications—the effect on the person's relationship to family, to the community, to the economic system, and so forth.) Persons were usually treated in these centers without regard to their wealth. Access to these centers was restricted, however, in that poor people living a distance away would not have been able to get there, both because of the cost of travel, and because family members would not have been able to sacrifice the time from their subsistence-level jobs to accompany the sick person. A more subtle obstacle to the healing centers for people on the margins of society was the centers' fundamentally conservative ideology. Their purpose was to cure diseases so that people could be reintegrated into the same social order and institutions from which they had come, and which may have played a part in the complex illnesses from which they suffered. Failing that, the centers provided a place where chronic illness would not disrupt others' participation in those same institutions. Social change or critique played no role in the healing centers, and in fact would have contradicted views of healing built around harmony and fitting in to one's world.

For people who could not get to the centers or who chose not to seek such help, the only option was to hope that one of the many itinerant healers came through town before the disease claimed the person's life. The itinerant healers were of two basic types, and the distinction between them is crucial to understanding Mark's interpretation of the healing in this passage. One type of healer was the "magician," whose reputation centered only on the ability to effect cures on various individuals. Like the physicians and healing centers, these healers aimed at enabling the sick, injured, or disabled person to become a fully functioning member of the established society. (This is the basis of the plea for healing of the man in the version of the story in the Gospel of the Nazareans cited above, which portrays Jesus as just such a magician.) In the accounts of magicians' activities, the social institutions and the religious systems of that society were taken for granted as structures to be accommodated or satisfied.

Another category of itinerant healer was the "charismatic prophet," whose mediation of healing was coupled with a challenge to those structures in the form of wisdom teachings or programs for political and social change. These prophets must be distinguished not only from the magicians, but also from the various messianic claimants whose programs were accompanied by signs that recalled events in Israel's history in which God was perceived as interceding on their behalf—the gift of manna, for example, or the dividing of the Reed Sea. While Jesus is portrayed in all of the Gospels as doing such "messianic" deeds, the healings attributed to him portray him rather as a charismatic prophet empowered by the Spirit of God, not only to heal, but also to bring about changes in the institutions and behaviors that reinforced a person's pain and exclusion from full participation in the society.

The account in Mark 3:1-6 is an example of the latter role, but with a twist. The story does not confront social or institutional barriers to the man's own participation in his society, but rather what appears to be an impediment to his being healed. That impediment is formed by implications drawn from the various rules implementing the commandment to keep the sabbath day "holy." Observance of the sabbath, circumcision, and table purity were crucial marks of group identity, especially for Jews living either in the Diaspora or in the internal exile of their own land under Roman occupation: Who they were as a people reflected their commitment to honor and obey God. Those commandments required elaboration if they were to be meaningful guides for the community's life. The collection of regulations concerning activities mandated or forbidden on that day were crucial to that end.

Prohibition of all work on the sabbath is at the heart of that observance. Sabbath rest commemorates God's own rest from the work of creating on the seventh day (Gen. 2:2-3; Exod. 20:8-11) and also God's freeing of Israel from forced labor in Egypt (Deut. 5:12-15)—theological underpinnings of the law that override almost every other consideration. According to the regulations that implement that commandment and make its observance possible, actions done to effect healing are specific expressions of work that is forbidden on that day, unless it is necessary to preserve life. Jesus' challenge to these regulations represents the act of a charismatic prophet in that his act of healing of what is obviously not a life-threatening condition recalls people to the life-affirming intent and function of the sabbath law that marks their identity: The day is kept holy by doing good, and not merely by avoiding specific proscribed activities.

Engaging the Text, Other Readers, and Our Communities

Jesus' role as charismatic prophet, with the healing functioning as a catalyst for the prophet's principal program of social and religious reform, offers one way to get a handle on this passage in our context. People for whom the magic element implied in Jesus' work as healer is an obstacle can find in the passage's lack of emphasis on the healing a reason to explore other dimensions. The issue of sabbath keeping and how time is set apart as holy touches both the contemporary longing for rest and renewal and the revival of interest in spirituality and ritual that permeates Christian communities and "new age" movements alike. In both cases, the passage encourages the linkage of spirituality and ethics—two arenas of religious concern often separated in contemporary practice—by means of the question attributed to Jesus in Mark 3:4. Similarly, people who would make belief in miracles (or even the receipt of physical healing) a litmus test of adequate faith, or who view this account as part of the proof of Jesus' divinity, would find their attention drawn to Jesus' authority as a religious and social reformer who empowers all dimensions of human wholeness. In our context, and perhaps in others as well, interpretation of this passage should include wrestling with the pastoral and theological issues raised by situations where God's help has been sought, but no healing ensued—where God seems to be arbitrary ("God had other plans for that person"), inscrutable ("we just don't understand how God has answered our prayer"), or even cruel ("God is teaching us a lesson by this suffering").

It would be important for readers from a context like ours to be attentive to questions raised about this passage by persons from cultures where itinerant healers or shamans are part of daily experience. For example, Sharon recalls readers from Indigenous communities in Central America asking, in relation to Gospel healing stories, whether Jesus was a *curandero*. If not, how did he differ from the *curanderos* in their culture? If Jesus heals because he is divine, does that mean they are too? For persons from such cultures, as for Jesus' contemporaries and early Christians, the question is not *whether* the healing occurred, but by whose power the healer worked. Commonly acknowledged criteria also allow these contemporary communities to come to agreement about the good or evil power evident in the healer's action (though clearly today those criteria are not the healer's observance of sabbath law). But what judgment is to be made when the person manifesting that power violates one of the commonly acknowledged criteria of goodness? That is the tension created in this text.

Relative to the issue of keeping sabbath, it would be important to talk with observing Jews about the meaning and means of keeping sabbath in their experience. One might ask Muslims about their ways to mark such holy times as Ramadan, or members of a Vietnamese community about the cultural and religious meanings of Tet. Some Christian individuals and groups are discovering anew the significance of Sunday observance as an expression of their religious identity. How do their experiences impact the reading of this text? Native Americans might translate questions about respecting holy *time* into affirmations about ways to honor the holiness of particular *places*. At issue is not collecting stories of unusual practices as a kind of spiritual or liturgical tourism, but rather learning from persons of other cultures in order to probe further the questions and concerns raised by the passage in one's own community.

Chapter 10

1 Corinthians 11:17-34

Locating the Readers and the Reading Context

Selecting the Biblical Text

We chose to include a passage from one of Paul's letters because of the special challenge to interpreters occasioned by the intimate link between a letter and specific elements of the ancient context. Not only such general factors as culture, religious context, social class, economic status, geography, and historical period come into play (as with any type of literature), but particular questions, problems, and practices are explicitly addressed in the direct communication between writer and recipients. Those underlying concerns must be identified if the response by the writer of the letter is to be understood appropriately, and not assumed to be the answer to a different question entirely. We chose this particular passage of 1 Corinthians because it explores ethical ramifications of liturgical practices—two areas of the church's life often considered to be unrelated.

Beginning the Journey at Home

The fact that this passage is found in a letter from Paul to the Christians at Corinth raises the question of the role letters have played for communities of interpreters, as well as questions about the role of letters in the ancient world. Even in the age of telephones, faxes, and electronic mail, most readers bring enough experience with letters to identify some of the particular concerns involved in interpreting part of a letter. For example, letters have specific senders and (usually) specific addressees. Letters addressed to "Occupant" or that are clearly composed of a form letter "personalized" by a computer that blends the letter with names on a mailing list command little attention. Letters differ according to the relationship between sender and addressee, and according to the occasions that prompt them: A letter to one's beloved and a letter to the Internal Revenue Service to clarify a problem in one's taxes will be as different in style and tone as they are in content. Such parallels in everyday experiences will help interpreters understand how important it is to know something about the sender and addressees of specific biblical letters, about their prior relationship, and about the specific events or circumstances that have occasioned the letter.

Particular experiences of modern interpreters with letters received or awaited can also affect the attitude with which they approach a section of one of the biblical letters. Are some members of a study group anxiously awaiting letters from loved ones from whom they are separated—children who have moved away, or family members away from whom they have themselves moved? If letters are long in coming, what circumstances underlie the delay? Tension in the relationship itself? War or other external crises where the others are living? Have official letters been the locus of hope or fear, such as important decisions by government agencies? Have letters from church officials carried a word of promise or dashed hopes for members in the community (for example, around women's participation in ministerial leadership)? Have letters—anonymous or signed—brought threats against them or members of their families? Have letters recently conveyed good news about such events as college admission, a new job, or an unexpected gift?

We share the modern world's decreasing reliance on letters for communication. We are much more apt to make a phone call or log-on to electronic mail when we need to be in touch with a friend or colleague. Despite the advantages of the immediacy of such exchanges, we still welcome letters, though, for the delight of rereading them, and for the knowledge of the time and effort they represent. Fred recalls the pleasure of receiving long letters from their son when he studied in England, and Sharon notes the emotional power of rereading a carefully preserved letter that her father, who has since died, had tucked into her suitcase when she left for a year of study in France. Both of us saw the dread of many of our friends who received letters notifying them that they had been drafted into military service during the war in Vietnam. We have felt both pain and comfort upon receiving letters from our own church officials, and upon hearing of the effect of such letters on others. We have known first-hand the horror of threatening letters from anonymous senders who know where we can be found. For us, therefore, letters carry authority and by the very nature of the genre command our attention.

Before moving into the specific passage, it might be wise to discuss two additional factors that would shape a group's or an individual's response to this text: previous impressions about Paul, and the role of the eucharist or holy communion in their experience. Paul has enjoyed both an enthusiastically positive and a strongly negative press in the churches. For many, he is seen as a theologian for all times, expressing in universally accessible language such theological affirmations as "justification by grace through faith" (in Romans and Galatians in particular) and the primacy of love (1 Corinthians 13). On both counts, Paul represents a welcome contradiction to the dominant values of competitiveness and self-centeredness that mark the world in which we live. On the other hand, we join with the many women who point to statements "against" women in letters attributed to Paul (such as 1 Cor. 14:34-36 or Eph. 5:22-24, even though the latter may well have been written by a follower of Paul), and with many in the African American community who cite Paul's failure clearly to oppose slavery (Philemon and, again, Eph. 6:5-8), as reasons to be suspicious of his statements on other issues as well, or perhaps reasons not to read the letters at all.

Relative to the common meal of the community, which is the specific subject of this passage, the role played by the celebration and theological interpretation of the sacrament of communion or the eucharist in the interpreters' church traditions will affect the issues they recognize as important in this text. People from highly liturgical traditions, for example, may find it hard to see more than the "words of institution" (11:23-26) that are cited in the communion liturgy as relevant to Paul's teaching on the supper. They may be inclined to dismiss the rest of the passage dealing with events and practices in Corinth as reflecting matters only of historical curiosity. On the other hand, neither of us comes from a part of our respective denominations where the eucharist held a central role in worship, and we have learned the power of that sacrament only in our adult lives. The ability of the bread and cup to express the unity of the community in covenant with God through Jesus Christ stands in marked contrast to the private "communion" between the individual believer and God that characterized our earlier understanding.

Encountering the Biblical Text:
Read, Feel, Question, React

The content of the passage itself gives rise to a number of questions. How did Paul learn about the Corinthians' practices relative to the supper? Clearly more than a breach of etiquette is involved in vv. 20-22, but what exactly is the practice that Paul criticizes? What are the roots of the "divisions," and how are those factions reflected in the problems surrounding the supper? From whom did Paul receive the "words of institution" (vv. 23-26), and how do they address the problem with the Corinthians' behavior? Paul's warnings in vv. 27-30 are harsh: What is meant by eating or drinking "in an unworthy manner," being "answerable for the body and blood" of Christ, or "discerning the body"? How do this example of Corinthian practice and the accompanying words of warning relate to the worship practices in various present-day Christian churches?

Reading Contextually:
Finding the Passage in Its Place

Locating the Social Context

The very fact that this passage is in a letter, as well as specific questions that arise from the passage, make discerning the social context and the occasion that prompted Paul to write a matter of great importance. In working with letters, therefore, it is usually helpful to investigate such matters early in the process of interpretation, prior to engaging in a close reading or other study focused on the passage itself.

Research into the Corinthian context yields a picture of Corinth as a port city on a major trade route in the Roman Empire, with all that such a role implies of cultural diversity, transiency of population, and economic and social competition. The lack of social roots and stability inherent in that setting was heightened by the fact that the old city of Corinth had been destroyed in 146 B.C.E., and its population slaughtered or sold into slavery. In 44 B.C.E. Julius Caesar reestablished the city, populating it with people from elsewhere in the Roman Empire, many of whom were newly freed slaves. As a result, in Paul's day Corinth lacked the stable, inherited social order that would have characterized cities with a longer history. Social position was instead the product of a complex interaction of wealth, legal status, gender, education, and ethnicity, with different factors being determinative on different occasions. Interactions among persons of higher and lower status were carefully prescribed, and status differences were generally reinforced by rules of etiquette and by a social code built around honor and shame. It was assumed that persons of higher status or those whose wealth allowed them to host the meetings or otherwise make larger contributions to the economically and socially diverse groups would enjoy special privileges. For example, at gatherings of trade guilds, which—like the suppers of the Christian communities—would have brought together people of different social ranks, the food one was served would correspond to one's station, with the wealthy dining lavishly, and the poor having only a minimal meal: In Corinth one knew one's worth even by the food on one's plate.

Part of Paul's work as a traveling artisan and missionary included establishing gatherings of Christians in small house-churches in Corinth (as in other cities on his route). He apparently kept in touch with those communities through exchanges of letters and through reports brought by other artisans, traders, and missionaries whom Paul met. A long agenda of issues raised by the communities themselves, and raised in Paul's mind by the reports he received, appears to have prompted the letter called 1 Corinthians.

Considering the Literary Context

Paul appears to have responded to the list of concerns one by one, interweaving ethical admonitions and theological interpretation to elaborate on his opening affirmations of God's grace and not human achievement or merit as the basis of the Corinthians' call and their life in Christ (1:1-9). The passage on the meal (11:17-34) addresses one of a group of issues related to public worship (11:2–14:40), about which there appears to have been misunderstanding—or inappropriate behavior—in Corinth.

A Close Reading of the Biblical Text: Steps in the Process

Preparing a Translation of the Text

Most of the differences in standard English translations of the passage reflect stylistic choices of the translators. Three points seem more serious. In vv. 24 and 25, various theological traditions relating to the manner of Christ's presence in the sacrament seem to be mirrored in decisions to read "as a memorial" (NEB), "in memory" (TEV), or "in remembrance" (NJB, NRSV). The other two points reflect translators' attempts to interpret the nature of Paul's charge against the Corinthians (v. 21) and the theological judgment he brings against them. Both of these problems are more complex than simply matters of translation, and they will be discussed below.

Identifying the Shape of the Text

The passage is designed to make clear to the Corinthians Paul's indictment of their actions (vv. 17-22), the warrant for his claim against them (vv. 23-26), and the consequences of their continuing in these practices (vv. 27-32). It ends with a brief concluding and transitional comment leading into the next major section of the letter (vv. 33-34).

The indictment itself begins and ends with Paul's lack of commendation of them (vv. 17, 22). Between are two charges of what happens when they "come together" (vv. 18, 20), apparently for community meals in the context of which bread and wine are set apart to be shared in a special ceremony. The first charge against them warns of "divisions," a problem Paul has raised earlier (1:10-17), but this time the divisions appear to be based on behavior at the supper itself, rather than on loyalty to different leaders as was the case in chapter 1. The second charge draws the theological consequences of their behavior, namely that—with or without the correct words of institution—they no longer eat the "Lord's supper," but only their private meals.

The words of institution of the supper, which are closely parallel to those found in the accounts of the last supper in the Synoptic Gospels (especially in Luke 22:19-20), are introduced as part of the tradition of the church said to stem from Jesus, and to have been received and handed on from believer to believer. They are cited without elaboration, indicating that Paul views them as common ground between the Corinthians and himself which ought to resolve the problem he has identified. Paul's conclusion about how their behavior and the foundation of the supper bring an indictment against them is that they are eating and drinking "in an unworthy manner," and thus are guilty of profaning the body and blood (v. 27), and of not discerning the body (v. 29). These actions have consequences for their immediate well-being and in the eternal judgment (vv. 30-32).

Refining the Questions

What exactly is happening at these meals that Paul condemns? Twice he raises the issue of the need to wait for the rest before eating (vv. 21, 33). At first glance it seems to be a case of bad manners—some start to eat the common meal ahead of time and fail to leave enough for latecomers. Paul's recommendation that those who are hungry eat at home (v. 34) sounds callous in light of his recognition that some in the congregation have no such option (v. 22). What seems more likely is that Paul refers not to bad manners in distributing a common meal, but to the meals whose menus differed according to one's social class. Special foods were thus served to some members in segregated banquets before the words of institution and prayer of thanksgiving set apart the distribution of bread and wine as the meal common to the whole community. Paul's judgment is that for some to dine lavishly while others go hungry is not a case of bad manners, but rather that it profanes the meal that should be a holy event in the life of the congregation. People who behave in that way both show contempt for the congregation and humiliate those who are poor (v. 22). The words of institution, which Paul and the Corinthians have in common, become the warrant for his argument against such practices.

Beginning in v. 26, Paul makes clear that this meal is not just a reminiscence of an event in the past, but rather that, like all events in their daily lives, this too has eternal consequences. The common meal is the act that makes clear their situation at the hinge between this age and the age to come. In the supper, both by the words spoken and by the meal shared, they proclaim and make present Christ's death "until Christ comes." The meal thus embodies both the community's deepest memory and the ground of its most precious hope. Paul elaborates on that interpretation in vv. 29-32. Keeping as one's own what is properly the common supper is summed up as eating and drinking unworthily, and thus as an inappropriate proclamation of the death of Christ. The theology of the cross so central to Galatians and Romans clearly undergirds this argument as well.

Paul concludes his argument by playing on the theme of judgment or discernment (vv. 27-32): One must examine one's own behavior at the supper, because in it is lodged eternal judgment before God. The illness and death that have occurred in the community are cited as evidence of that divine judgment, which is said to have disciplinary value, calling the community to account in time to turn from its ways and escape condemnation. The heat of this controversy appears to have led Paul to ignore the pastoral consequences of his words for any in that congregation who were suffering or grieving—to say nothing of the effect of those words on subsequent readers. The portrait of a vindictive God who punishes people directly and violently for ethical misconduct is neither a part of our religious experience or beliefs, nor a prominent theme elsewhere in Paul's writings. This escalation of language seems to be a final effort to convince the Corinthians of his point.

The bread and wine of the supper are not merely food, but also the vehicle by which those who partake of them become participants in one another. This result of a single "body" that must be discerned is introduced in v. 29 (as the various English translations attempt to suggest by their notes and use of an upper case "B" in "Body") and elaborated in chap. 12. The sacrifice identified in the words of institution is not the scapegoat driven from the community, but rather the sacrifice itself constitutes the organic unity of the community, and the one sacrificed is the eschatological judge of the whole world.

Engaging the Text, Other Readers, and Our Communities

Clearly the situation of a global institutional church torn by confessional and denominational divisions is different from that of the house churches of ancient Corinth. We usually do not mark the eucharist as part of a meal, and thus we do not experience transgressions against justice as issues of etiquette around a common table. The passage still confronts us, however, with an ethical challenge at the heart of liturgical practice and theology: Are the bread eaten and the cup drunk "in an unworthy manner," and the body of Christ not "discerned," when we live in abundance while global neighbors starve?

The contextual setting of the passage makes it clear that Paul's response to the Corinthians' behavior includes their conduct during those times not governed directly by the words of institution as well as during the event of the liturgy itself. Similarly in the modern context, the test of proper eating of the supper requires looking beyond the liturgy to ask whether the world's hungry have been fed. Exploring this passage thus pushes persons in a relatively comfortable, middle class context to try to understand the local and global dimensions of world hunger. If the group of those studying this text does not naturally include people who work to address the issue of hunger (representatives of organizations like Bread for the World and people who staff local food pantries, soup kitchens, or social service agencies, for example), as well as those who have known hunger first hand, their input should be sought. It would be important also to come to understand those institutional obstacles to the equitable distribution of food (political and economic manifestations of the discriminatory social customs of Corinth), and how overcoming them is involved in "discerning the body" in one's own context.

On another level, the test of proper eating of the supper pushes us to take a closer look beyond the holy table itself, at the organization and policies of our own local congregations and at the values they embody. Just as Paul accused the Corinthians of mirroring the social mores of their society, do our society's standards of worth dictate how persons are viewed and allowed to become involved in aspects of the life and leadership of the church? Do personal wealth or professional prestige dictate who holds office in the church, or whose opinions are heeded in meetings of the congregation or of committees? Are persons who are different from the majority of the congregation in their race or ethnicity, language, social class, degree of able-bodiedness, or sexual orientation made to feel welcome, or are they ignored until they give up and stop coming? Is the conduct of the church's life consistent with the affirmations of its liturgy, theology, and preaching?

Because of the importance of this section of 1 Corinthians in the liturgical practice of the Christian church, it would be important to reflect on the passage together with Christians from different confessional, denominational, and ethnic traditions, and with Christians from other parts of the world. How do these communities understand the link between sacrament and ethics—between worship and mission—in the life of their churches?

Central to Paul's argument against what had been reported about the Christians at Corinth is the recognition that to disregard the hunger of the poor is to opt out of the supper that belongs not to them but to Christ. That supper links the memory of Jesus Christ, the covenant that constitutes the "body of Christ," and the hope of life eternal—life so whole, authentic, and wholly attuned to the divine rhythms of love and justice that death itself cannot end it.

PART 3

Issues and Resources
in Interpretation

Chapter 11

Some Issues in Biblical Interpretation

Identifying the Issues

This roadmap has encouraged interpreters to explore the contexts from which they engage biblical texts, and to discover how their readings of these texts emerge from their social world and historical moment. As part of that process, the roadmap also guides interpreters into an encounter with other readers, particularly readers from diverse contexts, each of whom is also encountering the texts in his or her own context. In following this process we find that a number of questions emerge for us, and we assume that others are posing their own questions. Our experience is that questions arise from any process of reflection and study, and lurk in the background even when they are not raised explicitly.

The process outlined in this roadmap has led us to reflect on whether this attention to diverse readings and this challenge to discover one's own interpretation imply that any and all readings are "right." Does it mean that no reading can be judged wrong? Is each group and every person free to read the texts in their own way? In the introduction we have maintained that not every reading is "right." Still the questions remain: What makes a reading "right" or "wrong"? By what criteria do we decide? Who gets to determine the criteria, and who applies them? What do we mean by "right"? Is a "right" reading one that accurately reflects the text? Is a "right" reading one that is morally or doctrinally acceptable?

Closely related to questions about "right" and "wrong" in the context of the diversity of readings is the issue of biblical authority. If diverse readings are possible, how can the Bible be claimed as an authority within and by the community of faith? Which reading of the Bible is authoritative? Who determines that "right" reading?

Reflections on Our Context and the Questions

As we talked—and talked, and talked—about these issues, we suddenly realized that the roadmap itself might be a helpful guide in our efforts to think about these questions. Begin at home: That is the lesson of chapter 1. Acknowledge our own context, our own assumptions and desires. Seek to bring to consciousness those cultural dynamics that shape the very questions we are asking. In doing so, we quickly recognized that in part we do want to believe that there *is* a right reading.

Two factors impel us in that direction. First, the Euro-American academic world, which is one of our primary contexts, values the search for an objective, universal, incontrovertible interpretation of events and texts alike. We are driven to convince others, either by force of argument or power of position, that our reading is the correct reading. We would like to believe that the six readings presented here are better than and will supersede previous interpretations. While we recognize that the earlier consensus around one particular methodology (such as "historical criticism") and the exclusivity of the male Euro-American cultural context no longer reign unchallenged, we are still creatures of that world. Thus we tend to assume, even though we may not always recognize or admit it, that any temporary uncertainty and confusion is exactly that—temporary. If we can apply the appropriate process to the particular details, we will eventually distill the universal content. If we can abstract the universal truth from its specific expression, we can discern its eternally valid voice. Or if we can assimilate all the diverse perspectives, the sum of them will constitute a truly universal reading. Soon—and very soon, if Bible scholars will address the issues quickly and vigorously—a new consensus will emerge. We feel exhilaration in the prospect of this new accumulation of insights from multiple methods and wisdom from diverse contexts. We find satisfaction in the vision and hope of participating in some way in the formation of that new consensus.

Second, participating in congregations of Protestant denominations, we belong to church traditions that claim the Bible as the central authority, true and authoritative for faith and life. Working within that tradition, we have come to hold certain convictions—about issues of justice for example—many of which we understand to be based on and to have emerged from the Bible. We covet the assurance, based on the authority of the Bible, that those convictions are *just* and *right* and *authoritative* for the lives of all Christians.

There is, however, another current within our culture running parallel to that which pulls toward universal truth and authoritative readings, namely the current of individualism. Such an orientation tends to privatize religion into the spiritual task or quest of each believer. The popularized notion of the "priesthood of all believers" is invoked to claim that each individual can read the Bible for himself or herself. The awkward juxtaposition of these two tendencies of privatization and universalism within the church would seem to create a particular tension in the arena of biblical interpretation. On the one hand stands the ecclesial claim for Biblical authority; on the other is the spiritual practice of private interpretation.

Similar to the current of private interpretation in the church is the notion of the solitary scholar in the academy—an individual whose career is motivated by the desire to develop a peculiar interpretation that he or she must defend and refine. The successful development and promulgation of a unique reading defines the scholar's place within the academy. Running parallel to the tension created in the church between authority and private interpretation is the tension in the academy between the ideal of individual originality and the norm of universal, objective truth.

In looking at our own cultural context we come to realize the extent to which that context has shaped our very understanding of the problem: Either one believes that there is one true and correct (universal) reading, or one must allow that all readings are right. These two strands within our culture define the debate between a stance for absolute truth and an attitude of relativism. And yet, strangely enough, these two positions co-exist within the same society. Most of us, if and when we are honest, find that we hold both at the same time. How is that possible, we might ask? And why do we pose the question in these terms?

Since both of these postures exist easily within the dominant culture and are endorsed by it (or at least by segments within it), we can conclude that neither position offers a serious threat to the world of that culture. Furthermore, we concede that both offer a response to the issue of diversity. When the stance is that of striving toward the right or authoritative reading, criteria are established by which the correctness of a reading will be judged. Diversity of readers and different readings can be entertained, but they will always be judged by established norms defined by those in positions of explicit or implicit power. Furthermore, to be seriously considered, an interpretation must be presented in language familiar to those on the inside of powerful institutions or sectors of society. The defining image is that of a circle that can be expanded to include groups or perspectives previously excluded, but admission to the circle is controlled by those on the inside. A perimeter remains clearly defined, distinguishing between those inside and those outside.

But what about the posture of total relativism that would accept all readings, leaving each person or group to determine their own interpretation, each with equal claim to truth? Does such a posture not challenge the hegemony of the dominant culture? In a world governed by this perspective, each interpretation stands independent of all others and is accountable to none. The advantage is that each group can offer its own reading, so that the fact of alternate readings is readily acknowledged by all. But since all readings are considered to be independent of each other, they have no truth claims on one another, except for those that can be imposed by brute force and raw power. This means that alternate readings have no claim on mainstream or dominant interpretations. One can recognize various readings, even affirming them as appropriate for their own contexts. Or they may be considered "fascinating," and may even be incorporated or cited as interesting variations on the theme. But such a decision is always at the discretion of the individual interpreter or group.

The result is that, while this attitude allows for diversity, it subtly brackets that diversity, thus permitting the status quo to continue unchallenged in any fundamental way. Some readings inevitably will have greater power than others because they are the ones presented in the media, in pulpits, in print, and by persons in positions of leadership within the structures of church and academy. That power continues unchallenged, and the readings of the dominant culture can continue to function as if they had universal status. This process is reflected, for example, in language referring to "biblical interpretation," then to feminist biblical interpretation, womanist biblical interpretation, or *mujerista* biblical interpretation. Universal status is implied for biblical interpretation from one context—academic, male, Euro-American—

while all others are limited to their specific contexts. This language betrays the subtle way in which the posture of relativism still grants privileged status to one particular "relative" position.

The answer to the question of why these two postures so easily co-exist then becomes clear: As long as the question continues to be posed as an option between the two, the present hegemony will not be fundamentally disturbed. As long as the debate is posed in these terms, that debate is governed by the categories of the dominant culture and will continue to serve its interests. The question is framed in a form acceptable to it. To pose the question in terms of either the universal hegemony of one truth or total relativism is to be governed by the construct of *binary consciousness*. Binary consciousness is that lens through which the world is perceived in terms of either/or. One is either in or out; a reading is either true or false; there is either absolute truth or total relativism. But is that the only way to view the world?

Let us return to the exploration of our own cultural contexts. In addition to our shared experience of a common cultural context, we also have different experiences. Reading from the margins is a strand woven into the fabric of Sharon's world. As a woman studying the Bible in the context of a man's world—the theological seminary of the 1960s—she became aware that the supposedly universal readings of that context excluded her and her experience. She did not fit that world, and its readings did not acknowledge hers. To describe the dilemma in this way identifies two phases of the task. The first is the need to discover language that allows one to articulate one's "other world"—other than the dominant one, that is— and to read texts within and from that world. The second is the claim of that other world and of the readings of that world on the dominant culture. The first of these agendas could be achieved with no real threat to the dominant culture. Alternative readings could be developed, for example, within a women's group. Such readings could then be offered, either to be accepted or rejected by the dominant culture. Individual women might choose to function within both the world of the dominant culture and that of the women's group, becoming bi-lingual and bi-cultural, moving between the two and functioning within both, as if they were separate and unrelated cultures.

The second agenda, however, cannot allow the solution of simple coexistence of the different worlds. This agenda recognizes that the dominant culture has an impact on women (and other non-dominant communities). It states clearly that the way texts are read and the very choice of texts to be read shape the attitudes and actions of society toward women, and the attitudes and actions of women and men living within that society. Women, therefore, cannot simply articulate their own readings, as in the first agenda: Readings by women also make a claim on the dominant culture, and the definition of the issues is not left to the prerogative of the dominant culture. The authority claimed by women's readings is neither validated nor invalidated by the decisions of that dominant culture. The dominant culture and individuals functioning within that culture may determine their own response, but that response does not settle the issue. Their response is exactly that: their response. It is neither definitive nor universal in its authority.

Fred was basically at home in the dominant universe—though he might have preferred some remodeling—when he was confronted by other voices and worlds. How should he respond? Does he ignore and deny them? Does he listen politely, perhaps trying to include feminist readings, insofar as possible, within his dominant world construct? Does he acknowledge that feminist readings are probably important for women, and thus that they should be allowed to continue doing them? These are options he initially considered, but each of these responses assumes that the problem can be defined by the perspective of the dominant culture and presumes that power remains vested there. They do not address the task of reading texts within one's own context as it is now informed by the insights and claims of the readings of women. In other words, how is Fred to read the text within his own world as a man, but do so interactively with women? The challenge is to respond not simply to the readings of women as an abstracted and generalized category, but to the readings of particular women. Only in doing so does one begin to challenge the patterns of universalizing. This entails a move toward recognizing commonalities and differences in the readings of various groups of women, and between this diversity of readings of women and those of various groups of men. The *commonalities* make communication possible and value issues important. *Difference* makes that communication necessary.

Similar issues are posed for both of us in our encounter with other voices—most prominently those of African Americans, Africans, Hispanics, and Latin Americans—which constitutes another strand woven into our life experiences. In our encounters with African American and Latin American liberation theologians, we have frequently heard the claim for the "preferential option for the poor and the oppressed." We have also experienced resistance to this claim. Often the argument of those who resist that claim is that God grants preference to no one, but rather loves everyone equally, rich and poor alike.

The assertion of the preferential option for the poor unmasks the pretence of equality in such contrary positions. First of all, it identifies the fact that there are and always have been "preferential options." Power dynamics, ecclesial decisions, and academic protocol have always granted special privilege to certain interpreters, and thus to interpretations growing out of and reflecting their contexts. Second, that assertion itself realigns the power dynamic, establishing a new locus of power and investing persons and communities who are poor and oppressed with the right of authoritative reading. It does so by their own authority, not by appeal to the dominant structures. These interpreters deny the claim of the dominant culture to determine the authoritative reading and refuse to be bracketed out and dismissed. By naming the impact of the dominant culture, its power structures, and its ideologies on the lives of those whom that dominant culture would relegate to the margins, these readers refuse to participate in a relativist world in which their readings are said to have no claim on the dominant culture.

Finally we must acknowledge other strands that are woven into our cultural context, which would fall under the general categories of "postmodernism" and newer scientific cosmologies. These are both movements beyond the categories and assumptions of modernity that stem from the Enlightenment in the Western world—a worldview characterized by notions of scientific objectivity, disinterested reason, universal and timeless truth, and a focus on the individual. Though we will not elaborate here on the dynamic movement of postmodernism, we recognize that it forms part of our contemporary ethos, particularly that of academic culture, where postmodernist philosophy, for example, brings to center stage the issue of the "Other." Current scientific theories such as chaos and complexity theory provide images of connectedness within the cosmos that are quite different from those of earlier paradigms. Proponents of "fuzzy logic" or "fuzzy thinking" explore thought patterns that present alternatives to the binary world of computer languages and western consciousness in general. As a part of our culture, they provide helpful tools and fresh insights into our understandings of issues of diversity and authority, and into our notions of right and wrong. They participate in creating the ethos within which we have been alerted to some of the problems identified above. But we must acknowledge that they too belong to a particular culture, and specifically we must remember that they tend to be crafted within an academic context.

So where do we find ourselves? First, we recognize that diversity is not a new issue. Second, we understand that there are and have been different responses to that issue. We also begin to recognize that our approach to the issue itself is shaped by our cultural context. The dominant culture, which perceives itself as universal, tends to view diversity as a problem to be overcome. It will try by various strategies either to eliminate the diversity or to bracket and isolate it. By doing so, the dominant culture is able to continue to presume universal status for its own context and to grant its readings privileged authority.

Voices from non-dominant cultures, however, are fully aware of diverse and sometimes conflicting interpretations. Persons from non-dominant cultures know that context shapes perspective. A clue to this dynamic can be perceived in language patterns—for example, in the Latin American phrase "it appears to me," the African "maybe," the African American pattern of call and response, or the Euro-American woman's tendency to end statements with the intonation of a question. These are often perceived by the dominant culture as deference, or a lack of authoritativeness and assertiveness, but they are well-established patterns of interaction shaped within the cultures, not in response to the dominant culture. The speakers value these dynamics as an acknowledgment of their limited, context-specific perspective (while not denying the importance of that perspective, which is important enough to be shared), and as an invitation for response from other perspectives. Appreciation of such speech patterns grows out of a sense of relatedness and a desire for interactive community, and out of the search for understanding that emerges in that process of interaction. Such language patterns invite diversity rather than suppressing it. Authority is then found in those patterns of interaction rather than in the imposition of one perspective upon another.

The privilege of defining the problem, then, cannot be claimed by the dominant culture. The question of who defines the problem is itself a part of the problem. Voices that have been bracketed from the conversation and pushed to the margins refuse to be excluded and ignored. Interpreters from multiple contexts have taken their place at the table of discourse, and in so doing they have reformulated the questions.

Reflections on Other Contexts and the Questions

What is often perceived as the "problem" of diverse readings and normative judgments is not created by this roadmap, nor is it an issue that first arose from the tension between academic study of the Bible and religious instruction about the Bible. The emergence of interpretations from different contexts also has not caused the problem, for there has always been diversity of understandings. The problem is not the existence of diversity itself, but a response to the fact of diversity that seeks to resolve it into the quick hegemony of one voice or of a limited range of voices.

The Biblical Canon and Diversity

In fact, the issue of diversity does not emerge only in response to readings of the biblical text but is already present within the Bible itself. There are four distinct Gospels, two separate "histories" of ancient Israel (Joshua through 2 Kings and 1 and 2 Chronicles), and two distinct creation stories in Genesis. In addition one can talk about different theologies, such as those of Paul and James, or of Deuteronomy and Job. One response to that diversity has been to seek harmony among the variations, arguing that these are only slightly different perspectives. According to that response, what may appear as difference in the particulars is incidental, such that when we peel away the specific language and combine the different perspectives, we will discover the single underlying truth encoded in that language. Another response is to acknowledge different traditions or trajectories, letting each stand on its own terms. Following this approach, however, raises questions about the meaning of "biblical theology," or how the Bible views God and the relationship between God and humankind. Is there a single biblical theology or are there multiple biblical theologies? If the former, which theology or tradition becomes central, authoritative—*the* biblical theology? If the latter, how does the Bible function as an authority for faith or ethics?

The creation of the biblical canon is itself one response to diversity. In that process the church decided to include certain materials and to exclude others, thereby defining the limits of acceptable diversity: Four gospels were accepted, but others were rejected. Insofar as the canon does admit multiple viewpoints, it supports our concern for diverse perspectives, but at the same time it determines that there are wrong understandings. This latter aspect of the canon raises questions: Who is excluded? What perspectives are eliminated? Whose voices are silenced, and by whom?

This problem presents itself at two levels. On the most obvious level, choices were made among the various written documents produced in Israel and the early church, preserved in subsequent generations of those communities, and passed on in the early centuries of the church's life. A second level of the problem, however, must also be acknowledged. Many traditions of both Israel and the early church were not preserved and transmitted within the official archives. For example, most of what we learn from the Bible about the history of the divided monarchy comes from the perspective of the Southern Kingdom, Judah. Relatively little material in that account presents the perspective of the Northern Kingdom. Other documents that are mentioned in the biblical accounts—for example, the "Book of the Annals of the Kings of Israel" (1 Kings 14:19b)—have never been found. It is the perspective of the "winners" that dominates the official archives and the preserved records. On the other hand, there are many traditions, practices and understandings of the communities of Israel and the early church that were never recorded in written form. Writing itself was an act of power and privilege. The voices of marginalized persons—women, the urban poor, or peasants—rarely found literary expression. If their stories were written at all, they were recorded by authors who incorporated them within another story and subsumed them under a different frame of reference. Likewise, since only human beings express themselves in literary form, all texts grant priority to the perspectives of human societies over those of the myriad other societies functioning within the natural world.

How, then, do we understand canon? First, it is limited and finite in that these documents were written by particular people, in particular languages, in and for particular communities, and to address specific issues as the authors understood them. Furthermore, only the factors judged important or relevant from those perspectives are included in those documents. Both the range of issues addressed within the canon and the perspectives from which they are addressed are thus limited. So too are the types of religious practices described and the spheres of life within which God's activity is discerned. Little is said, for example, about the daily life of the household or about the activities of peasant workers. The expression of religious vitality by such persons is seldom if ever noted in the canonical texts. When these spheres of life are addressed in some way, they are presented and evaluated by others. In other words, the documents are not neutral or disinterested, either in the data collected or in its interpretation. Second, the process by which those documents were selected for inclusion in the canon was not neutral. The establishment of the canon involved a series of judgments made by the church in particular contexts and by specific, interested persons or groups. Despite those clearly contextual origins, the church considers the canon to have enduring value and authority.

What are the implications of this understanding for our engagement with the biblical texts? To view the canon as uniform and universal would suggest that the texts in it always apply to any given situation. The relevance and authority of each and every text are assumed or imputed. On the other hand, to view the canon as a particular witness to God's activity in the world, and to understand the canon as itself embracing diversity (even as it excludes some perspectives), is to distinguish between the authority or relevance of the Bible and that of any particular biblical text. Instead of viewing the relevance of canon in terms of its applicability, the reader engages the biblical traditions, acknowledging each of them as a particular and limited witness to God's activity in the world. That witness takes on meaning as it clarifies the reader's own context and is in turn interpreted by that context. From this point of view, commitment to a biblical canon does not absolve readers from moral judgments about that canon as it intersects their own life context.

The History of the Church and Diversity

In addition to diversity within the biblical canon and the additional voices that have been excluded by and from the canon, there has also been diversity of interpretations of the Bible within the history of the church. Even a cursory review of the history of the church will quickly reveal the variety of readings and reading methods throughout that history and at any given period. That diversity has been dealt with in a variety of ways. One response has been to grant representatives of one part of the institutional church (a confessional family, a denomination, or a local congregation) authority to determine the correct reading. Biblical interpretation was supposed to conform to and support church doctrine. More recently some have suggested that the locus of authority has shifted from church to academy. This shift has created tension between these two institutions, often resulting in a power struggle of one form or another over the authority to determine correct readings. To complicate matters further, of course, neither of these two camps is homogeneous, and neither speaks with a single voice in interpreting the Bible. Conflicts have developed both between and within denominations and churches over this very issue, and competing truth claims often characterize academic debate as well. Which of the many church institutions or factions has the power to determine correct readings? Which of the various methods and schools of thought competing for dominance in the academic world gets to be the principal voice in that arena?

In addition to these tensions within and between the dominant institutional structures of church and academy, there is another dimension to the problem of determining right readings. As we noted in chapter 1, there are also readings and reading communities that are not defined by the dominant institutional structures of the society, even though they live interactively with them. One example cited was the "Invisible Institution"—communities of enslaved persons who gathered to worship in the forest or "down by the riverside" on the plantations of the pre-Civil War South of the United States. The very name "Invisible Institution" identifies these communities from the perspective of the dominant culture. This is another way of dealing with diversity: By forcing such voices underground or refusing to recognize them, the dominant culture eliminates the diversity, and in so doing claims its own position as universal and right.

The fact that these alternative voices were invisible to or unheeded by the dominant society, however, does not render them non-existent, nor does it mean that their readings had no power or authority or that they were wrong. Persons worshiping within those communities of enslaved persons, and people in other times and other cultures who identify with them or stand in solidarity with them, readily acknowledge the existence and appropriateness of these alternative interpretations and their claims to authority. To such people, the institution is far from invisible!

These interpreters from the margins of the society, however, recognize that their readings do not and cannot stand in isolation from those of the dominant culture. On the contrary, the readings of the dominant culture that found scriptural warrants for the institution of slavery clearly had serious impact on the lives of enslaved persons. These persons knew full well that their own readings functioned within that reality and offered a challenge to it.

Even this brief discussion begins to illumine the interplay between issues of biblical authority and the dynamics of social and cultural power. It also begins to clarify the fact that the problem with a diversity of readings is not the existence of diversity, but the valuation of and response to that diversity, especially by dominant persons and groups. Do they see diversity as a problem that must be overcome or managed? Or does the real problem occur when dominant groups ignore, exclude, or otherwise silence genuinely diverse voices?

Reflections on "Right" Readings

These reflections on diversity still leave us with the question of what we mean by a "right reading." That word itself masks part of the problem, because it can refer to the *accuracy* of a reading or to its *moral or doctrinal soundness*. A right reading in the sense of an accurate one can be supported by such factors as analysis of the content of the text, of its grammar and vocabulary, and of the best data that can be recovered concerning the social contexts reflected in it. A right reading in the doctrinal sense coincides with the formal creeds or theological norms of a believing community. An ethically right reading assesses an action or a situation or prescribes standards of behavior that are consistent with moral values held by the readers or the readers' principal communities of reference.

These various right readings do not necessarily coincide, and therein lies a problem. For example, a correct reading of the household code in Eph. 5:21–6:9 assumes the existence of slavery as a social institution. If one's moral values include the affirmation that no human being can own another as property, however, that correct reading is not ethically right. If one were to say that the text itself calls for the overthrow of the system of slavery because we know that slavery is wrong, that ethically right conclusion would be a wrong (inaccurate) reading of that particular text. One is left, therefore, with the apparent dilemma of whether one should read the text correctly but to an end that is ethically wrong, or inaccurately but in a way that is ethically just and liberating. Clearly neither option is acceptable.

The diversity of texts and perspectives found within the canon itself provides a key for addressing such a situation. The household codes are not the only place in the Bible where issues of slavery, liberation, and justice are addressed. Though nowhere is the institution of slavery clearly called into question, the paradigm story of Israel's exodus from slavery in Egypt as God's saving act on behalf of God's people provides another moral voice in the conversation. The interpreter is then left with the question of how to assess and make moral judgments about the diversity of voices in the Bible as ethical words in the interpreter's own context, and not with the task of applying each specific text on its own.

To complicate the matter further, it is important to note that, for several reasons, the Exodus account itself has a morally ambiguous impact. First, despite the positive note it sounds relative to the end of Israel's status as slaves, the Exodus narrative does nothing to mitigate the patriarchal—one might even say "kyriarchal" or elite male—ideology of other biblical texts. The important roles of Moses' sister and of the midwives at the beginning of the story are subsumed under the focus on Moses, and Miriam's leadership—while celebrated briefly—is severely punished, while Aaron's parallel threat to Moses' hegemony exacts no consequences (Numbers 12). Second, the overall Exodus paradigm has at the other end of the journey the justification of conquest and genocide. These stories of Israel's colonization of the inhabitants of the land and the power of these stories in shaping history, such as the conquest of the "Americas" centuries later, make the Exodus narrative a painful story for Indigenous peoples in the western hemisphere, among others. Third, as some rabbinic commentaries on the

Exodus story have long noted, the Egyptians themselves evoke our compassion because of the suffering inflicted upon them by God, for the sake of God's redemptive intent for Israel. Fourth, the story tends to assume that other elements within the natural world are there simply to serve the needs of human society. The story of the plagues, for example, portrays divine intervention into the natural order for the sake of humanity. Thus, while the Exodus text does provide a counter-weight on the issue of slavery, it introduces other problems related to ethically "right" readings. It raises thereby the intriguing question whether a reading, such as a liberation reading of the exodus narrative, can be *both* ethically "right" *and* ethically "wrong."

It is important to note also that on some issues there is within the canon no diversity of perspectives explicitly about those issues, on the basis of which one might call into question problematic texts. For example, while there are very few explicit biblical references to sexual relations between persons of the same sex, and while it is clear that none of these texts speaks from the understanding of human sexuality found in modern social sciences, there is no "accurate" reading of a biblical text that can be said explicitly to endorse such relationships as an appropriate moral option. Similarly, despite occasional glimpses in the Bible of women in positions of leadership, which suggest that the historical practice of Israel and of the early church likely included a number of women in such roles, the prevailing ideology of the biblical texts in their canonical form is male-centered and normed by men's experience.

In such a circumstance, one may have recourse to earlier layers of the tradition that can be reconstructed from the text, or one can have recourse to extra biblical evidence in order to introduce alternative voices. Another way that communities throughout the history of biblical interpretation have dealt with the dilemma is by filling in the gaps of a story or telling the story with a new twist that changes its moral impact. In this process, which some have connected to the rabbinic writing of "*midrashim*" on the biblical text, characters in a text are portrayed in new relationships, events in a story take a different path at a key moment in the plot, a minor character is given a place of prominence, or the story is narrated from the perspective of a different character. For example, stories about the patriarchs and matriarchs in Genesis are enhanced by envisioning competing matriarchs—Rachel and Leah, for example—as supporting each other. The deposed Queen Vashti tells the story of the book of Esther from her vantage point. Mary and Martha *both* listen to Jesus' teachings, then Jesus and the disciples work with the two women to prepare the meal. Such retelling of biblical stories recognizes that any story is a literary creation reflecting the author's views, that all stories omit perspectives, and that no story is morally neutral. It plays with options: What if the situation were looked at from another angle, or in light of other values?

Such options, however, come from behind or outside the canon. If the moral rightness of a perspective that includes women as full and equal partners of men—or the moral rightness of an affirmation that homosexual relationships have as much potential for integrity and support for human wholeness as heterosexual relationships—is to carry the day, it will have to be at the price of reading *against* the biblical texts that specifically address these issues. Reading against the text in that way is yet another reading strategy, and one that finds theological if not textual support in the Bible. Thus, texts offering a vision of liberation and justice that encompasses God's activity within the world often require one to make moral judgments against the dominant structures of our societies, including their religious structures and texts, and on behalf of justice and various struggles for liberation.

The criteria supporting and denying such moral judgments are hotly contested, and the process of discernment called for is a delicate one. Most readers today would likely be in agreement that, in the case of slavery, biblical texts that support the institution must be judged to be "wrong" in the moral sense. The method by which this is done is not the issue. Whether one deals with these texts by dismissing them as reflecting the values of another social context or historical period, or whether one gets around the problem by reading the text as addressing a spiritual rather than a social meaning, makes little difference to the basic outcome on this question. The fact remains that, for moral reasons, virtually all readers today find some way around the text. For the other two issues cited, leadership of women and homosexuality, it is much less likely that agreement could be reached. Rightness, however, is not determined by general agreement or by majority vote. There was a time when there was general agreement within the dominant society that the institution of slavery was a biblically sanctioned practice, despite contradictory voices in the preaching of the "Invisible Institution" or in the witness of some Quakers and other abolitionists. Which was the right reading at that time in history? Who determined it? And by what authority?

There is still the question of whether one should seek to read against or otherwise get around any texts or set of traditions that offend contemporary moral sensibilities, even if there is general agreement about the offense. For example, an accurate reading of Amos 6:4-7 clearly indicts rich people for lifestyles that result in exploitation of poor people. The value system inherent in such oracles offends those who affirm that wealth and well-being are signs of God's blessing and recognize that many wealthy people are generous in sharing their wealth with poor people, and who therefore maintain that the wealthy should not be condemned as a matter of principle. We would affirm, however, that despite the discomfort they pose, such oracles that embody the "offense of the gospel" should not be dismissed, even though they contradict our dominant ethical values. Instead, they stand in judgment over those values. For example, it is important to note that the rationale cited above as undergirding objections to such oracles does not take into account analyses that conclude that by our very existence, we who are the wealthy minority of the world's people become exploiters of the poor—with or without our malicious intent. This text from Amos, as can be seen in the readings of Christian base communities and other similar contexts, illuminates that social and economic dimension of our existence in the world. Such offensive words, therefore, must be allowed to confront us and challenge our systems and our behaviors.

Determining which texts ought to be rejected as morally wrong and which texts should remain to confront and change us is complicated by the fact that even assessments about accuracy or correctness are not morally neutral. As the analysis of the readers and reading communities (chapter 1) and of prior encounters with texts (chapter 2) made clear, no reading is exempt from the influence of the readers' contexts. Furthermore, the perspectives and methods of socially powerful and dominant groups have dominated the field of mainstream published biblical interpretation. For example, it has only been with the recent work by Jewish feminist historians that centuries of stereotyping of the lives of first-century Jewish women has become obvious, and that the resulting inaccuracies—which, in turn, contributed to immoral attitudes and behaviors of many Christians toward Jews—have been addressed.

The preceding example raises yet another complication in this discussion. The words "first-century Jewish women"—and words central to other examples in this section of the chapter, such as "rich," "poor," "slave," or "homosexual"—already have meaning for interpreters who encounter them in connection with biblical texts. What anyone "knows" about them may or may not be consistent with first century understandings, but the words themselves invoke both specific persons and experiences of which one has direct knowledge—the poor person waiting each day at the bus stop or the lesbian couple who are one's treasured friends—and powerful learnings gleaned from such secondary sources as the church's teachings about the Jews' role in Jesus' death or film clips assembled by persons seeking to block civil rights legislation for persons who are homosexual. Consequently, a text does not receive meaning only through deliberate study or analysis, but rather it meets the reader with meanings already catalyzed. New information about the meaning of such words or of the text in which they are found in its community of origin can illumine our understanding, but that new information will not displace interpreters from their own contexts or erase completely the prior meanings evoked by or attributed to a text.

The discussion of how biblical references already carry meanings and references for contemporary readers also underlines the fact that all methods of critical investigation are colored by the social locations and ideologies of their communities of origin as well as of contemporary practitioners. Thus, the methods of historical study embody the value systems of European and North American universities and scholarly communities, central to which is the affirmation of both the possibility and the desirability of objectivity in one's research or analysis. However, when the disciplines of historical study are carried out by persons whose interests and curiosity direct their attention to other groups than those studied earlier—poor people, peasants, women, and children, for example—the different picture of the reality being studied makes clear that the objectivity or value neutrality of the disciplines was an illusion. At stake is not merely the addition of new data to make more complete a previously even more partial picture, but rather a change in the core subject being investigated. Investigation into the lives of the women living in a particular community, for example, changes the picture one gets of the functioning of public institutions dominated by men, as well as providing insight into those spheres of life where women spent most of their time. Study of peasant communities and of the poor classes in the cities provides information also about the richer strata of the society and different perspectives on the social systems and structures. To ask new questions uncovers a new reality, not just more information, and that shift has ethical implications.

While we can conclude from the above discussion the need for a healthy suspicion of all results, we do not intend to discount the significant contributions that derive from the use of the various methodologies. Nor do we want to suggest that skilled and careful use of the tools of research can be discarded. Whatever tools or methods are used must be employed with the greatest possible skill and thoroughness. Suspicion in no way excuses carelessness or sloppiness! What we do suggest is, first, that methods themselves— any and all methods—embody cultural and ethical assumptions to which we must be attentive. Second, the context within which the methods are used will also shape the understandings of the methods and the outcomes of the investigations. Third, decisions about appropriate methods are themselves shaped by the decider's context. The methods developed within the academic arena are not the only methods for reading texts, nor are contemporary methods the only valid approaches. Finally, whatever the method or methods followed, questions of accuracy and issues of ethical and doctrinal rightness must be addressed in relation both to the methods and to the readings that result from their use.

Concluding Reflections

In this chapter we have reflected on the primary ways in which the dominant culture has reflected on the issue of diversity. One strand of that culture has attempted to impose a unity on the world that excludes everything that does not conform to its definitions and standards. In other words, it seeks to create the world in its own image. The other strand of the dominant culture recognizes diversity within the world, but offers no vision of connectedness. Neither option is satisfactory. But these are not the only possibilities, and other cultures have much to teach us about how diversity is valued and engaged.

Our own belief is that the world in all of its diversity is a creation of God and locus of God's activity—as it were, the primary "text" of God. This means first of all that diversity itself is not a problem. In fact, to deny diversity is to reject aspects of God's world, and to seek to impose a single perspective is to usurp the role of God. In the second place this means that the world, in all its particularity and diversity, is a whole. No part is separated from any other. The text of the world as God's primary text includes many voices—those of humans and human societies, and all the other voices of the cosmos. The text of the whole cannot be reduced to any single aspect or voice, and no part speaks its message in isolation from the others.

The Bible, a witness to God's activity in the world, is a secondary text. The authority of the Bible lies not in itself, but in the God to whom it bears witness. Its authority emerges from the circular or spiraling process in which biblical texts engage the world of the readers, and the readers, in turn, engage the biblical texts. In that journey of heart, mind, and strength, in the company of many neighbors (Deut. 6:5; Lev. 19:18; Mark 12:30-31), they and we discern God's word in and for our world.

Chapter 12

Selected Resources for Biblical Studies

Any list of resources for biblical studies is out of date before it can be published. The field is exploding with new information from social scientists, historians, and archaeologists, and new insights from interpreters from a variety of social locations. For any resources you consult, it is important to try to determine *who* is doing the work, from *what social locations* they come, for *what purpose or audience* the work is being done, *what methodology* they are using, and *under whose auspices* (or financial or other sponsorship) the work is carried out. Keep in mind that no single resource—or even any collection of them—will give you *the* truth, but many can help you discern dimensions of truth and meaning in the text you are studying. In the list below we have grouped resources by categories, with a brief description of how each group can be useful and what particular questions or concerns you should take into account when using them.

Bibles

Every translation of the Bible is already an interpretation, and for that reason it is important to consult several of them (in addition to making your own translation of a passage from the original Hebrew or Greek if you are able to). For generations the Elizabethan English of the King James Version (KJV) set the standard for English translation. In recent years a number of other translations have appeared that use contemporary language more easily understood by modern readers, and that are based on older and more reliable manuscripts of the Greek and Hebrew texts. The Revised Standard Version (RSV) appeared under the auspices of the National Council of the Churches of Christ in the middle of the twentieth century. After several revisions of that original, a completely fresh New Revised Standard Version (NRSV) was issued in 1989, which took into account changes in English usage over the intervening decades, including the use of gender inclusive language referring to human beings. (An edition of *Gospel Parallels*, which presents the texts of Matthew, Mark, and Luke in parallel columns to facilitate their comparison, is also available in the NRSV, edited by Burton H. Throckmorton, Jr. [Nashville: Thomas Nelson, 1992]). Other principal English translations of the entire Bible include the Revised English Bible (REB), a revision of the New English Bible (NEB); the New International Version (NIV), translated by a team of evangelical scholars; the Jerusalem Bible (JB), the New Jerusalem Bible (NJB), and the New American Bible (NAB), translated by different teams of Roman Catholic scholars; and Today's English Version (TEV), produced by the American Bible Society for new readers or persons beginning to learn English. In addition, the Jewish Publication Society has produced an English translation of the Torah, Prophets, and Writings, entitled *Tanakh: A New Translation of The Holy Scriptures According to the Traditional Hebrew Text* (JPS). An ecumenical team of Protestant scholars has produced *The New Testament and Psalms: An Inclusive Version* (New York: Oxford University Press, 1995; a translation of the remainder of the Hebrew Bible may be forthcoming).

The Complete Parallel Bible (New York and Oxford: Oxford University Press, 1993), presents the NRSV, REB, NAB, and NJB versions in parallel columns. Readers able to use other modern languages will usually find a simplified translation by the United Bible Societies (similar to TEV), in addition to such classical translations as the *Reina Valera* in Spanish or Martin Luther's German translation.

Several of these translations are available in "study Bible" formats, with brief notes and cross-references to related passages of Scripture. The notes can provide helpful insights, but they should be used with caution and with attention to factors influencing the authors' interpretations. One of the most recently published examples, using the NRSV and featuring the work of more than sixty scholars (men and women, Jews and Christians, but, unfortunately, no persons of color) is the *HarperCollins Study Bible* (San Francisco: HarperCollins, 1993). *The Original African Heritage Study Bible*, edited by Cain Hope Felder (Nashville: James C. Winston, 1993), based on the KJV and including the work of about twenty African and African American authors (one of whom is a woman), highlights the relationship between biblical worlds and the history, cultures, and experiences of Africa.

Concordances

Both the original Greek and Hebrew texts and most major modern translations of the Bible have corresponding "concordances," or indexes listing every place where each word occurs. Concordances can be helpful resources for finding a particular reference of which one is able to recall only a few key words. They also allow one to explore the variety of ways a particular word is used, and the contexts in which it is found. Several words of caution should accompany one's use of concordances in word study, however. First, if one is working with any translation, it is important to remember that the same word in the new language can be used to translate several words in the original one, and, in turn, each word in the original language can be translated by several different words. An "analytical lexicon" (which identifies the word in the original Greek or Hebrew underlying a particular occurrence and provides an index of other entries used to translate that same original word) requires some practice to use effectively, but it can make the study of word usage more accurate. Even when one has identified occurrences of the same words in the original language, though, it is important to remember that different biblical authors may use a word with different meanings, and the same author may use the word differently in different contexts, so one should be cautious about building too large a case on data gleaned from use of a concordance.

Some of the concordances to the principal English translations are: John R. Kohlenberger III, *The NRSV Concordance Unabridged* (Grand Rapids: Zondervan, 1991); Richard E. Whitaker, *The Eerdmans Analytical Concordance to the RSV* (Grand Rapids: Wm. B. Eerdmans, 1988); Edward W. Goodrick and John R. Kohlenberger III, *The NIV Complete Concordance* (Grand Rapids: Zondervan, 1981); and James Strong, *Strong's Exhaustive Concordance* (KJV; Gordonsville, TN: Dugan Publishers, Inc., n.d.).

In addition to such published concordances, several computer programs exist that contain the text of the Bible (in the original languages and in a number of translations) and the means to identify occurrences both of individual words (like traditional concordances) and of phrases or groups of words. These, like all resources using the computer, change rapidly. If you work with a computer, you should

227

consult your usual suppliers to identify resources that would be most useful for your work.

Bible Dictionaries and Encyclopedias

These standard reference works are good places to begin to study key words, names of places or people, and aspects of the various societies and cultures represented in the Bible. In addition, they include articles giving background for each book of the Bible and a brief summary of its contents. Three such resources have been published recently, each including works by a large team of scholars. While each includes some articles by women, women's voices still represent a small minority, and few scholars outside the Euro-American community have been included. *Harper's Bible Dictionary*, edited by Paul J. Achtemeier (San Francisco: Harper & Row, Publishers, 1985), is a one-volume work published under the sponsorship of the Society of Biblical Literature. The *Anchor Bible Dictionary*, edited by David Noel Freedman (New York: Doubleday, 1992), is a six-volume work providing more extended discussions of most topics, but representing a less inclusive team of writers and editors than the Harper's volume. Both of these dictionaries include articles by a number of Jewish scholars as well as by Protestants (both liberal and conservative) and Roman Catholics. The four-volume *International Standard Bible Encyclopedia*, edited by Geoffrey W. Bromiley (Grand Rapids: Wm. B. Eerdmans, 1979), is a new work rather than, as might appear, merely a revision of the edition published early in the twentieth century. The editors and writers bring a conservative Protestant theological perspective to their work.

Bible Atlases

Another type of general reference work that can be helpful in orienting readers to the physical settings out of which the biblical books came and about which they speak is a Bible atlas. In addition to maps of the region, these books often provide information about the climate, the topography, plants and animals native to an area, agriculture, mineral resources, transportation routes, and other factors important in shaping the economy and social structure. Photos of the region and of archaeological sites and artifacts help the words of a text take on the textures of human lives. Two recently published Bible atlases that reflect recent discoveries in the area are: James B. Pritchard, ed., *The Harper Concise Atlas of the Bible* (San Francisco: HarperCollins, 1991); and *The Macmillan Bible Atlas* (New York: Macmillan, 1993).

Introductions to the Hebrew Bible and to the New Testament

"Introductions" to each Testament can be excellent sources of information about the historical backgrounds of the biblical books. Some incorporate the work of newer disciplines emerging in the fields of anthropology, archaeology, and economic and social history that provide insights into such concerns as the circumstances of women and the experiences of peasants, laborers, and others who are not part of the dominant groups and classes. These studies complement those that focus on such traditional concerns as political leaders and institutions, military policies, and the literature and practices of formal religious institutions. While every introduction represents specific ideological, political, or religious perspectives, many make neither those perspectives nor their methodological commitments explicit. Of the many such volumes that are available, these represent some that are easily accessible to beginning students of the Bible or especially helpful in the clarity and freshness of the perspectives they represent.

Significant for its integration of social and literary concerns is Norman K. Gottwald's *The Hebrew Bible: A Socio-Literary Introduction* (Philadelphia: Fortress, 1985). Jorge Pixley's *Biblical History: A People's History* (Minneapolis: Fortress, 1992) provides an overview of the history of Israel, with attention to issues in social history and to perspectives from outside the dominant groups of the society. Alice L. Laffey brings feminist critical concerns to the subject in *An Introduction to the Old Testament: A Feminist Perspective* (Philadelphia: Fortress, 1988). Alice Ogden Bellis includes womanist as well as feminist angles on introductory questions about the Hebrew Bible in *Helpmates, Harlots, and Heroes: Women's Stories in the Hebrew Bible* (Louisville: Westminster/John Knox, 1994), and her bibliography is useful in leading one to additional resources from those perspectives. Two introductions written by Jewish scholars provide an important and different perspective on the portion of the Bible common to Judaism and Christianity. They are *Sinai and Zion: An Entry into the Jewish Bible*, by Jon D. Levenson (Minneapolis: Winston, 1985), and *The Enjoyment of Scripture: The Law, the Prophets, and the Writings*, by Samuel Sandmel (New York: Oxford University Press, 1972).

Two introductions to the New Testament help to situate the reader in the varied contexts of the first century church and in the equally varied types of literature produced by those communities. The first is Pheme Perkins's *Reading the New Testament: An Introduction* (New York: Paulist Press, 1978); the second is Luke Timothy Johnson's *The Writings of the New Testament: An Interpretation* (Philadelphia: Fortress, 1986). More recently, Russell Pregeant, in *Engaging the New Testament: An Interdisciplinary Introduction* (Minneapolis: Fortress, 1995), provides a useful orientation to a variety of methodological approaches that are currently in use in New Testament scholarship. The work of an international, inter-religious group of women scholars has been gathered and edited by Elisabeth Schüssler Fiorenza in *Searching the Scriptures: Vol. 1 – A Feminist Introduction* (New York: Crossroad, 1993).

One-Volume Commentaries

One-volume commentaries are an accessible source of information about the Bible. Their disadvantage is that the discussion of any passage is of necessity brief, and the briefer the discussion, the more selective it will be about the issues treated and the perspectives represented. You may find that your specific questions are absorbed into general overviews. It is important to be aware of the social locations of contributors to these volumes, as well as to the editors' announced purposes. *Harper's Bible Commentary*, edited by James L. Mays (San Francisco: Harper & Row, 1988), was prepared under the auspices of the Society of Biblical Literature. One of the five associate editors and six of the seventy-seven contributors are women. Most of the contributors are Christian, and none come from the two-thirds world or are members of minority racial or ethnic groups in North America. The *New Jerome Bible Commentary*, edited by Raymond E. Brown, Joseph Fitzmyer, and Roland E. Murphy (Englewood Cliffs, NJ: Prentice Hall, 1990), includes nine women among the seventy-four contributors, all of whom are Roman Catholic. The same editors have also prepared *The New Jerome Bible Handbook* (Collegeville, MN: Liturgical Press, 1992), which contains condensed versions of articles found in the commentary.

Several one-volume commentaries deliberately bring a specific perspective to their task. For example, *The Women's Bible Commentary*, edited by Carol A. Newsom and Sharon H. Ringe (Louisville: Westminster/John Knox, 1992), brings together the work of some of the growing number of women biblical scholars in discussions of aspects of each book of particular concern to women; these North American scholars come from a variety of Jewish and Christian traditions, but only two come from outside the Euro-American community. Elisabeth Schüssler Fiorenza is the editor of *Searching the Scriptures: Vol. 2 – A Feminist Commentary* (New York: Crossroad, 1994), which is the work of an international, inter-religious group of scholars engaged in "feminist political interpretation for transformation" of a wide variety of writings not limited to formal canonical lists. W. Gunther Plant, Bernard J. Bamberger, and William W. Hallo bring a perspective from Reform Judaism to *Torah: A Modern Commentary* (New York: Union of American Hebrew Congregations [Jewish Publication Society], 1981/5741), in which they offer textual notes, commentary, and "gleanings" from various literary sources that have a bearing on each text.

Commentary Series

The volumes in a commentary series generally offer more detailed discussion of the biblical texts than can be presented in one-volume commentaries. Those series are hard to discuss in general, however, since most series embody a variety of approaches to the authors' assigned task (a factor that is particularly evident when volumes in a series appear over such a long period of time that the very assumptions of the discipline change over the course of publication). One new series that is particularly worth examining is *The New Interpreter's Bible* (12 vols.), which is being published by Abingdon Press, beginning in 1994 and concluding in 2000. This series includes contributors from all racial and ethnic groups—women as well as men. Most are from North America. Authors have been asked to address contextual concerns for both ancient communities and modern readers, and to pay attention to the use of the Bible in the church.

You should also be aware that many excellent commentaries appear as individual volumes, and not as part of series. If you have access to a theological library, therefore, you will want to examine the general collection by looking in the subject index of the computer catalogue or card file.

Journals

Articles in journals and anthologies are an important source of information about specific passages and about some of the questions that will arise in your study. Scholars who have recently completed graduate school often publish articles before they do books, and this group includes a greater percentage of persons from historically ex-cluded communities. Thus articles often provide a greater diversity of voices than one could find in commentaries and reference works. Even established scholars often publish their most recent work as journal articles, before they have completed enough research or other work to produce an entire book. Journal articles thus often provide more recent information. This is especially important in areas of study that are changing rapidly, such as cultural anthropology, sociological analysis, or the various literary criticisms. Finally, recently published articles can provide handy bibliographies of earlier works related to the topic you are investigating.

Finding out what articles are being published can seem like an overwhelming task, but several printed bibliographic aids can make the process manageable. *Old Testament Abstracts* and *New Testament Abstracts* provide brief summaries of articles (and some books) on biblical texts and related topics. Both series include indexes of biblical texts. In addition, you should consult the two volumes of the *Religion Index* (*Religion Index One: Periodicals* and *Religion Index Two: Multi-Author Works*). Such indexes and abstracts will put you in touch with such "classical" journals as the *Journal for Biblical Literature*, the *Catholic Biblical Quarterly*, and *Interpretation*, as well as with major journals published outside of North America. Latin American resources are indexed in *Bibliografía Teológica Comentada del Area Iberoamericana*, and you should be alert for similar resources from other parts of the world. In addition to printed resources, electronic databases can speed your research. Check with your library to find out what ones are available.

One problem with both print and electronic indexes is that they may take a while to catch up with the many new journals emerging all the time, especially in the two-thirds world. In order to be attentive to these important historically excluded voices, you should develop the habit of consulting regularly as many of these journals as you can. The following list is far from exhaustive, and it is changing almost daily. We mention these only to get you started on your search. The journals can be grouped into three categories: Journals specifically focused on the Bible; journals with a more general theological focus, or that represent a particular institution such as a denomination or a theological school; and homiletical resources.

In additional to traditional biblical journals like those mentioned above, you might want to consult the following journals that come from particular perspectives. *Biblical Interpretation* is published at the University of Sheffield in England, and it has been particularly diligent in seeking out contributors from a broad range of social locations around the world. *Daughters of Sarah* represents an evangelical feminist perspective and is written to be accessible to non-technical readers. If you read Spanish, consult *Revista de Interpretación Bíblica Latino-americana (RIBLA)*, each issue of which is thematically focused and brings together articles by Protestant and Catholic scholars from all areas of Latin America and the Caribbean.

Journals that deal more generally with theology, church, and culture sometimes include articles on the Bible. For most of those on this list, the title makes the journal's focus clear (and where that is not the case, we have included a brief identification in parentheses): *Voices from the Third World*; *Concilium* (Roman Catholic with an international, ecumenical focus); *Sojourners* (evangelical, social activist); *Feminist Theology*; *Journal of Feminist Studies in Religion*; *Journal of the Interdenominational Theological Center*; *Journal of Religious Thought* (Howard University Divinity School); *Africa Theological Journal* (Roman Catholic from Kenya); *Journal of Black Theology in South Africa*; *Journal of Hispanic/Latino Theology*; *Apuntes* (from the "Hispanic margin" of North America); *Vida y Pensamiento* (Latin American Biblical Seminary in Costa Rica); *Estudios Teológicos* (Roman Catholic from Guatemala); *Estudos Teologicos: Orgão da Faculdade de Teologia* (Lutheran from Brazil); *Revista Latinoamericana de Teología* (Jesuit, from the University of Central America [UCA] in El Salvador); *Jian Dao: A Journal of Bible and Theology* (from Alliance Bible Seminary in Hong Kong); *Asia Journal of Theology* (Bangalore, India); *Jeevaadhara* (an Indian journal of pastoral and theological concerns, with one issue per year on the Bible); *Taiwan Journal of Theology*; *Colloquium: Australian and New Zealand Theological Review*; *CTC Bulletin* (Commission on Theological Concerns of the Christian Conference of Asia); *East Asia Journal of Theology*; *In God's Image* (Asian feminist theology); *Japan Christian Review*; *One Body: Journal of Korean Immigrant Theology* (in Korean); *Pacific Journal of Theology* (Fiji and other Pacific Islands).

A number of resources for preaching are offered to pastors. They usually provide a study or commentary on the biblical passages assigned in the most common lectionary lists, and they may give suggestions for shaping a sermon, discussions of relevant pastoral and theological issues, guides for leading Bible studies, and prayers and other aids for worship. These resources should be used with caution, however, since their purpose is to push toward resolving the complexity of a text into a single focus for a sermon, rather than opening the reader to a greater variety of voices within the text and from the community of interpreters. Several examples of such resources with an ecumenical list of contributors are *Homily Service*, *Exegetical Resource*, and *Lectionary Homiletics*.

The Arts

The arts are an important locus of diverse voices in the conversation around biblical texts. Biblical stories, psalms, and other texts form the basis for music of many types (hymns, oratorios, cantatas, and spirituals, for example), and they have also found expression in drama, poetry, novels, and short stories. Along with academic historians who recover and reconstruct letters, diaries, and sermons that record some of the interpretations of the Bible by enslaved peoples, African American poets, novelists, and short story writers often incorporate such resources from their ancestors into their new literary creations. Museums and art history books bear witness to the importance of the Bible in the fine arts, and the Bible comes to life also in folk art and crafts from all parts of the world. For example, biblical texts, reproductions of art, and historical and theological commentaries come together in *Great Women of the Bible in Art and Literature*, with text by Dorothée Sölle, et al. (Grand Rapids: Wm. B. Eerdmans, 1994). Two recently published books provide a glimpse into the intersection of the Bible and art in Asia and Nicaragua, respectively: *The Bible Through Asian Eyes*, by Masao Takenaka and Ron O'Grady (Auckland, New Zealand: Pace Publishing, 1991; distributed through Friendship Press and the World Council of Churches); and *The Gospel in Art by the Peasants of Solentiname*, edited by Philip and Sally Scharper (Maryknoll: Orbis, 1984).

Academic Disciplines of "Biblical Criticism"

Persons who have studied the Bible in seminary or graduate school courses will have noted that both such traditional disciplines of "biblical exegesis" as source, form, and redaction criticism, and the newer types of literary criticism and social scientific studies, intersect with this roadmap at several points. While it is not necessary to be familiar with these academic tools in order to use this roadmap, you might well find that the two complement each other in some helpful ways. In any event, if you are using this book in the context of a class, you should follow your instructor's directions in preparing exegesis papers or other assignments.

If you want to study these academic critical disciplines, several resources will get you started. *To Each Its Own Meaning: An Introduction to Biblical Criticisms and Their Applications*, by Steven L. McKenzie and Stephan R. Haynes (Louisville: Westminster/John Knox, 1993), provides a review of the various disciplines and their contributions to biblical study. The revised edition of *Biblical Exegesis: A Beginner's Handbook*, by John H. Hayes and Carl R. Holladay (Philadelphia: Westminster, 1983) is a guide to the formal processes of exegesis. The "Guides to Biblical Scholarship" series published by Fortress Press consists of brief monographs on some of the principal methods, tools, and critical issues in biblical scholarship. Volumes in the series have been published over several decades, and recent ones deal with such emerging topics as sociological study, comparative folklore, and various types of literary criticism. Gene M. Tucker is editor of the Old Testament series, and Dan O. Via, Jr., is editor of the New Testament series.

While we have not listed resources that pursue all of these critical disciplines, we have included a sub-section dealing with "social world" or sociological studies. This is not in order to privilege those methodologies over others, but rather to identify some of the fruits of such study that will help you fill out the picture of the "social contexts" reflected in the biblical traditions and to which the biblical books were addressed.

Another important dimension of "critical" study of the Bible involves attention to readings coming from outside the dominant culture of Europe and North America. For that reason we have included a sample of such readings as the final sub-section of this chapter.

Social Worlds of the Bible

Studies in the fields variously identified as cultural anthropology, social history, or sociology of the ancient world intersect the field of biblical study as hybrids of complex lineage. Both the methods of investigation and analysis and the data being uncovered are changing at such a rate that even to define the discipline at this point in its history is close to impossible. Suffice it to say, this section lists some of the "classic" resources that provide information about and analysis of the everyday life of people living in biblical times, and the structures, institutions, movements, and ideologies that gave shape to their lives.

Some of the resources covering the various social worlds represented in the Hebrew Bible are: Norman K. Gottwald, *The Tribes of Yahweh: A Sociology of the Religion of Liberated Israel, 1250–1050 B.C.E.* (Maryknoll: Orbis, corrected 2nd printing 1981); Frank Frick, *The Formation of the State in Ancient Israel: A Survey of Models and Theories* (Decatur, GA: Almond Press, 1985); Robert R. Wilson, *Prophecy and Society in Ancient Israel* (Philadelphia: Fortress, 1980); Daniel L. Smith, *The Religion of the Landless: The Social Context of the Babylonian Exile* (Bloomington: Meyer-Stone, 1989); Paul D. Hanson, *Old Testament Apocalyptic* (Nashville: Abingdon, 1987). Carol L. Meyers's *Discovering Eve: Ancient Israelite Women in Context*

(New York: Oxford University Press, 1988) examines the contexts of women's lives in ancient Israel.

Resources covering the New Testament period include: Bruce J. Malina, *The New Testament World: Insights from Cultural Anthropology* (Atlanta: John Knox, 1981); John E. Stambaugh and David L. Balch, *The New Testament and Its Social Environment* (Philadelphia: Westminster, 1986); Gerd Theissen, *Social Reality and the Early Christians: Theology, Ethics, and the World of the New Testament* (Minneapolis: Fortress, 1992); Bruce J. Malina and Richard L. Rohrbaugh, *Social-Science Commentary on the Synoptic Gospels* (Minneapolis: Fortress, 1992); Luise Schottroff and Wolfgang Stegemann, *Jesus and the Hope of the Poor* (Maryknoll: Orbis, 1986); Wayne A. Meeks, *The First Urban Christians: The Social World of the Apostle Paul* (New Haven: Yale University, 1983); and Elsa Tamez, *The Amnesty of Grace: Justification by Faith from a Latin American Perspective* (Nashville: Abingdon, 1993). Ross Shepard Kraemer's *Her Share of the Blessings: Women's Religions Among Pagans, Jews, and Christians in the Greco-Roman World* (New York: Oxford University Press, 1992) explores the social contexts of women's religious practices during the period in which the New Testament was written.

Readings from Outside the Dominant Culture

Persons from outside of the dominant culture of the North Atlantic academic community bring increasingly numerous and significant voices to the conversation about biblical interpretation. This body of literature is growing too rapidly to document completely. We have therefore noted just a few of the major anthologies, not only for their intrinsic value, but also because their tables of contents and bibliographies will identify many of the scholars writing in the area. Their other works, in turn, can be identified through card catalogues, computer listings, and periodical indexes.

The expanded and revised edition of *The Bible and Liberation: Political and Social Hermeneutics*, edited by Norman K. Gottwald and Richard A. Horsley (Maryknoll: Orbis, 1993), is the signature volume of the new series "The Bible and Liberation" being published by Orbis. Three other anthologies that include voices from a variety of places in the "third" or "two-thirds" world are R. S. Sugirtharajah, ed., *Voices from the Margin: Interpreting the Bible in the Third World*, rev. ed. (Maryknoll: Orbis, 1995); John S. Pobee and Bärbel von Wartenberg-Potter, eds., *New Eyes for Reading: Biblical and Theological Reflections by Women from the Third World* (Bloomington: Meyer Stone, 1986); and Wendy S. Robins and Musimbi R. A. Kanyoro, eds., *Speaking for Ourselves: Bible Studies and Discussion Starters by Women* (Geneva: WCC Publications, 1990). The two volumes of *Reading from This Place*, edited by Fernando F. Segovia and Mary Ann Tolbert (Minneapolis: Fortress), address the agenda of contextual readings of the Bible. Volume 1: *Social Location and Biblical Interpretation in the United States* (1994), includes articles from outside of the dominant culture. Volume 2: *Social Location and Biblical Interpretation in Global Perspective* (1995), contains articles by scholars from other countries, many from the two-thirds world.

African biblical interpretation is best discerned in the many examples of theology written from various African contexts. Itumeleng J. Mosala's *Biblical Hermeneutics and Black Theology in South Africa* (Grand Rapids: Wm. B. Eerdmans, 1989), Gerald West's *Biblical Hermeneutics of Liberation: Modes of Reading the Bible in the South African Context* (Maryknoll: Orbis, 1995), and Alan Boesak's *Comfort and Protest: The Apocalypse from a South African Perspective* (Philadelphia: Westminster, 1987) hint at the variety of voices emerging from but one area of that continent. Teresa Okure's *The Johannine Approach to Mission: A Contextual Study of John 4:1-42* (Tübingen: J.C.B. Mohr [Paul Siebeck], 1988) brings a perspective of a Nigerian woman. As varied as they are, these examples only begin to reflect the diversity of contexts that make up Africa.

Carlos Mesters' *Defenseless Flower: A New Reading of the Bible* (Maryknoll: Orbis, 1989) defines biblical interpretation as part of Latin American liberation theology, and the journal *RIBLA* (cited above) identifies key biblical scholars working in this region. In addition, Ernesto Cardenal's *The Gospel in Solentiname*, 4 vols. (Maryknoll: Orbis, 1976–1982) provides transcripts of Bible studies done in a Christian base community in Nicaragua.

Theological discussions taking place in the countries of Asia are reflected in many books, but few of those available in North America focus specifically on biblical interpretation. Two anthologies of women's readings with that focus are *Reading the Bible as Asian Women*, edited by the Christian Conference of Asia (Singapore: CCA, 1986); and The Centre for Society and Religion, ed., *God, Women and the Bible* (Colombo, Sri Lanka: The Centre for Society and Religion, 1983). Kwok Pui-Lan's *Discovering the Bible in the Non-Biblical World* (Maryknoll: Orbis, 1995) explores issues involved in reading the Bible in a context where a variety of religions are practiced.

Within North America, the anthology *Stony the Road We Trod: African American Biblical Interpretation*, edited by Cain Hope Felder (Philadelphia: Fortress, 1991), introduced the academy and the church alike to the work of a community of African American biblical scholars whose numbers are growing rapidly. Three examples of biblical interpretation from the Hispanic or Latino Community in the United States are Justo L. González, *Santa Biblia: The Bible Through Hispanic Eyes* (Nashville: Abingdon, 1996); Jorge Maldonado, *Even in the Best of Families: The Family of Jesus and Other Biblical Families Like Ours* (Geneva: WCC Publications, 1994); and Virgilio Elizondo, *Galilean Journey: The Mexican-American Promise* (Maryknoll: Orbis, 1983).

Euro-American women were the first of the groups outside of the historically dominant community of Euro-American male biblical scholars to obtain access in significant numbers to graduate education and to opportunities to publish. Articles by both Jewish and Christian women from a variety of contexts are gathered in each of the following anthologies: Alice Bach, ed., *The Pleasure of Her Text: Feminist Readings of Biblical and Historical Texts* (Philadelphia: Trinity Press International, 1990); Adela Yarbro Collins, ed., *Feminist Perspectives on Biblical Scholarship* (Chico, CA: Scholars Press, 1985); Letty M. Russell, ed., *Feminist Interpretation of the Bible* (Philadelphia: Westminster, 1985); and Peggy L. Day, ed., *Gender and Difference in Ancient Israel* (1989). We cannot omit mention of two scholars and their works that launched the discipline of feminist biblical scholarship: Elisabeth Schüssler Fiorenza, *In Memory of Her: A Feminist Theological Reconstruction of Christian Origins* (New York: Crossroad, 1983); and Phyllis Trible, *God and the Rhetoric of Sexuality* (Philadelphia: Fortress, 1978).